Search Engine Soci

Second Edition

Digital Media and Society Series

Nancy Baym, *Personal Connections in the Digital Age*, 2nd edition

Mercedes Bunz and Graham Meikle, *The Internet of Things*

Jean Burgess and Joshua Green, *YouTube*

Mark Deuze, *Media Work*

Andrew Dubber, *Radio in the Digital Age*

Charles Ess, *Digital Media Ethics*, 2nd edition

Jordan Frith, *Smartphones as Locative Media*

Alexander Halavais, *Search Engine Society*, 2nd edition

Martin Hand, *Ubiquitous Photography*

Robert Hassan, *The Information Society*

Tim Jordan, *Hacking*

Graeme Kirkpatrick, *Computer Games and the Social Imaginary*

Leah A. Lievrouw, *Alternative and Activist New Media*

Rich Ling and Jonathan Donner, *Mobile Communication*

Donald Matheson and Stuart Allan, *Digital War Reporting*

Dhiraj Murthy, *Twitter*, 2nd edition

Zizi A. Papacharissi, *A Private Sphere: Democracy in a Digital Age*

Jill Walker Rettberg, *Blogging*, 2nd edition

Patrik Wikström, *The Music Industry*, 2nd edition

Search Engine Society

Second Edition

ALEXANDER HALAVAIS

polity

First edition published in 2008 by Polity Press
This edition first published in 2018 by Polity Press

Polity Press
65 Bridge Street
Cambridge CB2 1UR, UK

Polity Press
101 Station Landing, Suite 300
Medford, MA 02155, USA

ISBN-13: 978-1-5095-1682-7
ISBN-13: 978-1-5095-1683-4 (paperback)

A catalogue record for this book is available from the British Library.
Names: Halavais, Alexander M. Campbell, author.
Title: Search engine society / Alexander Halavais.
Description: Second edition. | Cambridge, UK ; Medford, MA : Polity Press,
    [2017] | Series: Digital media and society | Includes bibliographical
    references and index.
Identifiers: LCCN 2017024677 (print) | LCCN 2017037380 (ebook) | ISBN
    9781509516858 (Mobi) | ISBN 9781509516865 (Epub) | ISBN 9781509516827
    (hardback) | ISBN 9781509516834 (pbk.)
Subjects: LCSH: Web search engines--Social aspects. | Information
    technology--Social aspects.
Classification: LCC HM851 (ebook) | LCC HM851 .H343 2017 (print) | DDC
    303.48/33--dc23
LC record available at https://lccn.loc.gov/2017024677

Typeset in 10.25 on 13 pt Scala by Servis Filmsetting Ltd, Stockport, Cheshire
Printed and bound in the United Kingdom by Clays Ltd, St Ives PLC

For further information on Polity, visit our website: politybooks.com

Contents

Introduction

In 2016, German Chancellor Angela Merkel raised an alarm about the influence of search on the web: "Algorithms, when they are not transparent, can lead to a distortion of our perception, they can shrink our expanse of information" (Connolly 2016). While there have, over time, been many criticisms of the effect of search engines on society, this brings us to the very point of many of them: search reduces the amount of information available to us, and in doing so introduces bias.

Perhaps you come to this book wondering whether search engines are biased. They are. It would be impossible for them to be otherwise. Indeed, that is their intended function. A perfect mirror, reflecting the web and other knowledge spaces precisely, would serve little purpose. We want search engines to act as a filter, removing the less important stuff, so that we can apply our naturally limited attention to what really matters.

Matters to whom? That is perhaps the most important question we can ask about how search has changed our social lives. Over nearly a decade since the first edition of this book was published, a new focus has emerged around questions of algorithmic culture, on the power of hidden processes that shape our information space, and how economic and political relations are encoded into platforms and networks. Naturally, these questions have existed much longer, and have often been central to the study of large sociotechnical systems for decades, but the rapid integration of the internet into the everyday lives of most of the planet's population has given new rise to questions of how these often invisible biases might be affecting what it is to be a human of the twenty-first century.

Search engines and social platforms have quietly been at the forefront of algorithmic culture, reshaping the web, and, by extension, much of the way in which we interact with one another. No one has missed the rise of the largest search engine company, Google, as one of the new economic power-houses of the last few decades. But the focus has largely been on the ways in which Google has profited from advertising, or its seeming growth into a company that provides every-thing from education to automobiles, rather than the core technology that drove its growth. The search engine seems so unassuming, working quietly in the background, changing the structure of our lives.

The answer

Take a moment and type the following search string into your favorite search engine: "Google is your friend." Today, the number of "hits" for that phrase on Google stands at "about 882,000." The company is successful, but who knew it was so friendly? Even the abbreviation of the phrase – GIYF – receives over 100,000 hits. If you have picked up this book, you can probably guess the context in which this phrase is used. If not, a description may be found at justfuckinggoog leit.com, which reads, in part:

Google Is Your Friend

All Smart People Use Google

It Appears That You Are Not One Of Them

The search engine has become so much a part of our culture that there is a common assumption that we have found a cure for stupid questions. Folded into that assumption, we find a host of others: that even the unintelligent have access to and

can use a search engine, that a search engine will lead someone to a page that contains accurate information, and that
questions are best directed first to a machine.

Unpacking the black box of the search engine is something
of interest not only to technologists and marketers, but to
anyone who wants to understand how we make sense of a
newly networked world. Search engines and social platforms
have come to play a central role in corralling and controlling
the ever-growing sea of information that is available to us, and
yet they are trusted more readily than they ought to be. They
freely provide, it seems, a sorting of the wheat from the chaff,
and answer our most profound and most trivial questions.
They have become an object of faith.

We ask many things of search engines – what do they ask
in return? Search engines are at once the most and the least
visible part of the digital, networked revolution. The modern
search engine has taken on the mantle of what the ancients of
many cultures thought of as an oracle: a source of knowledge
about our world and who we are. Children growing up in the
twenty-first century have only ever known a world in which
search engines could be queried, and almost always provide
some kind of an answer, even if it may not be the best one.

The mirror

Search engines appear to be merely a functional tool, aimed
at making the real work of the web easier, but they have the
potential to reveal to us not only their internal structures, but
the structures of the societies that build them. In *Troilus and
Cressida*, Shakespeare (1912, p. 35) hints at why an examination of search engines is so enticing:

> And in such indexes, although small pricks
> To their subsequent volumes, there is seen
> The baby figure of the giant mass
> Of things to come at large.

Search engines represent the filters through which we view the content of the web, screens that allow us to inflict our own desires on the "giant mass" of the web, taming it and making it useful. At the same time, the view it presents is likely to shape future social values.

In his book *Information please*, Mark Poster (2006) reminds us of the change that has occurred: we once asked people for information and now we ask machines. He is interested in how this change to machine-mediated information affects our interactions. But it is all too easy to forget that the machines we are asking are constructed in ways that already reflect the conceptions and values of their makers.

What has changed

Much of the search landscape has changed since the first edition of this book, but a remarkable amount has remained the same. This is reflected in the content of the second edition, which retains much of the structure of the original, and many of the central arguments. But writing books about internet phenomena is a cursed task; books exist outside of "internet time" (Karpf 2011). In the months between completing the manuscript of the first edition of this book and its publication, Google had reversed their approach to sociable search, and a dozen other changes had happened to the search ecosystem. No doubt, by the time this is in your hands, search will have evolved in ways not anticipated by this second edition. Updates and other materials will appear at the book's companion site: ses-book.com.

I would like to thank those who read and responded to the first edition and particularly those who found the book useful to their own thinking and writing. There is nothing more gratifying than seeing the work of other scholars who were able to use my book as a point of reference or a foil. And I would like to thank my wife and my two sons, the youngest of whom was especially eager to know when this edition would be completed and I could focus my attention on what he considered more pressing matters.

We have come full circle in the years since the first edition. Many have thought seriously about search engines, "algorithms," and what they mean for our culture. But we are moving into a new era of search, one in which it disappears even more quickly from view. When search becomes invisible – answering factual questions without reference to the source, or deciding which of our friends provides the best content on social platforms – it becomes even more vital to watch, to test, and to understand how search and discovery technologies are changing us. Especially as the technology employs ever more complicated and capable algorithms, we too will evolve in our relationship to knowledge and to each other. We should do so carefully and consciously.

CHAPTER ONE

The Engines

How did we come to mechanize the process of search? How is it that it became something that is increasingly done *for* us rather than *by* us? It certainly did not happen all at once. Like most large sociotechnical systems, the process occurred gradually, and was influenced by a combination of technical innovation and the effect of existing structures of economic and political power. And, not surprisingly, it has also reshaped both industrial relationships and political influence in turn. The current state of the search ecosystem is the result of many years of evolution, and layers of encoding of our relationships to each other and to our collective knowledge. Search engines have politics that have been baked in over a long period of time, and that process deserves a deep archeological exploration, peeling back layer by layer.

This chapter cannot reach the depth such a historical treatment requires. It can, however, provide an outline of that history and an indication of the kinds of processes that have been built into search technology. Moreover, it can show how that suite of technologies made its way into the larger media ecosystem, shaping it in turn. It is tempting to treat the search engine as a free-standing technology, an invention that has made it easier to find things located on another independent technology, the World Wide Web. But even a cursory investigation suggests that the search engine, like most other technologies, is not something that can be treated without reference to a larger social context, and to evolutionary social and cultural changes. The search engine, far from being an isolated modern artifact, represents a touchstone of digital culture, and a reflection of the culture in which it exists.

The permanent loss of search engines is now almost unfathomable, but, were it to occur, we would find the way we communicate, learn about the world, and conduct our everyday lives would be changed. And so, we must look beyond the familiar "search box" and understand what it reveals and what it conceals.

Search engines today

A basic definition of the search engine might refer to an information retrieval system that allows for "keyword" searches of distributed digital text. That definition often remains our frame of reference, if we have one. If you ask someone what a search engine is, however, they are less likely to provide a definition than they are to indicate one of the handful of popular web search engines that represent some of the most popular sites on the web: Google, Baidu, or Bing, for instance.

And these sites are popular. As of 2012, more than half of Americans said that they used a search engine at least once a day (Purcell, Brenner, & Rainie 2012). Google is easily the most popular search engine today, and the various Google sites, including its search engine, are among the most visited sites on the web (comScore 2016). Google's dominance was already established a decade ago, and, despite inroads by Bing and Baidu, Google has continued to gain market share (see table 1.1). In 1999, Google was receiving 3.5 million search requests each day (Battelle 2005) and, while the growth has slowed in recent years, Google now receives at least a thousand times that number (Sullivan 2016), from more than a billion people each month. There can be little doubt that visits to search engines make up a large part of internet use, though it can be difficult to discover just how frequent that use is, and for what reasons.

One reason for this difficulty is that people often encounter

Table 1.1 Global search engine use as of September 2016	
Search engine	Global share (%)
Google	73.02
Bing	9.26
Baidu	8.74
Yahoo!	7.07

Source: NetMarketShare (2016). ComScore rates Google sites with a slightly lower share.

the large search engines through the façade of another site – that is, without intending to. So a search on a particular website may rely on Google to do the actual searching, or it may draw on an internal search engine. Both of these are a form of search, but may be measured differently by different research firms (Hargittai 2004). Many portal sites are also search engines, so just measuring the visitors, for example, to Yahoo! properties does not provide a useful metric of actual searches. (And even if you did, those Yahoo! searches could just be repackaged Google searches: Sullivan 2015.) Facebook is not usually considered a "search engine" even though it handles a surprisingly large number of search queries on a daily basis. And the traditional search box accessed via the web is itself giving way with the shift to mobile technology as the primary form of access (Schwartz 2016); by 2015, more than half of the queries Google received were from mobile devices (Sterling 2015). As hard as measuring the use of public search engines is, it is nearly impossible to measure search more generally: people searching their company intranet or their hard drive, for example.

Particularly over the last decade, there has been a rise in specialized search engines that seek to index not the entire web, but some constrained portion. This might be referred to as "vertical search," as opposed to the "horizontal search" of the general-purpose search engines, though this distinction has broken apart as the large search engine companies seek to acquire any novel approaches that might help them to win a share of submarkets. There remain certain areas that are in some sense naturally vertical, often because they index a part of the web that is not easily accessed (the so-called "dark web") or because they are otherwise defined by linguistic, cultural, or political borders, as in the case of Baidu or Yandex; but it is more accurate to say that search has grown increasingly *complex* in a number of ways.

Topically constrained search engines seek out only pages within a particular knowledge domain, or of a particular type of content. Some of these vertical search engines are focused on a particular industry. For example, an attorney in the United States might turn to open sources like FindLaw to provide news and information about their practice; to Lawyers.com to find an attorney within a particular practice area; to THOMAS, a search engine maintained by the federal government to track legislation; or to TESS to try to find out whether a proposed trademark is likely to infringe on an existing one – in addition to employing a number of subscription-based search engines for legal information such as those provided by Westlaw and Lexis-Nexis.

The inverse of this may be general search engines designed for particular kinds of users. The most obvious example of this is government surveillance networks. The US National Security Agency draws in massive amounts of digital information from all over the world, "nearly everything a typical user does on the internet," an estimated 20 trillion transactions in the US alone, and analyzes it using an indexing and query system called XKeyscore (Greenwald 2013). Companies also use sophisticated real-time search and analytics systems that sift through huge amounts of data (in 2010, Raffi Krikorian indicated that Twitter alone handled eight terabytes each day), and then provide that intelligence to private clients. A company called Echosec is one of several that correlate images shared via social media with their geographic location to infer emerging events ranging from military operations to natural disasters. The CEO of the company recently noted that it reminded him of the early days of search engines – a quickly evolving field where the query is more complex than a few keywords (El Akaad 2015).

While less constrained in terms of topic, academic search attempts to seek out a particular kind of document: one that adheres to traditionally scholarly constraints. At the most basic level, these sites are efforts to move databases that have traditionally been found in libraries onto the web. ScienceDirect, for example, provides reference to scientific literature for web users, and Google Scholar offers the utility of a large article and citation index provided by scholarly journals combined with other scholarly (and less scholarly) sources from the web, extending Google's tentacles into an important space for search. But there are dozens of others that provide access to open (e.g., BASE) or closed (e.g., DeepDyve) collections of academic articles. New ways of discovering this work – including through social networking platforms and large-scale analytics – will mean that this area will continue to evolve rapidly.

Academia is far from the only topically constrained space for doing search. While general-interest search engines like Google can be used to ferret out illicit files, a number of search engines specifically serve this particular niche. Torrentz.eu, which was shut down in 2016 after being in service for 13 years, was a meta-search engine that provided links to torrent files on various torrent trackers. And the "deep web" is partially defined by being those sites obscured from the major search engines, but they often have search engines of their own. For sites available via Tor, a routing system intended to provide a layer of anonymity, there exist more than a dozen search engines, including Ahmia.fi, Grams, and DARPA's Memex project. And data need not be illicit to be "deep." SunXDCC provides search for files shared via Internet Relay Chat. Search aggregators exist for things like local Craiglist listings, data to help to assess stocks, game cheats, coupons, and the meta-search engines that allow you to search across multiple engines.

In sum, while the general-purpose search engines provide access to the broadest range of resources, there remains space for search engines that are either deliberately constrained or that reach into areas where Google's "crawlers" do not dare to tread. Even more specialized forms of search draw together data that would not usually be considered "documents." Wolfram Alpha is not a web search engine at all, but an attempt to provide answers to questions. It can tell me what my most-liked photo on Facebook is, what the tensile strength of oak is, or what the plot of a mathematical function is. Zanran seeks to aggregate sources of numerical and statistical data from the web, so that a search for "age at death of US presidents" links to sites that provide that information in tabular form. These represent a basic parsing of information beyond keywords. Much of the excitement around the "semantic web" and microformats has dissipated, but the idea that structured information can be extracted and queried from large unstructured collections, like the World Wide Web, remains promising. Those who are trying to be noticed by search engines will frequently include metadata in their pages, including geolocation or indications of contact information. Efforts to develop protein and genetic material search systems go back at least a decade (Liebel, Kindler, & Pepperkok 2005), and a number of companies are now vying to be leaders in genomic search (Ossola 2015).

Thanks in large part to the shift to the mobile web, both searching for geographically constrained results and using geolocated data to constrain search have become vital. "Local search" has largely made local telephone directories a thing of nostalgia, allowing people to not only search for local businesses, but read reviews of those businesses written by their peers. Rather than competing with local search, many of the largest business directories ("yellow pages") have created their own local search engines, as have local newspapers and television stations. Sometimes, being created within the same locale is enough to make two resources related. The

Geo Search Tool (www.geosearchtool.com) or Google Earth can each help you find YouTube videos shot near the same location around the same time, providing a whole new way of thinking about organizing amateur video and other recording. And sometimes it need not be so explicit. Google has long localized results based on the general location of the searcher as revealed by their "IP (Internet Protocol) address." While it is not clear how Google and other search engines use geographic signals at present, a patent in 2015 by Google (US 20150339397 A1) describes a method for predicting the location of the device used for a search as well as where the searcher is likely to go next.

Sometimes it is not the content area that determines the search, but the type of media. Although large search engines, beginning with AltaVista, generally have had some ability to search for multimedia, it continues to present some of the greatest challenges, as well as opportunities, for those creating new search technologies. Structured "metatags" can be leveraged when present, but it is extracting meaning from the content itself that is more difficult. A number of efforts have been made to extract the content of photographs and videos, often using machine learning. By seeing how humans classify the contents of a large number of photographs, a system may learn to replicate this skill when presented with an unclassified photograph. For this to work well, it generally requires a large number of human-classified examples. One of the reasons Facebook's facial recognition system does well is that it can draw on a constant stream of human-assigned tags to help train it (Lachance 2016). As we move to devices that monitor the user's environment, they may be engaged in ongoing image recognition, which represents a kind of continual search (Simonite 2013). Rather than categorizing multimedia, it may be enough to identify items that are in some way similar, as Google's "search by image" does, or Shazam does when listening to a song in the environment and identifying it. Such similarity structures may prove to open doors to fundamentally different ways of searching and browsing music and video (e.g., the Songrium project: Masahiro, Goto, & Nakano 2014). As we move away from text-based documents and queries, search engines will be called upon to effectively extract information from these less structured forms of media.

As more and more of the world becomes internetworked, both the method of search and the world of searchable things extends beyond the purely digital. It would have been difficult to imagine, even a few years ago, that a search query would consist of the words "Alexa, where are my keys?" spoken while standing in your kitchen (Crist 2016). While the contours of the "Internet of Things (IoT)" are still being sketched out, it seems clear that search will reach beyond digitized documents and draw in real-time data from our devices, our social networks, and other sources, aggregating them into a usable search result. We are only just beginning to see examples of how they might play out. Early IoT-specific search engines, such as Shodan and Thingful, have focused on locating internet-connected appliances, and have found themselves at the center of discussions around privacy and security. And it may end up being the IoT devices themselves doing the searching (Carlton 2016) – what happens when your fridge needs to find the perfect ingredient for tomorrow's dinner party?

The line between a search engine and what has traditionally been called artificial intelligence is narrowing. In Steven Spielberg's 2001 film *A.I.*, the search engine is represented as a projected character known as "Dr. Know" ("Ask Dr. Know! There is nothing I don't."). A similar role was played by the holographic librarian named "Vox" in the 2002 remake of *The Time Machine*. Both depictions suggest a cultural recognition of search as a function that requires intelligence, and a feeling that machines can take on a part of that process. That idea is hardly new – for decades before the term "search engine" evolved, there had been interest in the relationship of search (often through structured relationships) to machine intelligence (Thornton & Du Boulay 1992). IBM has focused much of its recent energy on the Watson "cognitive computing" platform, and has sold it in part as a solution for enterprise search, revealing "trends and patterns hidden in unstructured content." Google is using machine learning to help to interpret user queries, employing an algorithm they call RankBrain to try to triangulate the meaning of a person's query (Clark 2015).

And it is not just artificial intelligence that can provide answers – some of the answers you need are probably known by another human. Yahoo! Answers was launched in 1995, and while it has lost ground, it still attracts millions of users each month, according to Quantcast. Other Question-and-Answer (Q&A) sites have grown over the last few years, including Quora and Stack Overflow, the latter of which provides answers to programming questions and, as of 2016, reaches 32 million people monthly. We might consider review sites, from restaurant and travel (like Yelp and Tripadvisor) to professional services (Angie's List and Healthgrades), as serving as a kind of curated search. Of course, these are just some of the explicit Q&A sites; implicitly, certain kinds of queries will be more effectively answered by others on Twitter or Facebook than they will be by a search engine.

At least for those of us who remember the time before search engines, they are defined by the query box on a web page. But search is both much bigger and much more complex than it once was. At one end, machine learning and analytics are drawing on almost unfathomable stores of unstructured data, finding patterns and connections within them that no human ever could. At the other end, individuals need to make sense of their "Personal Networked Spaces," digital information that relates directly to them and to their lives, right now, right where they are (Michel, Julien, & Payton 2014). Naturally, these tasks have existed before, but the size, extent, and diversity of the content of the web make it the ultimate target for such efforts. As a result, those who would have studied other topics in artificial intelligence, information design, library science, and a host of other fields have set their sights instead on developing better search engines.

Before the search engine

Some consider the greatest modern threat to be too much information, a glut of data that obscures what is really valuable. In his book *Data smog*, David Shenk (1997, p. 43) argues that computers are the "most powerful engines driving the information glut" by constantly drawing more data to our attention. While it is undoubtedly the case that the internet allows for the rapid delivery of ever growing amounts of information, it is also true that new computing devices were often created in order to manage and control increasingly complex environments. What once could be handled by a human, or a collection of individuals, became too time-consuming to result in effective control. So, in 1823, when the British government recognized the need for an effective replacement for human "calculators" to come up with tide tables at their ports, they funded an effort by Charles Babbage to design the first mechanical computer (Campbell-Kelley & Aspray 1996). Likewise, when the United States government found that it would take more than ten years to tabulate the decennial national census in 1890, they turned to Herman Hollerith, who founded the company that later became IBM, to create an automatic tabulating system (Aul 1972). That pattern of turning to information technology when faced with an overwhelming amount of data has occurred over and over: in libraries, in large businesses, and, eventually, on the World Wide Web.

It is natural to think of information technology as digital computing, since so much of contemporary information processing is relegated to networked computers. Computers are only the most recent in a long line of technologies that were created to allow for better control of complex collections and flows of information. The obvious example is the library:

once a collection of books and papers grows to a significant size, finding the appropriate piece of information in a timely manner becomes the subject of its own techniques, records, and machinery. Collections of documents can be traced back nearly as far as history itself has been recorded; were cave drawings the first libraries? As Kaser (1962) explains, many spiritual traditions conceive of the library as eternal, and the librarian as all-powerful. As early private collections grew larger, librarians emerged to organize and manage these collections. Because libraries were so important to many classical civilizations, the librarian was in a revered and politically powerful position which required special skills in collecting and manipulating information. In some ways, entrusting the organization of library resources to an individual – taking a large collection and making an individual or group of librarians the gateway to that knowledge – represented the first kind of search engine. And, as with later incorporations of that role, gaining control of the resource meant ceding some degree of power to the librarian.

Large libraries have always been a nexus of potential information overload, and so techniques and technologies evolved to help us filter and find information. Sorting and finding items within these collections required the creation and maintenance of information about the collection: metadata. The Babylonian library at Nippur had such records of the collection as early as the twentieth century BCE. The nature of the need was simple enough: the librarian needed to be able to discover which documents addressed a given topic, and then find where that document was physically located so that it could be retrieved for the person requesting information. Given that the subject of a work was often the issue most closely indexed to an informational need, the most popular indexes in the English-speaking world – the Dewey Decimal System and the Library of Congress System – provide a classification that is based on the subject matter of a book, so that books on similar topics are likely to be found in close proximity. Indeed, the role of spatial organization and information structure have been closely tied through most of the history of humanity: information architecture was once simply architecture (Latimer 2011).

Unfortunately, the number of dimensions of indexes that can be represented within spatial organization is limited, and the focus soon shifted from spatial organization to other forms. The use of computing systems in libraries has formed an important basis for how search engines now work. There is a long history of ideas about how to organize knowledge in the library, but the rise of computing in a library setting brought mathematics and linguistics to bear in new ways, and some of the core techniques now used by search engines were first used by library indexes. The field of Information Retrieval (IR) now bridges the closed library index and the wider collection of documents on the web (Salton 1975), and draws from many areas of computing and information science to better understand the information available over computer networks.

Public and private libraries were not the only form of data collections. The industrial revolution led to new forms of social organization, particularly the rise of bureaucracy, which required a flood of new paper files. Records and copies of correspondence were generally kept on paper, and guides emerged for suggesting the best ways to organize these materials, including the best ways to stack papers on a desk. Paper stacking gave way to pigeonholes, and the business titans of the early twentieth century made use of a fabulously expensive piece of office furniture called the "Wooton desk," which contained hundreds of pigeonholes and could be closed and locked, allowing for the secure storage of and access to personal work documents. The gradual development and innovation that led to vertical filing – a technology, perhaps unsurprisingly, developed by the inventor of the Dewey Decimal System – was a result of a data glut that began a century before anyone uttered the word "internet" (Yates 1982).

While subject-oriented classification made sense for the broad and relatively slowly changing materials of a library, it would have been useless when applied to the office of the last century. First, time was very much of the essence: when a document or file was created, changed, moved, or destroyed was often as important as the document's subject matter. Likewise, such records were often closely related to the people involved. Clearly this was true of customer records, and large insurance companies – whose very survival rested on increasing the size of their customer base – often drove innovations in business filing, right through to adopting the earliest electronic computers.

The earliest computer systems drew on the ideas of librarians and filing clerks, but were also constrained by the technology itself. While these earlier approaches provided metaphors for digital storage, they failed to consider the hardware constraints posed by the new computing devices and placed limits on the new capabilities of these machines. Computer programmers made use of queues and stacks of data, created new forms of encoding data digitally, and new imaginary structures for holding that data. Not housed in drawers or on shelves, these collections could be rearranged and cross-indexed much more quickly than their physical counterparts. Over time, this evolved into its own art, and database design continues to be a rapidly advancing subfield of computer science. Ironically, as more and more books are digitized, or physical books are stored in closed stacks and their storage and retrieval are automated, the physical library is beginning to look more like a database.

As the internet began its exponential increase in size during the 1990s, driven by the emergence of the World Wide Web, it became apparent that there was more information than could easily be browsed. What began as the equivalent of a personal office, with a small private library and a couple of filing cabinets, grew to rival and exceed the size of the largest libraries in the world. The change was not immediate, and, in the early stages, individuals were able to create guides that listed collections at various institutions, generally consisting of freely available software and a handful of large documents. Especially with the advent of the web, the physical machine where the documents were stored began to matter less and less, and the number of people contributing documents grew quickly. No longer could a person browse the web as if it were a small bookshop, relatively confident that they had visited each and every shelf. Competing metaphors from librarians, organizational communicators, and computer programmers sought out ways of bringing order, but the search engine, in many ways, was a novel solution for this new information environment.

How a search engine works

Before outlining the development and commercialization of search over time, it is useful to understand how a basic search engine works. Our interaction with the classic search engine, as users, is fairly uncomplicated. A website presents a box in which we type a few words we presume are relevant, and the engine produces a list of pages that contain that combination of words. In practice, this interface with the person, while important, is only one of three parts of what makes up a search engine. The production of the database queried by the web form requires, first, that information about webpages be gathered from around the web, and, second, that this collection of data be processed in such a way that a page's "relevance" to a particular set of keywords may be determined. By understanding the basic operation of each of these steps and the challenges they pose, an overall understanding of the basic technology may be reached. Figure 1.1 provides an overview of the process common to most search engines.

The process begins with a system that automatically calls up pages on the web and records them, usually called a crawler, but sometimes referred to as a "spider," "web robot," or "bot." Imagine a person sitting at a computer browsing the web in a methodical way. She begins her process with a list of

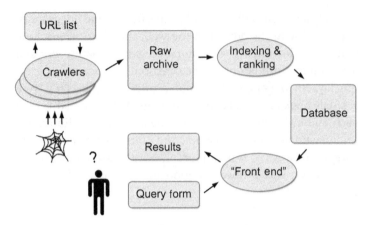

Figure 1.1 Conceptual organization of the typical search engine

webpages she plans to visit. She types the URL for the first of these pages into the browser. Once it loads, she saves a copy of the page on her hard drive, noting the time and the date. She then looks through the page for any hyperlinks to other pages. If she finds hyperlinks that are not already on her list, she adds them to the bottom of the list. Following this pattern, she is likely to record a large part of the entire web. Once complete, she would begin again from the top of her list, as there are probably changes to these pages and newly created pages that have been published and linked to since she began.

If the search engines really relied on individual humans to do this, it would take thousands of years to complete even a single crawl of the web. However, the operation described is not particularly complex, and creating a computer program that can duplicate this behavior is not difficult. Because the crawler is a relatively simple piece of technology, it has not evolved as much as other parts of the search engine. Even the smallest-scale crawlers are usually multi-threaded, making many requests at the same time rather than waiting for each page to be produced before moving on. They generally run not on a single computer, but on a large number of computers working in tandem. Most are careful to distribute their requests across the web, rather than ask for all of the pages from one server at once, since the crush of requests could easily overwhelm a single server, and most are "polite," taking into account webpage authors' requests for certain pages to be ignored. Nonetheless, these crawlers can sometimes make up a substantial number of the requests to a less-trafficked website. By one estimate, roughly half the traffic on the web is generated by these non-human visitors (Piejko 2016).

That does not mean that crawlers are all the same. There is an entire menagerie of crawlers out looking for new content on the web. On many pages, visits by web robots outnumber visits by real people. Some of these – going by exotic names like Slurp and Exabot – are gathering information for the largest general-purpose search engines, but others may be run just once by an individual. Small crawlers are built into a number of applications, including plug-ins for browsers and a bot used by Adobe Acrobat to create a PDF from a website. Because of small differences in how they are programmed, they behave slightly differently, following some links and not others, or coming back to re-check more or less frequently. Publishers of websites can exercise some level of control over Google's bot, through tools provided online, and most crawlers will obey a set of rules presented in a special "robots.txt" file a publisher may place on the server. But beyond these limited restrictions, the bots attempt to capture information from as much of the web as possible, as frequently as possible.

Following hyperlinks may not be enough. Large portions of the web are now generated dynamically, according to various requests from website visitors. Think, for example, of an online site that provides theatre tickets. The calendar, the pages describing available tickets, or even the seating maps may change depending on the show, the location of the person accessing the site, the current date, previous sales, and other variables. The modern webpage is probably not just generated dynamically by the server based on the content of a database, but built with HTML in combination with CSS and Javascript, and it often updates sections of the page on the fly (AJAX), creating a special challenge for the crawler (Mesbah, van Deursen, & Lenselink 2011; Google 2014).

Most crawlers make an archival copy of some or all of a webpage, and extract the links immediately to find more pages to crawl. Some crawlers, like the Heritrix spider employed by the Internet Archive, the "wget" program often distributed with Linux, and web robots built into browsers and other web clients, are pretty much done at this stage. However, most crawlers create an archive that is designed to be parsed and organized in one way or another. Some of this processing (like "scraping" links, or storing metadata) can occur within the crawler itself, but there is usually some form of processing of the text and code of a webpage afterward to try to obtain structural information about it.

The most basic form of processing, common to almost every modern search engine, is extraction of key terms to create a keyword index of the web by an "indexer." We are all familiar with how the index of a book works: it takes information about which words and ideas appear on any given page and reverses it so that you may learn which pages contain any given word or idea. In retrospect, a full-text index of the web is one of the obvious choices for finding material online, but particularly in the early development of search engines it was not clear what parts should be indexed: the page titles, metadata, hyperlink text, or full text (Yuwono et al. 1995). If indexing the full text of a page, is it possible to determine which words are most important?

In practice, even deciding what constitutes a "word" (or a "term") can be difficult. For most western languages, it is possible to look for words by finding letters between the spaces and punctuation. This becomes more difficult in languages like Chinese and Japanese, which have no clear markings between terms. In English, contractions and abbreviations cause problems. Some spaces mean more than others; someone looking for information about "York" probably has little use for pages that mention "New York," for instance. A handful of words like "the" and "my" are often dismissed as "stop words" and not included in the index because they are so common. Further application of "natural language processing" (NLP) is capable of determining the parts of speech of terms, and synonyms can be identified to provide further clues for searching. At the most extreme end of indexing are efforts to allow a computer to in some way understand the genre or topic of a given page by "reading" the text to determine its meaning.[1]

An index works well for a book. Even in a fairly lengthy work, it is not difficult to check each occurrence of a keyword or idea, but the same is not true of the web. Generally, an exhaustive examination of each of the pages containing a keyword is impossible, particularly when much of the material is not just unhelpful, but – as in the case of spam – intentionally misleading. This is why results must be ranked according to perceived relevance, and the process by which a particular search engine indexes its content and ranks the results is really a large part of what makes it unique. One of the ways Google leapt ahead of its competitors early on is that it developed an algorithm called "PageRank" that relied on hyperlinks to infer the authority of various pages containing a given keyword. Some of the problems of PageRank will be examined in a later chapter; here, it is enough to note that the process by which an index is established, and the attributes that are tracked, make up a large part of the "secret recipes" of the various search engines.

The crawling of the web and processing of that content happen behind the scenes, and result in a database of indexed material that may then be queried by an individual. The final piece of a search engine is its most visible part: the interface, or "front end," that accepts a query, processes it, and presents the results. The presentation of an initial request can be, and often is, very simple: the search box found in the corner of a webpage, for example. The sparse home page for the Google search engine epitomizes this simplicity. However, providing people with an extensive set of tools to tailor their search, and to refine their search, can lead to interesting challenges, particularly for large search engines with an extremely diverse set of potential users.

In some ways, the ideal interface anticipates people's behaviors, understanding what they expect and helping to reveal possibilities without overwhelming them. This can be done in a number of ways. Clearly the static design of the user interface is important, as is the process, or flow, of a search request. Westlaw, among other search engines, provides a thesaurus function to help users build more comprehensive searches. Over time, search engines have picked up certain interface elements, and kept them or left them behind based on response from those interacting with search. Type-ahead search queries, which pre-populate the search box with the top matching queries, were something experimented with by several search engines in the mid-2000s. Now they are a mainstay not just on the major search engines but on many other interfaces that draw on user input (Li et al. 2009). After declaring no interest in social signals for search (e.g., drawing on search results based on what friends produced or searched for), Google for a time provided indications of social results, including a feature they called "Search Plus Your World," which indicated how your social network was affecting which sites appeared in the results pages. Although by all accounts Google continues to include social signals, neither relationship nor authorship is indicated in the results pages any longer. As more traffic shifts to mobile devices, it seems likely that interfaces that are easier to use without a keyboard, including those that are voice-related and that incorporate the locative context, will be the most visible to those who search online.

Once a set of results are created, they are usually ranked in some way to provide a list of topics that present the most significant hits – sites that contain the keywords – first. The most common way of displaying results is as a simple list, with some form of summary of each page. Often the keywords are presented in the context of the surrounding text. In some cases, there are options to limit or expand the search, to change the search terms, or to alter the search in some other way. On some search engines, results are clustered by topic.

All three of these elements – the crawler, the indexer, and the front end – work together to keep a search engine's index continuously updated. The largest search engines are constantly under development to better analyze and present searchable databases of the public web. Some of this work is aimed at making search more efficient and useful, but some is required just to keep pace with the growing amount of content available online. The technologies used on the web change frequently, and, when they do, search engines have to change with them. As people employ document formats other than HTML (PDF-formatted documents, for instance), visual formats, or complex interactive sites, search engines need to create tools to make sense of these formats. The sheer amount of material that must be indexed increases exponentially each year, requiring substantial investments in computing hardware and bandwidth. As of 2011, Google data centers used as much electrical power as would normally provide for 200,000 homes (Glanz 2011). Someone visiting a skyscraper can quickly appreciate the work that went into building it, but few are aware of the work that must be continually done to make a search engine function.

Pre-web internet search

Once one has used a search engine, it seems obvious that it should exist, but the need for a general search engine during the early days of the web was neither immediate nor apparent. It usually is not until a collection of data grows too large to map in its entirety that the need for a search interface is made clear. Consider the average home library, which may fill only a bookcase or two. The books may be placed randomly, or by size, or by which are used more often or more appreciated, or by some idiosyncratic subject arrangement. At some point, however, a library grows to the point at which looking through everything to find the book you want is impractical, and at that point some form of indexing is necessary. Likewise, networked information started out as relatively small collections in relatively few repositories, and it was not until later that the need for different forms of indexing was made clear and tools were created to meet this need.

Early technologies used for finding files or users were often built into the operating system and, once computers were networked, it was often possible to use the same functions from a distance. Since long before the web has existed,[2] the Unix command "finger," for example, has provided information about a particular user, including when that user last logged on, and often some personal contact information. Its creator, Les Earnest, designed "finger" to aid in social networking at the Stanford Artificial Intelligence Lab (quoted in Shah 2000):

> People generally worked long hours there, often with unpredictable schedules. When you wanted to meet with some group, it was important to know who was there and when the others would likely reappear. It also was important to be able to locate potential volleyball players when you wanted to play, Chinese food freaks when you wanted to eat, and antisocial computer users when it appeared that something strange was happening on the system.

When computers were networked via the internet, it was possible to "finger" individuals from across the country or the world, to find out more about them. Eventually, it was used for other purposes, including distributing weather reports.

The first indexes on the internet were created by hand, often by the users of the systems as a guide to others. Consider some of the protocols in use on the internet before the emergence of the World Wide Web, beginning with "File Transfer Protocol"

(FTP), one of the first ways of moving files between computers. An early internet user would choose an FTP server from a list of public servers (a list they or someone else probably had downloaded from one of the servers on that list), and request a listing of files on that server. Often, there was a text document that could be downloaded that briefly summarized the content of each of the files on a given server. FTP continues to be used today as a way of transferring files, but the process of browsing through FTP servers in the hope of finding the document you were seeking was laborious and inconsistent, especially as the number of FTP servers increased. This increase also brought with it the rise of "anonymous" FTP servers, which allowed anyone to upload and download files to and from the server. While the increase in content was a boon to those who used the internet, it became increasingly difficult to locate specific files. As a result, what might be considered the first search engine on the internet arrived in 1990, before the World Wide Web had gained a foothold, and at a time when many universities had only recently become a part of the network (P. Deutsch 2000). This system, called "Archie," periodically visited the existing FTP sites and indexed their directories. It is probably a stretch to say that it "crawled" these sites, since, unlike today's web crawlers, it did not discover new servers linked to the existing servers. It also did not examine the full content of each of these pages, but limited itself to the titles of the files. Nonetheless, it represented a first effort to rein in a quickly growing, chaotic information resource, not by imposing order on it from above, but by mapping and indexing the disorder to make it more usable.

The "Gopher" system was another attempt to bring order to the early internet. It made browsing files more practical, and represented an intermediary step in the direction of the World Wide Web. People could navigate through menus that organized documents and other files, and made it easier, in theory, to find what you might be looking for. Gopher lacked hypertext – you could not indicate a link and have that link automatically load another document in quite the same way it can be done on the web – but it facilitated working through directory structures, and insulated the individual from a command-line interface. "Veronica," named after Archie's girlfriend in 1940s-era comics, was created to provide a broader index of content available on Gopher servers. Like Archie, it provided the capability of searching titles (actually, menu items), rather than the full text of the documents available, but it required a system that could crawl through the menu-structured directories of "gopherspace" to discover each of the files (Parker 1994).

In 1991, the World Wide Web first became available, and with the popularization of a graphical browser, Mosaic, in 1993, it began to grow more quickly. The most useful tool for the web user of the early 1990s was a good bookmark file, a collection of URLs that the person had found to be useful (Abrams, Baecker, & Chignell 1998). People began publishing their bookmark files to the web as pages, and this small gesture had an enormous impact on how we use the web today. The collaborative filtering and tagging sites that are popular today descended from this practice, and the updating and annotating of links to interesting new websites led to some of the first proto-blogs. Most importantly, it gave rise to the first collaborative directories and search engines.

The first of these search engines, Wandex, was developed by Matthew Grey at the Massachusetts Institute of Technology, and was based on the files gathered by his crawler, the World Wide Web Wanderer. It was, again, developed to fulfill a particular need. The web was made for browsing, but perhaps to an even greater degree than FTP and Gopher, it had no over-arching structure that would allow people to locate documents easily. Many attribute the genesis of the idea of the web to an article that had appeared at the close of the Second World War entitled "As we may think," in which Vannevar Bush (1945) suggests that a future global encyclopedia will allow individuals to follow "associative trails" between documents. The web grows in a haphazard fashion, like a library that consists of a pile of books that grows as anyone throws anything they wish onto the pile. A large part of what an index needed to do was to discover these new documents and make sense of them. Perhaps more than any previous collection, the web cried out for indexing, and that is what Wandex did.

As with Veronica, the Wanderer had to work out a way to follow hyperlinks and crawl this new information resource, and, like its predecessors, it limited itself to indexing titles. Brian Pinkerton's WebCrawler, developed in 1994, was one of the first web-available search engines (along with the Repository-Based Software Engineering [RBSE] spider and indexer – see Eichmann 1994) to index the content of web-pages. This was important, Pinkerton suggested, because titles provided little for the individual to go on; in fact, a fifth of the pages on the web had no titles at all (1994). Receiving its millionth query near the end of 1994, it clearly had found an audience on the early web, and, by that time, more than a half-dozen search engines were indexing the web.

Searching the web

Throughout the 1990s, advances in search engine technology were largely incremental, with a few exceptions. Generally, the competitive advantage of one search engine or another had more to do with the comparative size of its index, and how quickly that index was updated. The size of the web and its phenomenal growth were the most daunting technical challenges any search engine designer would have to face. But there were some advances that had a significant impact. A number of search engines, including SavvySearch, provided metasearch: the ability to query multiple search engines at once (Howe & Dreilinger 1997). Several, particularly Northern Light, included material under license as part of their search results, extending access beyond what early web authors were willing to release broadly (and without charge) to the web. Northern Light was also one of the first to experiment with clustering results by topic, something that many search engines continued to develop. Ask Jeeves (which became Ask. com) attempted to make the query process more user-friendly and intuitive, encouraging people to ask fully formed questions rather than use Boolean search queries, and AltaVista provided some early ability to refine results from a search.

One of the greatest challenges search engines had to face, particularly in the late 1990s, was not just the size of the web, but the rapid growth of spam and other attempts to manipulate search engines in an attempt to draw the attention of a larger audience. A later chapter will address this game of cat-and-mouse in more detail, but it is worth noting here that it represented a significant technical obstacle and resulted in a perhaps unintended advantage for Google, which began providing search functionality in 1998. It took some time for those wishing to manipulate search engines to understand how Google's reliance on hyperlinks as a measure of reputation worked, and to develop strategies to influence it.

At the same time, a number of directories presented a complementary paradigm for organizing the internet. Yahoo!, LookSmart, and others, by using a categorization of the internet, gave their searches a much smaller scope to begin with. The Open Directory Project, by releasing its volunteer-edited, collaborative categorization, provided another way of mapping the space. Each of these provided the ability to search, in addition to browsing their directory structures. Since the indexed material had already been selected, often by hand, as being of general interest or utility, searches on these sites could be very effective. Eventually many of these directory-based portals became major players, particularly Yahoo!, which experimented with a number of search engine partnerships, beginning with combining Inktomi's search technology with their existing directory in 1998, and eventually acquiring some of the largest general-purpose search engines, including AlltheWeb.com, AltaVista, and HotBot.

The early development of search engines was largely centered in the United States. By the middle of the 1990s, the World Wide Web was beginning to live up to its name, and sites could be found in many parts of the world, but American sites in English continued to make up the bulk of the web. Around the mid-1990s, the number of web users and websites exploded in Europe, as well as Hong Kong, New Zealand, and other countries. While sites were increasingly hosted "worldwide," the hyperlinks from them either led back to the US or remained within the hosting country. They only very rarely linked to a third country (Halavais 2000). Likewise, users in these countries tended to purchase items from local merchants rather than taking advantage of the global web-based marketplace (Jupiter Communications 1999). Just as search engine competition was heating up in the United States, many around the world were asking why they should use a search engine that was not suited to their own culture and language. The World Wide Web tended to reinscribe existing global flows of information, even as it presented some alternatives.

The rise of regional search engines is often left out of the history of search, but, by the mid-1990s, many countries and linguistic groups were relying on services tailored to their own languages and interests. Early examples included the Swiss search.ch, an Israeli engine called Walla, France's Voilà, and the Russian Rambler. More recently, non-English-language search is again in the news, with China's Baidu attracting a strong global following, joined by Yandex in Russia, Naver in Korea, and others focused on Japan, Sweden, Israel, the Czech Republic, Iceland, and more.

By the mid-2000s, search engines had re-ordered the web, making it search-centric. While the anachronistic phrase "surfing the internet" remained, the dominant paradigm was no longer moving from site to site in a sea of hyperlinks, but rather searching for specific items, or browsing through particular guides. In the late 1990s, Jacques Altaber, an official at CERN (Conseil Européen pour la Recherche Nucléaire), the organization that first supported the World Wide Web, suggested that the web would become a new sort of operating system, the platform on which an ever greater proportion of our communication and information tasks would take place (James 1995). By the mid-2000s, search engines became central to that operating system, moving from a useful tool to a powerful focal point of collective attention. Today, although the search box is losing its primacy as the "front door" of the web, the influence of the search engine continues, just beneath the surface. Even when visible, search has largely been taken for granted. Now that it has begun to recede beneath various interfaces, working behind the scenes of our everyday interactions online, it retains that influence while becoming even more obscured.

Many of those who initially developed search engines did so because they had a need and answered it. Many successful search engines were designed by students, and some of those pioneers now work in what has become a substantial search engine industry. The author of Wandex, for example, eventually worked for Google, and the creator of the original WebCrawler moved on to work on a blog search engine called Technorati, each improving on the technology of search. But WebCrawler is emblematic in another way. It was developed in 1993, a year that was important because it marked the commercialization of the World Wide Web, and, with it, the search engine. By 1994, WebCrawler had two commercial advertisers sponsoring the site, and, in the middle of 1995, it had been acquired by America Online as part of their effort to bridge to the web. The story of the development of the search engine is tied inextricably to the commercialization of the online world, and although there continue to be a number of important search engines that are supported directly or indirectly by government or research funding, the search engine wars of the 2000s were driven by the potential profit of online advertising.

The rise of the search engine coincided with the dot-com bubble, especially during the late 1990s, and large sums were invested in developing new and existing search engines and competing for a share of the search engine market. Over time, many of these search engines were acquired by their competitors, and the field narrowed somewhat. By the early 2000s, Google had come onto the scene and rapidly seized a large proportion of the global search market. At present, Google remains the most popular destination for those who want to do a search. There remain other search engines, of course. Microsoft began offering MSN Search in 2005, followed by Live, and then Bing. Others around the world are seeking to capitalize on the search infrastructure of the web, and the potential profits that come with the ability to shape attention and traffic. But Google remains synonymous with search.

Commodifying search

The story of search is not simply a technological one; the rise of search goes hand-in-hand with the commercialization of the internet. This is despite the fact that search on the open web is almost universally offered as a free-to-the-customer service. Certainly, enterprise search – providing a search engine for services within an organization – is sold to businesses, universities, and others. But for the giant search engines we are most familiar with, search is provided without charge. And yet the digital economy revolves around search.

With $16.3 billion in profits in 2015, Google's holding company, Alphabet, was the eighth most profitable business among the Fortune 500, and Google's revenues have continued growing at a relatively stable rate since the company's birth. It has long been the dominant search engine, but that reach continues to grow. It has faced a range of antitrust suits, particularly in Europe, and the ultimate effect of these remains an open question. How is it that a company whose core product is free has been so profitable? The most obvious answer to that question is that Google may be a leader in search, but it is more centrally an advertising company.

While Google makes money in a wide range of areas, including selling mobile hardware and search appliances for enterprise search, and provides services (Gmail, Chrome, YouTube) or does research in an even broader set of contexts, the vast majority of its income comes from selling advertising on its own sites and on partnered sites. In this, it is not entirely different from over-the-air television, which is often in the business of "selling eyeballs to advertisers." Some of these sales are, of course, directly related to their search business. Like many companies, Google places advertising "adjacent" to real search results. But it has also made it much easier for small businesses to bid for advertising in a range of spaces by offering a reverse auction on keywords, a model that now makes up a large part of web advertising as a whole. And, as part of this process, it collects and uses information about its users to target advertising better. There is a significant economic motivation for drawing as many users as possible to its properties, and traditionally search has been an attractive way to do this (see Hillis, Petit, & Jarrett 2012, p. 36).

The major driver of the search engine wars was a recognition that search drew traffic. Less obvious is the power of search to shape traffic: not only does it draw in users, but directs them to other parts of the web. As we will see, the search engines have the power to grant fortunes and to take them away – it is as if they are the builder of roads, stoplights, and front doors for every business online. Naturally, it is vital for search companies to maintain the credibility of their search, and so – at least in the case of general search – they insist that their results are in some sense the "naturally" best match for your query. Nonetheless, the acute attention they garner from both people who are searching the web and companies that are seeking to reach customers makes them a source of significant economic value.

All of that attention has been "baked into" the algorithms that drive search. In particular, one of the earliest sectors of profitable sales online was pornography, and there was significant financial incentive for drawing visitors to websites with adult materials. Search engines were placed in the position of resisting the influence of companies and individuals who sought to lure visitors to such sites, and, again, this affected and shaped the algorithms and the approaches that were embedded in search. A case could be made that a large part of Google's success was in producing a process that was more capable of resisting such attempts.

For better or worse, the worldviews of those search companies and the engineers who shaped search are made a part of the search process. Some of the competition in search results is because those worldviews are not as universal as people within the bubble of Silicon Valley might imagine. Some alternative search engines limit results to those documents that do not tread into moral or religiously objectionable material (including HalalGoogling.com and Yippy.com), or, on the other side of the coin, there are search engines (including Boodigo.com) intended for those who find the most popular search engines restrict pornography too much. A number of sites, most notably DuckDuckGo, trade on the notion of protecting the user's information and not providing it to advertisers (and likewise not shaping results based on previous searches). And, as noted, a number of search engines have successfully developed indexes that serve particular linguistic or cultural communities, often with some support from governments in the area. While these examples are intended to exploit areas in which the generalized search engines do not meet customer needs, the search engine giants have significant advantages in having the largest web index and the ability to respond quickly to large numbers of visitors.

The enterprise search market has also provided space for search engines on a different scale. Early on, it seemed as though the largest search purveyors would also dominate this area, leveraging their large-scale efforts (Hines 2007), but a number of vendors have emerged offering a range of products. Enterprise search often must pull from different sources of data (including various databases, email, and potentially both shared and personal disk drives), must manage different levels of access and security, and in some cases must provide a form of backup or archiving, either to protect organizational data or to respond to regulatory requirements. Particularly as these systems integrate with analytics and draw in new kinds of machine learning, it may be that they provide a proving ground for technologies that will then move to general search engines, rather than the other way around (Simone 2015).

Not listed in the above menagerie of search engines is Facebook, which now handles more than 2 billion searches per day (Constine 2016). Like Google, it is developing machine learning – they call their system Deep Text – to analyze the content and sentiment of posts and make them more searchable (Murphy 2016). This is not the general search represented by Google, Bing, and Baidu, but the frequency of use makes it just as important to consider, especially when the nature of search has shifted so much toward social platforms over the last decade. Search engines became central to the web because resources were so widely distributed and difficult to find. Social platforms have changed that, and for many people their link to the rest of the web is via social platforms. In 2016, 62 percent of Americans got their news via social media, more than a 20 percent increase over the number in 2012 (Gottfried & Shearer 2016). More generally, platforms like Facebook, Twitter, Reddit, and others serve, as the motto for Reddit notes, as a "front page of the internet," and the kind of browsing of the web that used to happen individually now happens more collectively. In some ways, a search of Facebook *is* a web search, with the millions of words Facebook users type each day serving as a kind of index of the web and beyond. Major search engines have included social signals in various ways in order to produce better search results, but those social connections – which have always been important – have now taken on a much greater importance, and future innovations in search will probably rely heavily on the kinds of meaning that can be extracted from social platforms.

Search and society

Search engines were developed as a response to a particular social problem, a problem that did not exist in the same way in the past. The signature technology of the last few decades has been digitization: the ability to transfer communications media into a format that may be transmitted via computer networks. As a result, more information is available in more places than ever before. This embarrassment of riches has necessitated new ways of filtering, sorting, and finding information. This is an old story – necessity as the mother of invention – and it is tempting to leave it at that. Indeed, the technical problems are challenging and exciting. It would be wrong to assume, however, that the social and cultural needs that led to the creation of search engines no longer are of import. Perhaps more than ever, our evolving ideas of what a search engine should do shape its development, either by creating new needs (finding video content, for example), or in some cases by resisting change in favor of familiarity. It is important, if we want to understand the technology better, to understand the social and informational environments in which it is deployed. Social context makes search what it is.

Understanding how people use search engines can also give us a seemingly unobtrusive way of learning about society's interests in the aggregate. Encouraged in part by Google's Zeitgeist pages, which provided an indication of search terms that had become suddenly more popular in a given week, John Battelle (2005) presented search engines as a source of a sort of global "database of intentions," providing what could ultimately become a fine-grained map of our interests and personalities as individuals and groups. In other words, by learning how people behave when using search engines, we may come to understand how they behave in general. Since that suggestion, social scientists' interest in what has come to be called "big data" has grown exponentially, and the idea that micro-expressions on the social web might be analyzed to better understand sociality is no longer novel. Searching for answers is perhaps the most human of social activities, and we can now study it in ways we have never been able to in the past.

In part, this is because watching the search process online is fairly unobtrusive. The problem is that we are observing a moving target. How most people searched for new information in 2000 differed significantly from how they did so in 2015. By 2030, we will have again changed the schema with which we discover new information. We are living through a period of extremely rapid change in how we interact socially, and search is the bleeding edge of that. How we decide what we need to know, how we find material that will address that information deficit, and how we evaluate and make choices based on those discoveries are all changing nearly as quickly as the topographies of interaction online do. So, while search engines and search mechanisms more broadly offer a window on information-seeking and decision-making, the bigger question is how they are changing the way we relate to the world and think about discovery, because the change in search technology is important, but not nearly as important as how we are changing as searchers.

No new technology leaves us unchanged, and often the changes are unexpected and unpredictable. More than two millennia ago, Plato was already making the case that communication technologies changed who we were, and not always for the better. Rather than enhancing memory, he argues in the *Phaedrus* (2002), writing subsumes it, and reduces the abilities of those who read rather than remember. Someone visiting a university library in the early 1980s would still have found a card catalog, and would have been able to observe more of the inner workings of the search process. This has now been replaced by a popular acronym, JFGI: Just Fucking

Google It. The effort of seeking out an index and evaluating potential resources has been replaced by pressing a button and "feeling lucky." As with earlier technological advances, this is not a tool with simple consequences. The double edge of technology – and particularly of communication technology, since communication is at the core of our social interactions – represents one of the most pressing reasons we must examine the role of the search engine not just in society, but in permeating our social lives. The following chapter examines how we use search engines, and how they have, in turn, changed us.

CHAPTER TWO

Searching

Search changes who we are. Understanding how search affects us requires that we have an explicit understanding of how humans search and why. Rather than an activity that happens relatively infrequently, as part of a process of research or to answer a specific question, search is central to what makes us thinking humans and allows us to work socially. To understand this, we need to understand what people do when they are actively searching, as well as the context in which search occurs. Search is so much a part of who we are as people and as societies that it often remains unexamined. This is particularly unfortunate when the task of searching and the place of search have changed so rapidly over the last few decades.

There are at least three questions we can ask about the search process. The first of these deals with the concrete issue of how people enter items into a search engine query box and how they interpret the results. This interaction at the interface level is of particular interest to the designers of search engines, and tells us a lot about search engines, the people who use them, and how we all think about our world. The broader question is why people search, what motivates them to look for certain material on a search engine, and whether they are in some way satisfied by what they find. Finally, we might ask whether the mere existence of a search engine changes what people want to look for, and their social values and expectations. That is, do the motivations surrounding search change with the existence of particular kinds of search technologies?

A more complete understanding of the search engine requires that we look at search from a variety of perspectives.

The perspective of the "user" is an obvious starting point – or at least should be. Often the design and evaluation of search is done from the designers' perspectives or using metrics of interest to the researcher (Spink 2002). Rather than trusting designers' innate understanding of the problem of the search process, and their internalized models of who might be using their system, user-centered design requires an iterative process of understanding what the user expects and creating systems that help to satisfy users' needs and desires.

There are problems with this approach, one of which is assuming that users do not also change to adapt to systems. Douglas Engelbart, who may be considered the father of the user interface, long argued that information systems and users co-evolve (Engelbart & Lehtman 1988). His work at Stanford, which brought about the mouse, hyperlinking, word processing, and dozens of other elements of the modern interface that we now take for granted, was oriented toward tools that would augment "the capability of humans to deal with tough knowledge work and to process effectively the large volumes of information with which knowledge workers must deal." He suggested that, as a community became accustomed to particular interfaces, they created new needs. New online services lead to new capabilities among the user base, and new desires to be fulfilled. It is not enough to react to the user, or create systems that respond to existing needs; the designer must understand the current user, and at the same time anticipate how the system might change the user.

The perfect search

Even if the perfect interface does not exist in real life, it persists in our dreams. This dream interface usually comes in two forms. One form is the conversational agent that is as good as a real librarian. We met Vox and Dr. Know in the first chapter, and, more recently, Spike Jonze's *Her* (2013) provides a version of that dream. When asked how she works,

"Samantha" replies: "Well, basically I have intuition. I mean, the DNA of who I am is based on the millions of personalities of all the programmers who wrote me, but what makes me 'me,' is my ability to grow through my experiences. So, basically, in every moment I'm evolving, just like you." When her "user" notes that this idea is really weird, she assures him "you'll get used to it." Because, while it is strange to think of a computer having this ability to evolve, it is perfectly natural for us to accept this from the (other) people we interact with. In this view, the machine and the human learn together, and build from experience. Rather than being limited to a single query and a specific answer (though this is also possible), the system adapts and probes and questions, trying to fill in gaps and discover answers. Search is done through conversation. Unfortunately, even this sort of ideal of a search engine as an intelligent conversational agent is not perfect. Our interactions with humans can be at least as frustrating as our interactions with machines, and communication is always marked by imperfect understanding.

Perhaps, then, the ideal device is one that knows what you mean: a perfect brain–machine interface, a search engine that knows what you are thinking. This is hardly a new dream. The ability to communicate to another person exactly what you mean has been an objective of just about every philosophy of every culture. Umberto Eco, in his *Search for the perfect language* (1995), recounts some of these attempts, from recovering lost "original languages," to constructing logical grammars for philosophy or model universal languages. There is some of this dream of a philosophical language in current efforts toward the construction of "ontologies" and the "semantic web." This is not the first time new technologies were considered the gateway to "angelic speech," or mind-to-mind communication. The radio, for example, was seen as a way to link up minds so that a new global understanding might be reached (J. D. Peters 1999). H. G. Wells (1938) imagined a "World Encyclopedia" that would provide common understanding across topics, and as a result lead to world peace. In this view, the ideal search interface does not need to draw inferences from the keywords you provide or engage you in conversation; it knows just what you mean.

The difficulty is that the searcher does not always know precisely what she means; if she did, she would have little need of searching. The word "search" suggests that a person is interested in finding something that has been lost. People do use search engines for this, particularly to "re-find" information that they may already have encountered on the web, but more often they are hoping not to "find" but to "learn," or to "discover." Perhaps, then, the ideal search engine does not just understand what you desire, but knows what the user wants even when she does not know herself. That is a conundrum, but may not be an insurmountable challenge. Social signals may provide this kind of suggestion for those who do not know what they do not know. Search technologies capable of doing this also tend to undermine personal and social will in pernicious ways.

At present, though, effective search requires that the searcher commands the experience necessary to identify appropriate query terms and utilize multiple approaches to arrive at a set of results, and then to rapidly evaluate those results to determine which are most likely to provide the appropriate and accurate answer. Given the lack of a "perfect" search engine, much of the quality of the search experience today relies on the knowledge, skills, and abilities of users who come to the search engine. Accessing the web is now easier than ever, although it is certainly easier for some than it is for others. Even as the network continues to reach out across the globe, a second-level digital divide becomes clearer, between those who are skilled users of the internet and those who are not. Different people have different aptitudes and different patterns of use when it comes to searching the web, and so it is a more useful resource to some than it is to others (Hargittai 2002a).

A large part of that has to do with digital literacy more broadly: being good at searching requires more than being able to use a search engine well, even if web search is seen by many as the most prominent part of digital literacy (Alexander, Adams Becker, & Cummins 2016). A good searcher needs to have a mental model of how the web is organized, and how the search engine relates to that structure. She needs to be able to critically analyze the problem she is seeking to address, and be able to evaluate, summarize, and make use of the resources she finds. In other words, use of a search engine is one important part of a broader repertoire of searching skills, which in turn is part of a broader range of literacies. There are reasons to be concerned about the variability of such skills, particularly given the kind of effect this has on educational, occupational, and health outcomes. There are some hopeful signs that digital literacy is improving across the board (Eshet-Alkalai & Chajut 2009), and, at the same time, search engines have reduced the need for some of the technical knowledge previously required to use them most effectively. But the question of matching skilled searchers with capable tools will always be with us.

Searching skills

It is commonly believed that searching requires no skill at all, and even now people tend to believe that "digital natives," those who grew up with web access throughout their childhood, have had sufficient exposure to search engines to have natural expertise. While young people may not remember a time before search engines, we have known for some time that this does not mean that they are particularly adept at using them (Heine 2007). In fact, many have next to no understanding of how the web is structured, how material ends up there, or how to alter a search query to produce better results (Rowlands et al. 2008). Instead, the web is seen by many as simply some sort of extension of Google. Some of the things many of us now do when we have a question to answer are second nature; because these behaviors are so ingrained, we fail to remember that they are not part of the average seeker's collection of skills.

There are really two dangers here. The first is assuming that, because these "digital natives" are members of a generation that has been immersed in digital networking, they represent the cutting edge of its use. This would suggest that those who have different schema for seeking, for example, academic information are merely behind the times. The other mistake, perhaps unsurprisingly the one made by experienced librarians and scholars, is to assume that the web and search engines are always less appropriate tools for finding reliable information. It does not take much insight to notice that college students today are likely to turn to a large search engine to make initial inquiries on academic topics, rather than to the library catalog or databases. Those who teach high schoolers have suggested that the availability of search engines has changed substantially what it now means for them to do research, with students very likely to use Google in a typical research project (94 percent of teachers agreed), and far less likely to use textbooks, newspapers, or library databases (Purcell et al. 2012). As of 2009, more than 40 percent of the material college students used for research assignments came from general-use search engines like Google (Primary Research Group 2009). This can cause a significant disconnect between those who have traditionally been guardians of knowledge and new students.

In practice, students use the internet because it is convenient, and because it often provides them with current information in a format that is easily accessible. They are more likely to do this in their homes than in school, either because access at school is more difficult, or because they have more freedom to discover on their own at home (Levin & Arafeh 2002), though, particularly at earlier ages, lack of availability and close monitoring of their activities can also condition their home use (Ferguson et al. 2015). Unfortunately, despite the popularity of using search engines to find school-related information on the web, students may have more confidence in their ability to find and evaluate information than is warranted. In one survey, for example, while 92 percent of the users were confident in their searching abilities, 62 percent were unaware of any distinction between paid search results and unpaid results (Fallows 2005). It makes sense that students are using search engines more, and it is fair to expect that searching information systems will be an important part of their work experiences as they get older. For that reason, among others, it is important to think about search engine use not just as an auxiliary skill, but as an important part of a new literacy.

The skill most likely to affect the success of a search, at least when it comes to the traditional desktop, general search engine, is the ability to choose the appropriate search phrase. How can you know which terms, or combination of terms, best target the information you are after? To know how to choose the best search terms, you must understand how the search engine indexes the web, and pick terms that exploit this process. First, you must understand that search engines, at their core, represent an index of terms on the web; that, for the most part, they do not attempt to summarize pages, for example – at least not yet. Understanding search engines as indexes means that the searcher is able to create a mental model of a webpage that meets their needs, and then can pick the search terms that are likely to be present on that page.

The searcher is likely to be even better prepared if they know that most search engines look for words, and sometimes phrases, that distinguish the page from other pages – that is, particularly uncommon phrases. Finding a single uncommon term is not an easy prospect. There are a limited number of terms in any language. English is particularly rich in this regard; the second edition of the *Oxford English Dictionary* contains just over 228,000 words, to which you must add hundreds of thousands of technical terms, borrowed terms from Latin and other languages, and proper nouns. In short, English alone probably contains several million potential search terms. But the web contains at least several billion English-language pages, each of them with a collection of these words. It is clear that the word "the" is of no use at all in answering any sort of specific question. Short, common words like "the" or "to" are generally considered "stop words" and ignored by search engines precisely because they are so useless.

In addition, most search engines look for words that "matter." If you look at the index at the end of this book, you will find that it does not contain most of the words on this page. The author and publisher have selected words and phrases they think are most distinctive of a discussion, and excluded words like "excluded," because they are so general as to be useless. Search engines actively exclude only a very small number of words, but most engines give added weight to terms and phrases that appear frequently on a given page, and comparatively less frequently on the rest of the web. This allows for the results to reflect pages that are less likely to mention a term "in passing." Even knowing this, however, single terms are unlikely to be particularly successful in returning useful results.

Marc Prensky (2004) suggests that "pretty much every Digital Native can program to some extent, even if it is only setting up and personalizing his or her cell phone, or using 'and' or 'or' in search engines." On the contrary, it is clear that, while expert searchers once used these "Boolean operators" and other constraints on their searches (Hogan 1998), the vast majority (at least 92 percent) of everyday searchers were unaware of these operators, let alone more specialized ways of tailoring a query. (Boolean operators allow search engine users to tailor searches that systematically include or exclude results containing particular keywords or matching other criteria.) It may be that, once again, we are applying pre-search engine experiences in information retrieval to a new system. In 2003, Bernard Jansen tested out the hypothesis that searchers would have more success when using complex queries, and determined that the use of Boolean operators is "generally not worth the trouble for the typical Web searcher." As a result, explicit ways of constraining search either have been removed, or are often not obviously available to the average user.

One of the best ways of constraining a search is to use multiple search terms. As noted above, any English-language word is likely to show up on thousands, or even millions, of individual pages, but by combining even two words, a searcher can reduce the number of results significantly. Several years ago, a game emerged around this principle, called "Googlewhacking," in which the aim was to find two terms that appeared together on only a single page.[1] The difficulty of that task illustrates the reason for using multiple search terms.

On average, most people who enter a query on a search engine follow it up with another query or two, modifying their search in order to achieve a better result (Jansen, Spink, & Saracevic 2000). In many of these cases, the user is merely retyping the query, or adjusting spelling. In others, they realize that they need to provide a further restriction in order to narrow the results they have received. Someone interested in buying a large jungle cat might type the query "buy a jaguar" into Google.[2] Perhaps unsurprisingly, most of the initial results will be about an automobile. They would recognize this and type, perhaps, "buy a jaguar –car" if they knew that the minus sign excludes search terms, or they might type "buy a jaguar animal" if they didn't know that. Experienced searchers expect their searching to be iterative, refining keywords and engaging in focused browsing until the search goals are met (Hölscher & Strube 2000). In some cases, the search engine can help to refine the search in some way or even suggest potential avenues for limiting the results.

Expert searchers recognize that search is not only an iterative process, but one that is rarely linear and requires seeking out the concepts that surround a problem or question (Webber 2002). In other words, the query and search strategy is likely to change as more information becomes available. That information is unlikely to come from a single "winning" source, but is a result of gathering, evaluating, and comparing information from a range of sources. Bates (1989) has famously termed this approach to information-seeking "berrypicking," and differentiates it from the classical model of information retrieval. Even basic information-seeking online is a complicated process, and since it is unlikely that a single interface is best able to provide support for the variety of types of searches and searchers, a diversity of different search engines and techniques is crucial.

Some searchers assume that, when they use a search engine, especially when a search results in hundreds of thousands of pages, the search engine has indexed the entire web. Many, however, recognize that search engines differ significantly in the amount of the web they have successfully indexed. At the peak of early search engine innovation, Bharat and Broder (1998) found that only 1.4 percent of the pages managed to make it into all four of the most popular search engines; the rest were present on one or more of the engines, but not all. For those inexperienced with search, a single search on a large search engine may seem like enough. In fact, the same query on several search engines independently, or through a "meta-search engine," can yield a wider range of results.

Even the most complete search engine is likely to have missed much of what is called the "deep web" or "dark web." That might even be a good thing. As one group of early search engine pioneers noted, "It is safe to say that at least 99% of the available data is of no interest to at least 99% of the users" (Bowman et al. 1994), and, as a result, a general-purpose search engine probably does not need to index the entirety of the web at once. Some estimate that fully 80 percent of the content on the web is hidden from the general-purpose horizontal search engines (Ratzan 2006), while others suggest that proportion is much, much larger, estimating that, for every page in a major search engine's index, there are 500 missing (Sullivan 2000). Especially if the latter estimate remains true today, the sheer size and rate of growth of the web is enough to suggest why search engines have an incomplete index, but there are several other reasons, as well.

The search engine's crawler must usually be able to follow a hyperlink to arrive at and index a page; if the page is not hyperlinked from another HTML page somewhere on the web, it is unlikely to be indexed. Anything other than HTML – including document formats (Adobe Acrobat or Microsoft Word, for example), applets and other executable files, archived ("zipped") files, video, and audio – presents a novel challenge to a search engine, and that challenge is even greater when there are hyperlinks within those documents. Things like live feeds, links to virtual worlds, or even robots that can be controlled from the web (see, e.g., Schulz et al. 2000), are very difficult to anticipate and make sense of in the context of search. Much of the material available through the web can only be accessed through local searches on individual sites. Consider, for example, all of the pages available from a public library's web portal. There is probably a page for each book available in the library, but these pages probably do not appear as results from a search on a general-purpose site. For Amazon, where such links help their bottom line, a more complete crawl is desirable.

Finally, a large proportion of the web is explicitly excluded from web crawlers. This can occur in at least four ways. First, many websites require a username and password to view some or all of their content. Sometimes this login information is even free of charge, but general-purpose search engines are usually unable to obtain an account in order to index these "walled gardens." Second, some sites employ the "robot exclusion protocol," which explicitly instructs search engine crawlers to ignore some or all of the pages on a site. Third, some pages present different information depending on the location of the viewer. By noting the IP address of the visitor, the web server can determine what country or city the visitor is coming from and change the language and content of the site accordingly. Although it is frowned upon by search engines, some even present a completely different set of pages to the crawlers from those that appear to the user. Fourth, documents on the site may not be accessible using traditional web protocols, either because they are in a format other than HTML or because they are routed through a different protocol from traditional HTTP (using the TOR Onion Router, for example).

Expert searchers know about the deep web, and know – at least within particular domains – how to access it. This approach brings back the "shopping mall" model, and requires familiarity with specialist search engines and directories. That familiarity is likely to come only with experience or focused exploration. If the average web surfer is looking for information on an individual, she is likely to key that person's name into a general-purpose search engine in the hope that something will come of it. With more experience, she might turn to search engines dedicated to the task (Zoominfo, Spock, Spokeo, Pipl, or one of many others), search social networking sites like LinkedIn or Facebook, or check industry organization or company membership directories. The even more experienced might access proprietary networks and public records compilation services. While metasearch engines are drawing some of this material together, it is likely that the deep web will be with us for some time to come (Sherman & Price 2001).

Throughout the search process, the user is likely to be evaluating results, allowing the nature of the search to evolve as more information is located. The precise strategy differs from searcher to searcher, but as most search engines provide some form of summary of the results, the evaluation begins there. Ironically, part of that evaluation stems from trust in the search engine itself. The mere fact that a search engine has suggested a site lends it credibility. Eye-tracking studies have shown that we are drawn to the top of the first page of results, and may ignore results that are lower on the page, let alone buried on subsequent results pages (Guan & Cutrell 2007). That trust extends to the sites themselves, and if a search engine leads a user to a page that is not at all relevant, many users – especially inexperienced users – will continue to browse that site, assuming they were sent there for a reason.

There is evidence that, although education is important, sophisticated search behaviors are most directly a result of practice: users with more experience with search are likely to be more sophisticated searchers (Howard & Massanari 2007; Liu et al. 2013). It is important to keep in mind that, even as search engine users are changing, there will probably always be not just a range of skill levels, but a diversity of approaches to search. Just as teachers are coming to understand that their classrooms are filled with students of not just differing abilities, but different orientations to the material, those interested in search need to recognize a spectrum of skills and approaches (Gardner 1983). As people become more experienced searchers, rather than approaching some idealized vision of a search engine user, they tend to adopt more complex and individualized approaches to their search activity.

A diversity of search

Researchers readily admit that searchers on the web are probably more diverse in background and in intent when compared with users of early information retrieval systems (Jansen, Spink, & Saracevic 2000), but the prototypical search experience is still thought of as academic, in part because that is what those designing information retrieval systems are most familiar with. As a practical matter, searching for material in order to write a paper represents a fairly specific, and relatively infrequent, use of search engines. Andrei Broder (2002) has suggested that, in addition to the traditional informational searches, searches may also be navigational (e.g., wanting to find a site with music reviews) or transactional (e.g., finding where to buy a cheap moped). Though some work has been done to try to understand the relationship between concepts and the choice of keywords, this is likely to be different when looking for an academic source than it is for many other contexts.

Consider a specific example: just before a long trip, a colleague's daughter managed to get her head stuck in a toilet training seat, and he had to try to figure out how to free her. Rather than turning to relatives or a doctor, he did what many would in recent years: he turned to a search engine. A quick search for "potty seat head stuck" yielded a number of results, including instructional videos, and several suggestions for removing the seat. This and other minor emergencies are averted on a daily basis thanks to both the production of diverse amateur content for the web, and the ability to find it. The web tells us how to do things. Finding this information is often as easy as searching for the process you wish to learn about – like "replace shower fixture" – and most web users have sought such information (Madden 2005).

Many searches are related to planned action: for example, deciding where to travel, whether a restaurant is good, if it is a good idea to use a particular method of organizing an office, or which automobile to buy. This sort of information gathering in support of a decision is a very common use of the web. The process is likely to involve not seeking an exact solution to a problem, but rather gathering a set of sources and information that can then be evaluated and analyzed by the searcher. Alison Head and Michael Eisenberg (2011) looked at how college students researched solutions and information for everyday life, rather than to complete academic work. Though they gather information from a range of sources, the web has become an important source of information about everyday life needs. They discovered that college students found themselves seeking out news and current events, making purchases, in need of health-related information, seeking employment, planning travel, finding friends or experts, and solving everyday domestic problems, among other issues. While college students represent a particular demographic, those genres of search cut across most other demographics as well. One survey suggests that when people of all ages have a "need in the moment," 87 percent first turn to search on their phones (Gevelber 2016). The students often turned first to Google (sometimes followed by Wikipedia), to answer their questions. Decomposing a complex search problem into its constituent elements and analytically mining the web represents what we commonly think of as "critical thinking," and search patterns may represent this. But many effective searches also bring in more intuitive approaches that reflect pressures of time and attention common to every search task, and the expertise brought by experience (Klein 1999).

Researchers are also interested in the process of "re-finding" information that has been sought out and discovered in the past (Aula, Jhaveri, & Käki 2005; Capra & Pérez-Quiñones 2005). Search engines have often retained a history of an individual's searches, and sometimes provided that information to users, or, for privacy reasons, allowed them to delete the record. On the web, the traditional way of remembering a site was to bookmark it, but users have increasingly relied on the web search engines rather than a personal or shared bookmark file. If someone is able to remember enough about a particular page, it makes sense that they should be able to conduct a search that is very specific. As more and more of the world is in some way represented on the web, the process of remembering will also become linked to search in interesting ways. It might be valuable to think of "re-finding" not as a subset of finding, but the other way around. The search for new information may be profitably conceptualized as "re-finding" pages that you never encountered before. How is it that we model the page we are looking for, and how does our experience as a search engine user shape that model?

A related approach is ongoing, real-time search, and although this shares a great deal with the process of search, it rarely goes under that name. The idea of "web analytics" has subsumed what would once have been considered search, and still remains part of the broader question of search and findability. For those engaged in online analytics, the question is rarely one of finding a needle in a haystack, but rather of understanding the overall form and structure of the haystack itself. In these cases, it is not re-finding existing results, but reusing searches that have worked in the past, and making sense of the results both as a whole and in comparison with past results. As we shall see, the future of search is bound up closely with this particular genre of search behavior and is the subject of a great deal of current research and development, especially as humans have become less and less involved in the process.

In these types of searches, and in many others, it can be helpful to search by similarity to previously discovered pages. On some search engines, a result may be followed by a link to find "more like this." Given the difficulty of interpreting the average searcher's queries, a great deal of research seeks new ways of finding conceptual similarity among documents, to allow for this sort of query-free searching. The picture that emerges shows search to be a complex process, a process that becomes even more complex as the kinds of answers people expect become more involved. There remains a place for simple search interfaces, and there seems little doubt that the largest search engines will continue to develop these, particularly for the mobile user. At present, the interfaces for expert searchers are less capable than they could be. By understanding expert searchers, and their needs for querying, extracting, recording, and recombining data iteratively, we may also better understand how to support the less sophisticated searcher as well.

Tracking searches and searchers

One of the difficulties in modeling a perfect search strategy is that the search engines are, themselves, in a constant state of flux, and at least some of that flux is hidden. An industry has grown up around understanding just how search engines are operating at any given moment. At one point, when updates were less frequent, webmasters referred to the "Google dance," during which the latest iteration of Google's search algorithms would decide which pages would receive more privileged placement in search results. Now, they have largely given up on the practice of naming and charting Google updates, as the search engine is constantly changing and trialing new kinds of signals.

At the same time, major search engines have continuously changed the way their systems worked in order to respond to pressures both from those who would seek to exploit the search engine to present their own pages in the best light, and from users who demand more accurate results even as the information environment becomes more complex. There is no ideal search strategy because search engine developers are trying to make the engine better fit how the user is already searching.

The problem is how to understand just what the user is doing. One of the first sources of such data is "Transaction Log Analysis" (TLA). Most interactions on the web are recorded in some way. When a person visits a website, that site records a set of information: usually the time of the visit, the user's IP address, some basic information about the user's browser and operating system, and what page referred the user to the current page. Search logs provide the same kind of data, but also include information about what queries are entered. At a basic level that is all a log contains, but more information can be inferred from these individual entries. A path can be constructed that indicates attempted and successful searches, changes in keywords and the like, for example (Jansen & Pooch 2000).

Simply looking at the queries that users generate can provide some information about how people search. This may be part of the reason that a ticker at Google headquarters shows real-time queries of the search engine on one wall. The first challenge to understanding these queries is the sheer volume of the data. One such early analysis, for example, attempted to make sense of half a billion queries on the AltaVista search engine (Silverstein et al. 1999). While the broad category of "big data" has only recently gained popularity, search engine data has always been at the edge of the computing and networking capabilities available.

These transaction logs may be enhanced in a number of ways, many of which come under the umbrella term "web analytics." Most search engines now track which links the user clicks, allowing them to link queries to the results the user finds most interesting. This kind of tracking of implicit decisions is particularly important for search engines, as it is possible to infer the relevance of the produced results by seeing which items the user clicks through (Joachims et al. 1997). The use of cookies provides even more extensive opportunities for tracking what users are doing when they search. Since Google provides a federated login to all of their services, it also means that they are able to track user behavior across applications. A large number of websites use Google Analytics, a free web analytics package, as well as advertising through AdWords, which presumably provides Google with even more information about what users are doing even when they are not visiting Google-branded sites. This sort of tracking by DoubleClick, the web advertising company, raised privacy concerns years ago. DoubleClick was eventually acquired by Google. At present, user behavior is closely analyzed by a number of online platforms, and often combined across platforms to create a surprisingly detailed dossier of individuals' online habits.

Although transaction logs, even in their most enhanced state, usually reside on the host machine, in some cases transactions are recorded on the client side. This can provide a much clearer picture of how a single user makes use of the web, and their strategies for finding information. Companies that provide ratings and traffic data often rely on client-side (or proxy server) logs of representative – and sometimes not-so-representative – web users to determine which sites are particularly popular. Those logs, when employed by researchers, provide the advantage of tracking exactly where users go on the internet, as they move from site to site. This provides a much broader context for examining the search process across sites. For example, it allows us to better understand how search on a search engine is often followed by searches on internal sites (Ortiz-Cordova, Yang, & Jansen 2015). Despite increasing concentration in the use of a single search engine, search continues to be a multi-platform activity.

Many such logs provide even more detailed information, including recording the content of viewed sites, keystrokes, mouse position, or the use of applications other than the web browser (Westerman et al. 1996; Arroyo, Selker, & Wei 2006; Menchen-Trevino & Karr 2012). Each of these approaches has the advantage of being relatively unobtrusive. In the case of server-side logs, most users do not even know they are being tracked, though well-publicized releases of search logs may change this awareness. It is reasonable to assume that users might behave in different ways when they recognize that they are being observed, and so this sort of analysis "in the wild" remains a particularly widely used source of information. While the information may be unbiased, it can be somewhat diffuse, and requires a great deal of inference if you are interested in users' intents.

Greater availability of eye-tracking hardware has provided a new tool for understanding how people interact with the search engine interface. Eye tracking allows the researcher to determine what elements of a page draw the searcher's attention, and in what order. Much of this work supports a concept called "information foraging," which argues that searchers are particularly sensitive to cues ("information scent") that suggest that their next step will lead them closer to the information they are seeking, without wasting their time (Pirolli & Card 1999). Eye-tracking studies demonstrate where attention rests as a viewer scans a webpage. On results pages, the eye is generally drawn to a "golden triangle" at the upper left corner, paying the most attention to the first result on the page, and gradually less to each of the subsequent results (Granka, Joachims, & Gay 2004). This miserly defense of attention seems to be a learned behavior, and more common among more experienced searchers (Aula, Päivi, & Räihä 2005).

Few of these approaches move beyond the screen to effectively observe the searcher directly, rather than just documenting her transactions. User-centered design has pushed developers to take into account the physical contexts and intentions of their users and how they behave when they interact with the computer. Sophisticated use of log data can allow researchers to infer some of the context for searching (e.g., Adar et al. 2007) and to detect broad patterns (Beitzel et al. 2004). Unlike log data, which can be collected relatively easily and automatically, and surveys, which often rely on accurate self-reflection, direct observation of users engaged in search activities is expensive, time-consuming, but can ultimately be very valuable. Eszter Hargittai (2002b) and others have led efforts to make sense of the process of search from a perspective that goes beyond the interface level, and seeks to understand the motivations and social imperatives that shape the experience of search. As she notes, logs fail to provide data about how people react to events in the interfaces – the degree, for example, to which they are satisfied or frustrated by their searches. As we will see in the next chapter, search is inherently social, and so to understand search, you must understand the social context in which it occurs.

The adaptive search engine

When given a question to answer, more than a quarter of adolescent searchers typed that exact question into a search engine, rather than coming up with keywords (Guinee, Eagleton, & Hall 2003). From the perspective of more traditional information retrieval systems, such an approach is naïve and ineffective, but that model of information-seeking was changing even before the web came along (Belkin, Oddy, & Brooks 1982). The use of fully formed questions in a search engine query is now a mark of experience (Liu et al. 2013). Search engines have answered the challenge by creating engines geared specifically to question-asking (Ask.com), and by assuming that search terms are only part of a phrase when specifically constrained. By 2013, Google had rewritten its query system to focus on this kind of "conversational search" and dubbed its new algorithm "Hummingbird."

Hummingbird was in part the outcome of more than a decade of research and design dedicated to the idea of "semantic search." As noted in the first chapter, search engines have long started with an index of the terms on a page, and particularly those that occurred more frequently in the target text than they do on the web as a whole. (This is often called tf–idf: term frequency – inverse document frequency.) This approach lent itself to "gaming" the search engine by including a large number of false keywords on the page, a strategy called "keyword stuffing." A number of approaches have been used to mitigate this, but the idea of a semantic web – an idea that had been promoted as early as 2001 by the founder of the web, Tim Berners-Lee (Berners-Lee, Hendler, & Lassila 2001) – found its home in semantic search. Basically, the idea was that the semantic content of the web, the basic concepts and their relationships as described by web documents, should be made easily legible not just to machines but to humans. The actual explicit coding of semantic data proceeded very slowly, but search engines have sought to extract the implicit semantic content both from webpages and from user queries. For Google, Hummingbird was a culmination of such efforts, which drew on the semantic modeling that was already happening and made it better suited to what is often called a natural-language or conversational interface. (Google titles the ability to search the web via voice, introduced in 2013 for the web via the Chrome browser, "conversational search," and the introduction of Google Home in 2016, along with similar capabilities on Android phones, allowed people to ask these questions without being in front of a screen.) Humans do not need to learn to find better keywords if the search engines learn to better understand how humans organize knowledge and ask questions.

Natural-language question answering represents a large-scale trend in search online that runs parallel to traditional search engines. In fact, question-and-answer sites are sometimes referred to as "human-powered search." Sites like Stack Overflow, which provides answers to programming problems, not only have become wildly popular, but the skill of asking questions well and the complementary skill of answering questions effectively have come to represent special value among certain communities. The *New York Times* reported that some programmers were including their Stack Overflow badges in résumés in order to demonstrate that they were capable of asking and answering questions effectively (Carey 2012). A more general question-answering site, Quora, attracts people like a former US president and Canadian prime minister, one of the founders of Facebook, and many other celebrities, politicians, scientists, and artists. As of 2006, it had roughly 100 million monthly active users, roughly a third that of Twitter. Other sites, including Jelly and Cha Cha, similarly seek out experts online to provide credible answers. Of course, that problem of capturing expertise and locating experts has long been the domain of knowledge management within the organization, but by moving it to the web, it forms a new kind of online search.

This approach also narrows the space between the original hand-curated web directories, searches for information held by particular people, and searches of people by people. Especially in the last case, a phenomenon in China, called "human flesh search," has attracted significant attention (F.-Y. Wang et al. 2010). Rather than a particular website, this describes episodes in which individuals are found, and sometimes harassed, through the gathering of information by users on a number of different platforms. It has been used particularly in rooting out corruption and scams. It bears a resemblance to what is often called "doxing" in the western context: releasing private information about an individual, including phone numbers, addresses, and other personally identifying information. While search engines are becoming ever better at ferreting information and connections from documents, the ability to coordinate and collect human expertise remains an area that is likely to continue to be exploited moving forward, and search engines will become better at identifying and leveraging human expertise.

The evidence suggests that in some ways users continue to want the same things from search engines that they have always wanted: answers. On the other hand, their interactions with search engines evolve even as the search engines change. We can turn to the most basic source of data, the queries themselves, for some evidence of this. A group of researchers compared queries on the Excite search engine in 1997, 1999, and 2001 (Spink et al. 2002). There was a shift during the period from seeking pornography to finding information about commerce, shopping, and work. Contrary to what you might expect, it did not seem that users became more adept at using the Excite search engine during this four-year period. The style of people's queries changed very little over the period, and their willingness to dig beyond the first page of results was reduced. The authors conclude that search engines need to improve, in order to "assist users with query construction and modification, spelling, and analytical problems that limit their ability or willingness to persist in finding the information they need." An ethnographic study of college students' search habits (Duke & Asher 2011) likewise noted that Google's pervasiveness had changed students' expectations: "Google's simplicity and single search box seems to have created the expectation among students of a specific search experience within the library: in particular, a single search box that quickly accesses many resources and an overreliance on simple keyword search" (p. 72). Not just keywords, though – as Google has improved its ability to respond to searches, Helen Georgas (2014) has noted "a high reliance on natural language searches." The result is that, as another study reported, "students are confident about their online research skills; clearly, this has little to do with their success in finding relevant scholarly sources" (Bloom & Deyrup 2012).

Search engines continue to slowly evolve to meet the needs of the searchers. One of the greatest challenges to search, and something that is fairly obvious when studying search logs, is that people incorrectly spell keywords related to their search. One way to help users find what they are looking for is to help them to use keywords that are correctly spelled, and therefore more likely to appear in the target documents. Simple spell-check against static word lists represented a good first step, but spelling errors were even more common for items like the proper names of people and places. Google has harnessed our collective ability to spell, and, by grouping near-misses, can suggest a more popular spelling.

This approach extends to other areas. Over time, and billions of queries, it may be possible to notice certain consistencies among query terms. Someone searching for "John," "Paul," and "George," the engine could suggest, may also want to include "Ringo." By tracking which links are clicked, search engines can provide something akin to a voting system. If the top result for a search for "Mars" is consistently avoided, it is likely that, despite whatever algorithm led to it being placed at the top of the results list, it is not much use to searchers, as a rule, and so it may be demoted or removed.

A significant portion of search engine research now focuses on understanding the web, in addition to the searcher. Rather than merely creating an index that indicates what terms appear on various pages, or what the link structure might suggest about the importance of a page, these efforts try to discover what concepts are important on a page, and how this concept or topic might relate to other pages (e.g., Dittenbach, Berger, & Merkl 2006). The Text REtrieval Conferences (TREC) have turned an eager eye toward the web over the years, and support efforts to provide for understanding of web content in order to aid searching.

These kinds of redesign of the search engine's processes and interface are generally a long-cycle response to user behavior. Even the development of vertical search engines to meet the needs of a perceived subgroup represents this sort of slow evolution. There is also the more immediate response to individuals' particular contexts for a search, or their searching history. Broadly, we can refer to these as "personalization": an ongoing response to users that focuses on their individual needs.

In particular, the rapid increase of mobile users of search engines allows for the user interface to respond "on the fly." Because mobile search behavior tends to be different from search behavior at the desktop, and because it is becoming the standard (Google has suggested that their focus is on maintaining an index specifically for mobile users, and will update their index for desktop-based searchers less frequently: Ratcliff 2016), understanding how it differs from desktop search and how to react to those differences is important (Church et al. 2007). At a very basic level, many search engines make use of alternative interfaces to present themselves differently on a small mobile device from how they might be presented on a larger display, but they extend this to include information that is more likely to be geospatially relevant, and provide results pages that are more easily read on a mobile device. These uses of contextual cues provide ways of reducing the complexity of search and predicting what wanderers might need to look for online at a given moment. Localmind, an application that was acquired by AirBnB, provided local Q&A for questions that were directly related to the user's location. As Josh Catone (2009) notes, Twitter already forms a basis for local search, but there are more advances to be made in search that intersects with continuous movement through our everyday spaces. In the coming years, mobile search is likely to be a significant driver in developing new ways of accessing complex information while on the move, from conversational interfaces to augmented reality, and research that better understands the needs and capabilities of those users is sorely needed (Goh, Lee, & Razikin 2015).

Search engine personalization allows the engine to be reconfigured on the fly. In some cases, the searcher can customize the engine by directly altering how it appears and functions. A number of experiments have sought active user involvement in shaping the interfaces directly. On the Aftervote metasearch engine, for example, which was available in the late 2000s, users could indicate whether they wanted beginner, intermediate, or advanced interfaces, as well as how to weight the results from various search engines, whether to blacklist certain sites, and how results are presented. However, active personalization is generally ignored by users seeking rapid answers to immediate questions. Personalization can also occur without any sort of direct input from searchers (Pitkow et al. 2002), and this has become the norm.

Google News, for example, monitors which stories people select and provides similar stories on its "recommended" portion of the page. Search personalization represents one of the most active areas of research, but, as with search generally, by privileging certain sources over others there is the danger that a searcher may become trapped by her own search history.

Nonetheless, some of the cognitive work of "re-finding" is reduced when the search engine remembers for you.

The mind of a search engine

In 2015, Google introduced RankBrain as part of its indexing capability, a system that draws on machine learning to better interpret visitors' queries and match them with pages. Machine learning is basically a process by which computers can use a network of relationships in order to learn to recognize related patterns over time. This has often been dependent on extracting particular "features" from the data to be categorized. Once these features – elements that can effectively be used to make distinctions in the data – are identified, they can be used to classify patterns and make good estimates of similar items. So, for example, if you wish to create a system that can recognize a person's face from among many hundreds, you first would want to identify a way to automatically detect the shape and location of the eyes, the nose, etc., so that these could then be used as a group to compare with earlier examples (Brunelli & Poggio 1993). As machine learning approaches improved, much of the focus was on identifying the most important features in a collection of data and seeking ways of extracting them and using them to classify items.

Particularly over the last decade or so, there has been an increased interest in a different set of approaches to machine learning, usually coming under the umbrella term "deep learning" (Arel, Rose, & Kamowski 2010). One of the early applications of such approaches, and particularly a family of models called convolutional neural networks (CNNs), was to the problem of recognizing images. Rather than creating tools to explicitly detect edges and shapes, given enough examples, CNNs are able to generate the best approach to detecting the features that matter most. As a result, deep learning approaches can often be applied to problems where there is a large collection of complex (high-dimensionality) data that needs to be sorted, classified, or otherwise understood. This closely describes the challenges of internet search.

Because these technologies are generally hidden from the user, there is little recognition of this quiet revolution across domains. While the ideas behind deep learning remain outside much of the public discourse, it has come to wider attention through Google's release of the Deep Dream application in 2015 (Mordvintsev, Olah, & Tyka 2015). When CNNs (in this case a framework Google called Inception that had been developed to help to classify images for its Image Search) have been trained on visual data, they can be run, effectively, in reverse, to reveal what is being detected across an image. The psychedelic results, which often yield dogs and other animals even when dogs are not present in the original image (because of the early images the network was trained on), led to wider interest in at least one area in which deep learning was being used.

But this approach can be used to find patterns within a range of domains, especially those for which there are very large numbers of individual examples, and where sufficient processing resources are available. In particular, deep learning approaches have been successfully used to more easily recognize human speech, to make sense of and translate written work, within recommender networks, and in a range of bioinformatics applications. Naturally, they are also well suited to web search-related tasks. RankBrain is the most widely known example, but a number of web platforms are seeking to leverage deep learning to better structure search. This includes not just the search in the traditional sense of query and results pages, but also the more passive form of search that appears in the construction of news feeds for web platforms like Facebook, Twitter, Instagram, or Pinterest. Across the computing industry, there has been an extraordinary effort to apply these new approaches to artificial intelligence. In 2016, Google, Facebook, Amazon, IBM, and Microsoft formed a partnership to share standards (and likely to lobby governments), while Apple has struck out on its own and one of the best-funded efforts, OpenAI, is backed by Elon Musk, a relative newcomer to the area. It seems likely that the future of most companies that are built on the social internet will rely not just on breakthroughs in the application of artificial intelligence to solve new kinds of problems, but on making those systems more efficient and quicker. When, for example, Facebook needs to deploy billions of AI-driven agents, the computing power required is enormous (Higginbotham 2016).

While at present forms of deep learning are being added to existing search processes, it is very likely that they will in turn change what it means to search. Given at least two widely held dreams of future search – the conversational agent and the predictive mind-reader – deep learning and related approaches that rest at the intersection of statistics and artificial intelligence will have an increasing role to play. Conversational search will feel more natural to use, and be better able to figure out what you are trying to look for. Predictive search systems will probably not be called "search engines," since they "recommend" and "curate" rather than react to individual queries. Search engines that find within the behavior of millions of users will be able to discern needs that a human observer would be unlikely to detect. At least in some respects, our future platforms are likely to know us better than we know ourselves. In turn, that means that what we know about how search is happening, as well as the set of skills we might develop around search, are going to change as well.

The adaptive society

Google's corporate history notes that, when founders Larry Page and Sergey Brin were initially looking for a buyer for the technology that would become Google, one portal CEO told them, "Our users don't really care about search" (Google

2007). In retrospect, such a comment appears staggeringly myopic, but it was probably not inaccurate. Users did not care about search until they learned what it was and came to depend on it. The changes that have come about with the rise of the search engine have been wider than search skills or search engine prowess. We are essentially information-driven creatures, and when the primary way in which we navigate our informational world changes, it is fair to assume that those changes will pervade other parts of our culture.

We now spend some part of our day connected to systems that aim to anticipate our informational needs and reduce the necessity for us to learn to find information ourselves. The availability of a search engine and easily searched data makes traditional forms of information organization seem tedious and dated. The vertical file that brought the industrial revolution into the office is slowly giving way to the power of search. Using files, like using maps and newspaper indexes, is not a natural skill, and, as our search engine expertise increases, we may lose some of our familiarity with those earlier technologies of findability. Our mobile devices tell us which street to turn on to get to the psychiatrist, even if we cannot correctly spell her name or profession. (Although Varnhagen et al. 2009 found that children who were better spellers were more successful in their searches.) Unfortunately, these earlier ways of knowing may have appealed to different kinds of knowledge.

An article in the *San Francisco Chronicle* described the operations of that city's new citywide information line that could be reached by residents and visitors dialing 311 within the city limits (Colin 2007). Initially intended as a way to have a single phone number for all city services, many of the calls were not so easy to connect to a city department. The article explains the calls as modern human nature molded by search engines: "Anonymity. Technology. Excessive information gathering. The elements of 311 are very much those of the Internet age (do people still say that?), and in ways the service resembles a kind of Google hotline just for San Francisco. As with Google, it seems the service can give rise to the questions, rather than vice versa." There can be little doubt that search engines have made the web more useful and provide a valuable service, but to return to the question asked by Plato in the *Phaedrus*, what have we lost with these changes?

There are many answers to that question. Martin Nussbaum, a partner in a large New York law firm, recently spoke about his experience with information technology in legal research. He said he was enthusiastic about the way in which technology makes it possible to quickly and easily search for relevant material when preparing for a case. Although not necessarily happy about how information technology had affected other elements of being an attorney, he saw this change as clearly positive. But, upon reflecting on his early days as a new attorney, in the physical law library of his firm, he remembered that there was once more of an opportunity for serendipity, discovery, and learning that may not be as likely with the new searchable sources. This nostalgia for the stacks is widely felt.

Serendipity was inherent to the initial metaphor for traversing the web: surfing. The metaphor suggested that while you may be moving through the information, there was room to turn around, or take detours, and that the topography of the information encouraged these actions. In the case of Wikipedia, a new term has emerged for the process of wandering from entry to entry: *wikipedestrian*. There is a particular knowledge that is obtained only through exploration that is, even when goal-oriented, open to peripatetic friction. There is room for the web *flâneur*, who has gained an understanding of an area not through the accumulation of facts, but by making a large number of wrong turns.

Serendipity is enjoyable, but it is also important to innovation, Robert Merton argues in his fascinating history of the concept, entitled *The travels and adventures of serendipity* (Merton & Barber 2003). Although searching for materials may seem to be antithetical to serendipity, which has more affinity with browsing than with searching, the above description of "berrypicking" suggests it is a part of the experienced searcher's retinue of skills. Consider someone who goes to a search engine hoping to find a particular product; unless it is the first "hit" on the search engine, and the searcher visits only that site, they are likely to spend some time browsing through the results (Rowley 2002). In other words, searching retains a significant amount of browsing. Indeed, a good system for searching should incorporate what Smith (1964) termed "systematic serendipity." John Palfrey (2015) has noted that there is virtue in a "new nostalgia" for libraries, one that encourages risk-taking and ensures that information browsing will not remain the purview of private corporations and their algorithms. One of the greatest dangers of search by artificial intelligence is that our own search intelligence will atrophy.

Another answer to Plato's question is that students – from kindergarten through graduate school – are using recorded knowledge in new ways. Many people see these as diminished ways, and teachers complain about cut-and-paste essays hastily assembled out of web-based resources. As with serendipity, this is a two-edged sword. Expert users of search engines are able to assemble a much wider range of resources from their armchair than students might have been able to in the university library a decade ago. The kinds of sources they use are clearly changing, but whether these represent somehow a diminution of students' research capabilities remains an open debate. Students rightly question why they should be responsible for memorizing facts that are frequently discoverable on the web at a moment's notice. On the other hand, the availability of such information quickly and easily may make it more difficult to create the kinds of connections that lead to deeper knowledge and wisdom.

If we assume that all knowledge can be available on the web, and that such knowledge can be effectively indexed, the idea that we are becoming search-engine-minded is not troubling.

If, on the other hand, we take it as a given that knowledge is not just a process of accumulating facts, but involves the experience of learning by doing, the idea that answers are always as near as our favorite search engine is problematic. We understand that the educated person possesses a mastery of latent knowledge, "similar in kind to the inarticulate knowledge of knowing one's way about a complex topography, but [with] its range enhanced by the aid of verbal and other linguistic pointers, the peculiar manageability of which enables us to keep track of an immense amount of experience and to rest assured of having access, when required, to many of its countless particulars" (Polanyi 1998 [1952], p. 103). Many decry the lack of technical education and of computer literacy, and, as we have seen, a secondary digital divide exists between those who are able to find information online and those who are not, but at the same time we must seek to avoid the totalizing effects that the fact-oriented search engines seem to encourage.

Arno Penzias (1989) links intelligence to the ability to ask "questions which illuminate." In this, he is hardly alone; the idea that real wisdom comes from finding and asking probative questions is a fairly common one (Arlin 1990). Given that, should we not be concerned by a machine that changes our daily experience of asking questions? It is not too strange to think about the ways in which our technical environment affects our everyday interaction. The popular press is rife with examples of how instant messaging is bleeding over into other forms of communication. If we become accustomed to asking questions of search engines in ways that are necessarily different from those we might ask of another human, can there be any doubt that this will change the way in which we think and interact with one another? How does "search" intersect with "society?"

CHAPTER THREE

Sociable Search

That the term "social search" is redundant has not reduced its popularity. Particularly when we think about the "bias" of the search engine, the most pressing bias is the social soup in which the search engine swims. Every part of the search engine relies on social relationships, expectations, and popularity. Search engines distil the social behaviors of their users, the socially defined structure of the World Wide Web, and our collective creation of knowledge in order to meet other social needs. The idea that search could be anything but social is absurd.

Nonetheless, the term "social search" appears widely, referring to technologies that draw explicitly on connections among people in order to find information more effectively. This chapter addresses this more common view of "social search" – which we might define roughly as the intersection of social networking platforms with search engines – rather succinctly, and then moves on to what we might call the broader social context of search: how does the search engine interact within the broader social spaces of search and discovery, and how is that changing? And, perhaps just as important, may we move search beyond collaboration and toward conviviality?

If search engines have always been social, they are now more sociable. While "social" and "sociable" share the same Latin root, meaning "to unite," the latter connotes a certain degree of companionship, a friendly form of interaction. Judith Donath (2004) pioneered the use of the term "sociable media," which she defines as those media that "enhance communication and the formation of social ties among people."

She distinguishes this approach from ideas that focus on information retrieval. Rather than increasing the flow or accumulation of information, sociable systems perform best when they fulfill the social needs of the community, allowing for the appropriate distribution of attention and social interaction. There already exists a literature surrounding "social navigation" (Munro, Höök, & Benyon 1999; Svensson et al. 2001), but "sociable search" goes beyond systems designed to help groups make sense of an information source, and toward building social capital within search communities.

As with many functions now performed automatically, the process of indexing the web was initially performed by individuals exercising their own judgment. It takes only a glance behind the curtain to recognize that current search engines, while their processes may be automated, still perform in large part through the collection of latent human judgment applied to the content of the web and the value of particular pages. Most search engines now rely implicitly on the links drawn from blogs and other websites, just as web surfers explicitly follow those links. But there has been a revival of openly engaging human judgment in the process of web search. Blogging has spawned a host of social software that is designed to help to connect people together, and those connections mean new ways of finding experts and locating expertise.

As many people look to the future of search, their focus falls on social networks and information sharing. This idea of the social nature of navigation can be traced back to the "trails" of hyperlinks Vannevar Bush (1945) suggested more than 70 years ago, but there remains the pressing question of how best to harness that social component. One particular area in which this becomes important is the functioning of informed democratic processes: public engagement in policy and political campaigns. Sociable search has gained a particular foothold in this venue.

As the Rolling Stones remind us, there is always a tension

between finding what you want, and getting what you need. The emergence of sociable search suggests that we need to find not just information, but each other. Search is important for the individual who wants to be part of a larger social conversation and provides a tool for gaining social efficacy, but a tool capable of linking people together to build social capital and develop collective intelligence is even more important. Searching and browsing represent closely tied forms of finding information online, and sociable search seeks to combine them to discover new ways of navigating our online worlds. Social interaction and social processes distort the contours of search, reinscribing the existing power relationships and accepted knowledge into a new digital framework. Searching before the search engine was likewise conditioned by social context, and the search engine is ultimately a social machine.

Social search

Everything has always been social, but when that word is added in front of everyday activities, it generally connotes "interaction with others via the internet while engaging in some other purposeful activity" or, perhaps more concisely, "social networking + x." This is likewise the case with search, where "social search" generally suggests three related ideas: internal search on social networking platforms, external search engines indexing social networking platforms, and social networking platforms being used as a "signal" to indicate what material on the web is likely to be of particular social relevance.

Sometimes "social search engines" refers to search engines focused on retrieving information from social networking platforms. Search engines like Social Mention and Smashfuse provide search that specifies contributions to social networking platforms. Often mated with "listening" platforms (like that provided by Radian6), these vertical search engines provide users with a tool for interrogating and monitoring social network conversations. But this is a fairly narrow application of the term.

People increasingly use search engines to find things that interest them on the wider web. As of 2014, for example, about as many people ended up at news articles via Facebook as did via search engines (Mitchell, Jurkowitz, & Olmstead 2014). We may not think of the way people use Facebook, often as a repository of collaboratively filtered material from the rest of the web, as "search," exactly. Typing a query into Facebook's search box does, however, cleave more closely to traditional definitions of search engine use. In 2016, Facebook handled more than 2 billion searches per day (Constine 2016), which would – if we considered it a search engine – put it in third place behind Google and Baidu.

Social networking platforms remain one of the more challenging targets to index, due to their scale and the speed with which they change. Often a search is intended to produce results that have to do with an emerging event, and so indexing has to move at the speed of the collective contributions. This has been a challenge for sites like Facebook, which has tried with varying success to create a search system. Its "Graph Search," which debuted in 2013, represented search that drew explicitly on the "social graph" or connections among its users. While it was used, especially by more experienced members of the site, it provided an interesting example of integration between social and search, allowing users to connect content to their own social networks and draw semantic connections to the outside world via a connection to Bing (Spirin et al. 2014). It allowed for structured filtering of information found within Facebook. For example, you could find "people who have friends who live near Phoenix, Arizona and like ice hockey." While Graph Search was popular among "power users" and marketers, it gradually gave way to keyword-based search that is more familiar to everyday users, though certain queries in the structure used by Graph Search still work, and there are ways to access its functionality outside the normal search box.

In 2016, they replaced their "trending" indicators with a new system called Search FYI (Facebook 2016). In part, this was probably a response to criticism around human-curated site-wide trending lists, but the algorithm quickly pushed fake news and other items that seemed unlikely as trends to the fore. It seems likely that Facebook, Twitter, and other sites that draw on massive user contributions will continue to innovate as more and more of the demand for search moves from the traditional web to these platforms.

What is most commonly meant by "social search" is the use of data from social networking platforms to help to inform and rank search results. This is basically a form of search personalization, re-ranking the search engine results not according to personal characteristics, but rather the broader relationships of a searcher, and the interests of her larger social network (Carmel et al. 2009). By 2007, Google had done an abrupt about-face on social search, and began incorporating social signals into its search engine results rankings. Google Social Search was officially announced in 2009, and allowed users to see pages that were related to their connections on various social networks (Siegler 2009). The use of social signals increased when Google made another foray into social networking platforms and introduced Google+. (Orkut, an earlier social networking experiment that was launched before Facebook came into being, was officially shut down in 2014, and a number of other efforts by Google – Buzz, Reader, Wave – have not had staying power.) Indeed, while Google+ is not particularly popular as a social networking site, it is still updated by those who hope to influence Google's search results. The first use of social signals showed up prominently in the search engine results pages, but have largely disappeared. There is speculation that they may be used as one of the many signals that make up Google's ranking algorithm, though Google indicated in 2014 that neither Facebook nor Twitter had any special influence on ranking (Schwartz 2014).

Others have made similar efforts at courting social networks as a part of the search engine interface or to better understand the relationship of web content to social networks. Naturally Google, the most prominent search engine, is particularly important here. But Microsoft's Bing search engine made bolder attempts to include social networks in its search interface, seeking to integrate it with Facebook and Twitter, tying content to selected bloggers, and experimenting with a number of other social network-related interface elements. Today, however, the Bing search results, like Google's, are largely bereft of social connection. Baidu Space, an effort from the Chinese search engine to create a Google+-like social information and networking site, was rolled up in 2015, though the forum system called Baidu Tieba remains. Baidu's search engine indexes the latter, but does not appear to use it to produce signals for ranking results.

There remain a number of experiments that draw explicitly on social connections to help index the web. Several scholarly papers are based on implementation of socially mediated search (Horowitz & Kamvar 2010; Smyth, Coyle, & Briggs 2012). Generally, these draw on the idea that those sites that have been selected by a user's friends and acquaintances – or, better yet, authoritative members of the broader social network – are more likely to be judged relevant (Kim & Park 2013). It seems that, even if the major search engines appear recently to be less interested in the role of social connections in search, there remain research and design questions that will draw attention for some time. As Trattner et al. (2015) note, "the action of searching has become a social process on the Web, making traditional assumptions of relevance obsolete and requiring new paradigms for matching the most useful resources that solve information needs."

These two forms of social search – searching social networks and combining social network information with the search process – seem to have disappeared as quickly as they came. By 2014, a post mortem in *Techcrunch* ran with the headline "Good riddance to social search" (Lardinois 2014). But, of course, search remains a deeply social process, even if search engines no longer explicitly reflect that. As long as the people using the search engines and other technologies of discovery are themselves social, search will continue to be social.

Search context

The above descriptions of social search ignore the fact that most searches are in some sense social. Yes, part of the reason for this is that we are social animals and the sociotechnical systems we use are inherently social. But it is not difficult to see that even what we think of as the most basic search – an individual entering a keyword query in the Google search box – exists within a social context.

Evans and Chi (2009) outline this context, examining the way in which 150 users conducted a search. They deliberately asked questions about the temporal context of these searches. What were you doing just before the search? What motivated you to conduct the search? What did you do with the information once you found it? There has been significant work on how searchers construct a strategy and, at least when they are more experienced, engage in iterative queries to drill down to the information they need. Comparatively less has been studied when it comes to how this search process meshes with the everyday lives of those who use a search engine.

Before conducting the search, the motivation for the search is established, a framing for what kind of problem the information found on the web might address. There is also some preliminary strategy for searching, some set of keywords or questions that might lead the person to information they imagine might address a defined area of ignorance. During the search, the searcher may begin to adjust their model of the problem, engage in some level of sense-making, and begin to evaluate the sources of information as they encounter them. After the search is completed, users often integrate this new knowledge with beliefs and knowledge they already have. Part of this process may include re-presenting this knowledge in a way that might be useful to others or storing it in a way that means it can be re-found more easily at a later date.

At each of these stages, social interaction is likely to occur. People are likely to begin with questions to family, friends, or co-workers. They may send a message to someone they feel is knowledgeable in the area. A significant part of their preparation is probably to rely on direct or indirect interaction with acquaintances. Similarly, they are likely to involve others in the sense-making process. How often have you heard the phrase "I read on the internet the other day that. . .?" Once users have this information, they are likely to draw on the people around them to help to assess the credibility of what is found, and to help to integrate it with other things the user and those in the user's social network know about the world.

This is particularly true of searches that are related to understanding and planning events that are part of a person's everyday life. If you are planning a trip, or deciding what neighborhood to move to, or researching guitar techniques, these activities are likely to look different from a traditional academic search. They are likely to extend over a period of time, rather than consisting of a single search process that occupies all of the user's attention. Head and Eisenberg's (2011) investigation of young people's search patterns found that they often stretched over several days and involved seeking out confidants and expert resources. The emotional (seeking out information about a family member's cancer diagnosis) and physical (in another case, the young person was seeking out meat curing procedures, which if incorrectly done could have led to real health risks) effects of these searches can be much higher stakes than are usually found in academic assignments. And while 95 percent of their respondents turned to search engines, with Google often being their first step in a search, fully 87 percent turned to family and friends for advice and information as well.

At each of these stages, there is the opportunity to intervene with new search tools. In many cases these might "pave cow paths," enabling and enhancing the kinds of interactions that are already taking place. Alternatively, it may be that the better approach is to look for contexts in which traditional search can enable and enhance existing social processes that lead to new knowledge (Hecht et al. 2012). Finally, there may be spaces in which new forms of social interactions with large knowledge collections can occur. There are interesting experiments around web annotation that, if adopted widely, are likely to change how people interact socially with texts. These tools now appear within familiar applications, like the Kindle e-reader's crowd-based annotation functions. But even where there are opportunities for new technologies to support collaborative search, it is likely that users will continue to create their own collaborative assemblages. It is not unusual to see a group of people with mobile devices in hand, engaging in conversation while they search out an important piece of information (Morris 2013), or, at a larger scale, members of a class or other lecture audience seeking out a useful date or source, with the first person sharing it and others adding to the conclusion with their own search results. When not physically collocated, groups of searchers are likely to rely on email or telephone to communicate their results. We will continue to see efforts to integrate these processes, but often those structures that are created on the fly with the technologies at hand are adopted because they are familiar and effectively support the search process.

Of course, there is a social context that extends well beyond the immediate pre- and post-search interactions. Searches are shaped by worldviews, by the context and framing that we internalize from our social context. And what we find is likewise pressed through that social filter, so that two people who receive and process the same search results are likely to reach radically dissimilar conclusions, and perhaps even engage in radically different behaviors because of it. These "lay ontologies" (Calori 2002) and "lay epistemologies" – a form of "common sense" built up out of a lived social existence – mean more to a search process than does the ability to arrive at appropriate queries or keep good records of the search process. We often find what we look for, and both what we look for and what we find are shaped significantly by our social milieu.

Collaborative filtering

As we have seen, search engines often draw on tacit interactions – the structure of the web, searchers' clicks through results pages, and the like – to improve their search capability. There are groups of alternative systems that instead draw on explicit reviews and coding by large groups of site members. This kind of distribution of a large project has been termed "crowdsourcing" (Brabham 2008), a play on the word "outsourcing" that refers to online structures that promote mass collaboration. Not all tasks are amenable to this kind of distribution; many kinds of tasks do not continue to benefit from each new person added to the team working on the problem. For some projects, more people can actually increase the amount of time it takes to complete the task (Brooks 1995). But search is the classic task that usually benefits equally from each new person added to the problem. Distributed approaches to computing have found early application in the search for extra-terrestrials and in analyzing permutations of protein folding (SETI@Home and folding@home, respectively). Just as those projects leverage small amounts of computing power from a large number of machines to search problem spaces, collaborative systems provide an infrastructure for aggregating the small judgments of a large number of individuals.

This form of structured, distributed browsing tends to be

especially good at discovering new sites that meet a general user need. As we have seen, search engines are meant to be as flexible as possible, but often assume that a person has a fairly clear search goal in mind: something like "I want to find the most likely cause of a rash on my arm." In practice, many people turn to the web to find out "What are some amusing images of cats that I have not yet seen?" or "What is something on the web that can entertain me?" or, more generally still, "What news items are interesting to people like me?"

Collaborative filtering sites are designed to provide answers to the questions above in a way that requires little action on the part of the user. We could look at a number of levels of such personalization. At a very basic level, a person chooses the newspaper that best suits them, or turns to a television channel, even without knowing the content, because they suspect that The Cartoon Network or Cable News Network will present them with content that they will be interested in. Personalization often refers to a step beyond the choice of channel. Work in the early 1980s at the Massachusetts Institute of Technology aimed to create a *Daily Me*, a newspaper that reflected the specific interests of each reader (Brand 1987). Generally, these systems discovered readers' interests by asking them to identify a set of topics. This process, as one researcher has suggested, is in many ways analogous to a search engine query (Bender 2002). Both represent a kind of editorial function, creating a "front page" of stories from a world of possibilities, based on explicit criteria provided by the user.

This sort of explicit filtering is fine, but assumes that users are willing to indicate their preferences, and that they actually know their preferences, neither of which is necessarily true. Collaborative filtering allows for those who share similar interests to collaborate to discover relevant materials, with very little individual effort. Some of the first successful online collaborative filters were designed to screen comments in a discussion that were not particularly interesting, helpful, or amusing. Slashdot represents a blog that has for some time provided, as their motto makes clear, "News for Nerds. Stuff that matters." The process by which that news was gathered differed very little from the filtering process at, for example, a daily newspaper. A small number of editors examined news submitted by the readership and others, and decided which items should receive a short abstract and be placed on the front page. These articles often received hundreds of comments within a short space of time. Some of these comments were well informed, or at least amusing, but were buried by hundreds of non-relevant, erroneous, or redundant comments. Rather than editing the comments, the creators of Slashdot left this up to randomly selected visitors to the site, who were asked to rate some of the comments, either increasing or decreasing each comment's overall score by one. This collaborative method allowed readers to look at only the best comments, by viewing only those that were above some selected threshold, and to ignore the large number of less worthy comments. This process, while it clearly established authorities, seemingly did so without reference to the traditional markers of authority that tend to hold sway in other contexts (Poor 2005).

Slashdot, like a number of influential blogs, has the ability to uncover websites that would otherwise have remained an obscure part of the millions of rarely visited sites, and quickly direct a flood of traffic to them. Search engines can also shape traffic, of course, and attracting attention from search engines remains a goal many webmasters strive for. But filter sites like Slashdot can open up a flood of traffic in a very short period of time. This led to something users called the "Slashdot Effect." Small websites quickly became overwhelmed by the flash crowds caused by a link on a major filter site, and often shut down under the duress (Adler 1999). This continues to occur occasionally with many of the major filter sites, including Reddit, though changes in content distribution on the internet (wider use of shared platforms, server caching, content delivery networks, etc.) make it less common than it was during the first two decades of the web. Arriving on a search engine results page is important to those who create content for the web, since it assures that visitors will discover their page, but given that collaborative filters provide the equivalent of one results page for all of their users, appearing on the front page of a major filter site can represent a massive change in the collective attention, bringing a once obscure webpage quickly to the fore.

Reddit represents the latest iteration of a long history of such collaborative filtering sites, including Slashdot, Kuro5hin, Fark, Digg, and others that allow for the community to vote for the most interesting links and comments. It bills itself "the front page of the internet" and has found itself at the center of a number of controversies that have demonstrated how badly collaborative filtering and searching can fail. Perhaps most notably, the site mistakenly identified the bombers of the Boston marathon in 2013. While investigators in this case, as in many cases, sought information from the public, Reddit served as a hub of discussion and analysis, and the community ultimately identified someone who bore no responsibility (Tapia, LaLone, & Kim 2014). Despite this error and others, Reddit manages to arrive collaboratively at sites that are important both to the smaller sub-groups on Reddit ("subreddits," of which there are roughly a million) and to the site as a whole.

All of this works under the assumption that preferences in one area are likely to translate to tastes across topics, so the opinions of peers can help to guide us to useful resources. This is generally the case. Sociologists have long noted that homophily, the tendency of like-minded people to "flock together," tends to be self-reinforcing (McPherson, Smith-Lovin, & Cook 2001). If two people have similar backgrounds and preferences on a range of matters, they are likely to have similar tastes in other areas, leading to even greater congruence. Collaborative filters like Reddit represent an interesting example of a kind of agonistic field that does away with many of the obvious markers that allow for distinctions of taste, and is reduced mainly to the explicit ranking of various choices. By reducing some of the cues that might otherwise interfere with collaborative work, as well as the transaction costs normally entailed in such collaboration, these systems represent an opportunity to incorporate a more diverse and resilient group of searchers, even within topically or interest-constrained collections of users (Chi & Pirolli 2006). It is too soon to know how exactly affiliations created via social filters – "implicit cultures" as they have been termed (Blanzieri & Giorgini 2000) – affect other areas of social experience, though their use in the political sphere suggests changes in a number of institutions are likely.

There are several of these kinds of filters, in addition to Reddit, often with slightly different operating processes, addressing different aims, and catering to different languages and cultures. StumbleUpon, Digg, i-am-bored, and netvibes, for example, may appear to have slightly different functions, but serve the same ultimate role: concentrating attention on sites that have been identified collaboratively.

Bookmarking is essentially a search technology, a way of re-finding information (Yanbe et al. 2007). By opening those bookmarks to others, bookmarking systems recapitulate the phylogeny of web search. One of the earliest methods of finding one's way around the web was to rely on someone's published list of bookmarks. By allowing users to see one another's trails of bookmarks, we are engaged in a never-ending process of social remembering. The collaborative bookmarking sites that were especially popular in the early 2000s (Delicious, StumbleUpon, Diigo, etc.) resulted in what was sometimes called "folksonomies," an alternative to the top-down organization (even when collaboratively created) of taxonomies (Vander Wal 2005). The individual web surfer may have had no intention of creating an overarching organizational structure, but in attaching idiosyncratic tags to a given bookmark, she helped to associate it with other pages, and associate herself with other surfers. This process, when taken collectively, resulted in what Weinberger (2007) refers to as the "externalization of meaning," a way of attaching metadata as commentary and connecting ideas explicitly. Although tagging sites explicitly with metadata has largely died off, experiments in web annotation and other forms of implicit categorization and commentary abound, and many of the same processes of collaborative finding continue to exist in community sites.

There has been some discussion regarding whether these new forms of social search are preparing to unseat the major search engines, and particularly the Google juggernaut. At first, this seems to be a comparison of two very dissimilar kinds of services. Search engines are designed as indexes, allowing for particular terms to be located anywhere on the web. "Sociable search" instead acts to aggregate evaluations of content, or collect sites that are favored by communities. While this may describe their operation in the purest form, in reality they lean much closer to one another. Both sociable search and traditional search engines browse the web seeking appropriate pages to index, but search that is enabled by social networking seems to uncover relevant pages that general-purpose search engines leave behind. Search engines, recognizing that indexing alone is not enough, also attempt to measure the community's evaluation of a site, inferring such information from link structures and other facets of the site, but, again, by explicitly taking into account the searchers' social networks, results are even more effectively ranked (Mislove, Gummadi, & Druschel 2006). Both sociable search and traditional search require the generation of summaries of the pages, though it seems again that sociable search may have an edge here (Boydell & Smyth 2007). Like most large sites, bookmarking sites and collaborative filters generally provide the ability to search their contents in a more traditional way, and, more and more frequently, pages from the major social filter sites like Reddit are showing up at the top of search engine results pages of Google and other general-purpose search engines. In practice, both perform the same function – concentrating public attention – either by rating indexes of the web, or by indexing ratings of the web.

Reddit and similar websites may not be actively seeking community as their goal, just as social bookmarking sites like Delicious do not have that intent. But by making the actions of their users transparent to a certain degree, they provide the opportunity for sociability and the creation of social capital. Erickson and Kellogg (2000) have described this property as "social translucence," a certain degree of visibility among those who are using a resource. Being aware of other users of a system allows for better coordination of effort, and increased trust. Search engines trade on the ideal of trust – we need to know that they are neither unintentionally nor intentionally aiming to mislead. But the indirect observation of self-interested and cooperative users of collaborative filtering and bookmarking sites provides a basis for building trust that traditional search engines will find difficult to match.

Of course, collaborative filtering is also like search engines in that it biases the information passed through it. Reducing the "groupthink" of group filters and limiting unintended filtering often becomes a design issue. While voting on comments represented a solution to Slashdot's problems with large numbers of bad, off-topic comments and attempts to spam the site with links, the site soon found it necessary to create a meta-moderation process for voting on the moderators' votes. Reddit has had to continuously tweak the algorithms that determine what appears on the front page to likewise reduce attempts at manipulating that feed. Some of that meta-moderation may be hidden in algorithms, and other parts may be much more subtle, and represent a process of social learning or acculturation of new users so that they contribute in ways the community appreciates (Halavais 2009). So, just as other search technologies do, collaborative filtering introduces both intended and unintended bias in the sites promoted to the sites' members.

It seems likely that the use of collaborative filtering will continue to become integrated within a larger ecology of findability. At present, only the most experienced users of the web are participating in these collaborative systems. Over time, a larger proportion of users are likely to be collaboratively filtering, but this will not eliminate the need for more proactive searching to fulfill specified needs. Much of what occurs on these systems is perhaps better considered as social browsing, while social search makes use of social relationships to augment traditional searching processes (Freyne et al. 2007). Elements of sociable search already exist in many search engines, and it appears that there continues to be an ongoing convergence toward these types of systems.

Social networks and search for expertise

Social connections are already central to most search engines, if only implicitly. The PageRank system, for example, infers the quality of a site based on social judgments. It never asks humans directly which pages are most authoritative, but, as Jon Kleinberg (1999) notes, hyperlinks "encode a considerable amount of latent human judgments," and researchers have long noted the similarity between social networks and hypertext (Kumar et al. 2002). While collaborative filters and other forms of sociable search may rely to some degree on latent judgments, they are usually fairly overt in how opinions are recorded. Sometimes, however, the information you are seeking has yet to be converted into a format that can be easily consumed by those who have a question: sometimes the best way to get at expertise is to query not the search system, but the expert herself.

This spectrum of collaborative filtering extends beyond finding information, and bleeds into finding information for people, about people, and ultimately connecting with those people. Major social networking systems, sites like Facebook or LinkedIn, allow people to search for user-supplied profiles and connect to others in the network. And many of these systems provide various ways of tapping into the individual knowledge and abilities of others on the network, by prompting users to make connections or introductions, by inferring relationships between people, and by providing an easy route to their expertise.

Again, the idea that social networking systems are in some way related to search may seem odd at first blush, but, as we have seen above, search has always been tied to social networks. Collaborative filtering and bookmarking systems provide some degree of social translucence, allowing for the effects of social networks to be more clearly recognized. At the same time, social networking systems like Facebook often seem to lack a *raison d'être*; once someone has identified their friends, it is not immediately obvious how that network might be employed. One of the most natural ways of making use of that network is to find information. There is a good chance that someone affiliated with you is more likely to be able to provide relevant referrals. By mining our social networks, we provide some basis for finding and evaluating resources on the web (Kautz, Selman, & Shah 1997).

Social networking systems also tend to promote the kind of social information-seeking we do every day. For many types of problem, we seek the human repository of expertise and knowledge. Why would we become an expert on a topic if it is possible to find an existing expert? There has been quite a bit of research questioning how we find people who are likely to know something, and how this extends to electronic networks (Adamic & Adar 2005). The task of searching a social network is structurally similar to searching the web at large. People are in some ways like webpages: they hold information, they are connected in various ways, and those connections lend them a certain degree of prestige or authority. Understanding how we search our social networks, then, gives us some indication of how we might search the web at large. But understanding how we search our social networks in other contexts can also help us to search our social networks online (J. Zhang & Ackerman 2005). Indeed, searching our social network for experts before we search the rest of the web can often help us to reach our goal more quickly, and create a community of searchers (Ribak, Jacovi, & Soroka 2002).

The search capability of many social networking systems is really two sides of the same coin: finding information about people you know, and finding people based on certain characteristics. First, social networking systems often provide an environment for searching for information about people. The names of some of the early online dating sites – Match.com, Friendfinder, MatchMaker – hint at this search function. Of course, there are a number of new vertical search engines that focus on finding information about people as well, but the social networking and dating sites have provided such a function for some time. Typing someone's name into a general-purpose search engine is unlikely to yield biographical information or a résumé. That biographical information is more likely to be found on LinkedIn or Match.com. These represent a sort of replacement for the Rolodex of the past, and there is some evidence that this is the more common use of systems like Facebook, rather than to locate people that are unknown to the searcher (Lampe, Ellison, & Steinfield 2006).

These services also provide an important complementary function: the ability to search by characteristic and find a group of people who match a particular search query. There were certainly pre-internet analogs for such reverse searches – as in, for example, of criminal records indexed by criminal history and modi operandi that could yield a pool of suspects – but the ability to do this more easily and for a broader number of people has far-reaching effects. Searches in this context are often narrowly tailored. A user might want to index any mention of "cats" against dating profiles, replicating a traditional indexed search by term, but often searches of profiles consist of characteristics that are measured along an established set of scales, from age, to religion, to physical appearance. In the case of employment databases – both those operated by large corporations, and public sites like Monster.com – the characteristics of greatest interest are often the skills, knowledge, and experience of the people who are indexed. As more business is conducted in ad hoc groups and networks, searching for appropriate expertise becomes more frequent, and more important. Finding the right expert within the organization, or outside it, is a way of finding a "site" of information. That process can be helped by systems that allow for people search, and social networking systems are a natural place for this to occur (Becerra-Fernandez 2006).

We have already seen that search engines have difficulty with the "deep web," but the deepest part of this is what we might call the "wet web": the information that remains stuck in people's brains, the tacit knowledge that has not been recorded in indexable form. A good search can uncover a great deal of information, but knowledge and wisdom are notoriously difficult to separate from their human hosts. Given this, a complete search should yield not only text, images, video, and other forms of information, but people with particular expertise.

The most obvious way of doing this is by creating a market for answering questions, and several such markets exist. As noted earlier, Stack Overflow and Quora, as well as longstanding examples like Yahoo! Answers or Baidu Knows (Baidu Zhidao), demonstrate the new importance of Community Question Answering (CQA) sites. Generally, these sites allow individuals to ask a question and then for either the information-seekers or any participant to rate the various answers. In some cases, this is all that is provided, while in others, points are awarded, and the market is largely reputation-based. For a time Google provided a paid answers exchange, as have others. All of these systems attempt to gain expert opinion without the unneeded overhead of locating and hiring an expert. Outside consultants can be expensive not only because their expertise comes at a premium, but because of the expense of finding and interacting with them. For a single question, that expense is frequently overwhelming. By providing the infrastructure for asking questions and having them answered, such systems remove some of the organizational barriers to reaching the knowledge in other people's heads.

In many cases, the questions asked are not particularly esoteric, and might be found in some form on the internet. Popular questions on the Yahoo! Answers site, for example, include those about traveling on airplanes with infants and the title of a half-remembered book. This is information that is already out on the web and indexed, but it requires human help to determine what is credible, filter out the less important elements, and synthesize it into a concise whole. People generally find it easier to assess the credibility of answers when they come from people they already know and trust (Morris, Teevan, & Panovich 2010), but they also turn to these sites to get alternative perspectives, first-hand experience, and to simply have the opportunity to interact with others (Jeon & Rieh 2013). Indeed, the introduction of these multiple perspectives may lead students to be more critical of sources than they might be if, for example, a search engine provides a ranking with an authoritative first item (Salmerón, Macedo-Rouet, & Rouet 2015).

In some aspects, this echoes other ways in which the web is being used to commodify and trade the labor of knowledge workers. Several websites provide the services of locating and hiring outsourced technical labor. By acting as a kind of global eBay of labor, even for relatively small projects, this provides new ways of generating value and selling it on a relatively open market. This commodification of expertise is happening at precisely the same time as many people are gifting their intellectual labor, on small and large scales, to collaborative projects with a public benefit. Wikipedia continues to stand as an example of something created by the accumulation of millions of man-hours of donated expertise and expression, and the blogosphere, though less centralized, provided another such example (though in recent years it has become slightly harder to find those blogging for a public audience for free).

This all suggests changes in the way that society creates, shares, and evaluates knowledge. To what degree is "truth" determined by findability and the endorsement of peers? How do structures that allow for filtering and assessment shape that truth? Other trends in social computing, particularly those focusing on user-created content, are driven in part by our focus on search engines as a means for discovering materials, rather than relying on traditional institutional sources of authority. What does this new form of authority mean for the process of thinking collectively, and for our ideas of how to evaluate the credibility of sources?

(Re-)Finding community

All of this suggests a move from goal-oriented searching for information, to a desire to build both explicit and tacit connections between people. The idea that either is possible in an online world is ridiculed by some. After all, an individual sitting in front of a computer screen certainly appears to be about as anti-social as can be. Moreover, the kinds of social interaction that person engages in online seem to lack both fidelity and depth. In this view, relationships of trust and reputation are simulated in the online world, represented and quantified as a score, and available to all. While from the perspective of traditional ties this may seem diminished, it allows for transactions that would otherwise be impossible.

The eBay rating is the perfect example of this. Why should you trust someone on eBay enough to send them money? You have no reason to believe that they are human, let alone trustworthy. However, a number next to their name indicates the track record of this user within the marketplace, and by clicking this you can discover how others have ranked the person. Despite not knowing anyone, you have some level of shared trust that allows for a financial transaction to take place. This in some ways represents the apex of capitalism: buyer and seller in a frictionless environment of exchange, with attention and reputation reduced to scores.

In the next chapter, our focus is drawn to the idea of an attention economy, but social platforms create economies of reputation as well. Cory Doctorow has also written about such economies. In his novelette *Down and out in the Magic Kingdom* (2003), characters live in a world in which the money economy has disappeared, replaced by "whuffie," a currency of reputation. In reality, there is not yet a single currency for reputation, and it is sometimes difficult to differentiate attention from reputation. If someone is listed as a friend by 1,200 Facebook members, does this mean they have a particularly strong reputation or that they manage to draw attention to themselves for other reasons? Does that distinction really matter, when either has been commoditized and is tradable, and the mere ability to measure the degree of connectedness makes it worthy of pursuit – the ultimate portable wealth in an era of "liquid modernity" (Bauman 2000, pp. 153–4). Of course, much is missing in this one-dimensional trading floor, but the ability to create a more perfect, flexible market of exchange is gained.

It would be fair to assume that such explicit trust networks crowd out what – perhaps confusingly – has come to be called "social capital." In 1997, Langdon Winner decried the loss of small community bookstores in the face of online retailers like Amazon.com, noting that bookstores were more than merely a place to buy books: they were a place to meet and talk about ideas. Pierre Bourdieu has defined social capital as "the aggregate of the actual or potential resources which are linked to possession of a durable network of more or less institutionalized relationships of mutual acquaintance and recognition" (1986, p. 248). That is a very broad definition, and the term has been interpreted in a dizzying number of ways, many of them at odds with one another (Foley & Edwards 1999). Many share the idea that mass society and mass culture atomize the individual, and under these conditions it is unlikely that she will protect and nurture the institutions of democracy. The challenge is to find ways of maintaining and building sociability, or, in William Kornhauser's words, "if men are to remain civilized or become so, the art of associating together must grow and improve in the same ratio in which the equality of conditions is increased" (1960, p. 32). Amazon.com has gradually introduced social interaction of various sorts on their site, though it may remain a pale shadow of what was available in a small local bookshop. By creating structures that both exploit and build the connections between individuals, there is a potential not only to allow citizens to find information – a vital ingredient of good government – but also to build the informal institutions that ensure the continuation of that government.

The goal-oriented exchange behaviors of the marketplace can lead to abbreviated social links, but it is not necessarily the case that these quantified relationships replace deeper civic engagement. That claim has been made most famously by Robert Putnam, who has argued that the decline in groups like bowling leagues in the United States is emblematic of the replacement of our more sociable leisure-time activities with more individualized pursuits like watching television (1995). There is something puzzling in the idea that bowling can support the development of strong civil society, but – as in the case of Digg – the process of collaboratively working through news and events to uncover the most interesting is seen as antithetical to the same kind of development of strong ties.

In both cases, the idea is that sociability leads to conversation, conversation to deliberation, and deliberation to some form of political consensus and action. Michael Schudson (1997) suggests that the idea that conversation alone is the germ of democratic participation is probably too simple; conversation is hardly unique to democratic societies. He argues that democratically oriented conversation is "not essentially spontaneous but essentially rule-governed, essentially civil, and unlike the kinds of conversation often held in highest esteem for their freedom and their wit, it is essentially oriented to problem-solving." Not all conversations that occur online, from distributed blog conversations to the chatter on YouTube, would rise to this level. But cooperating to build an understanding, working together toward collective knowledge, provides the grounds for forming tacit connections and the skills necessary to work collaboratively toward problem-solving. At the same time, there is real concern that using friends to help us to find truth has led to significant disagreements about what constitutes a true statement, and often self-enforcing groups of online connections can create a consensus around the veracity of information found that is at odds with traditional views of truth.

Search never stands alone. It is inextricably embedded in the social relationships found online, and both helps to shape them and is shaped by them. Understanding the full spectrum of search activities provides a picture of online sociality. Understanding this process requires understanding how networked technologies of attention shape those interactions, and the central role of search in shaping attention.

CHAPTER FOUR

Attention

The telephone may have been invented by Alexander Graham Bell, along with a host of contemporary competitors, but what we think of as the telephone today owes a great deal to a pioneer who may be less familiar. Bell found a way of carrying voice over a telegraph line. When it was first put into use, lines would be run directly between locations that needed to share information, generally between the factory and office. Eventually, networks were created. Some of these were actually broadcast networks: designed to distribute news and entertainment to many telephones at once (Marvin 1988). The more popular private, point-to-point use required human operators to connect people who wanted to talk to one another. At the turn of the nineteenth century, Almon Strowger was one of two undertakers in Kansas City, Missouri, and the other undertaker's wife worked as a telephone operator. Not surprisingly, his rival's mortuary received most of the calls from the recently bereaved in search of funeral services. Frustrated, he devised the Strowger switch, and slowly telephone systems did away with operators in favor of direct dial capabilities (Brenner 1996). This pattern is familiar: just as the telephone switch attempted to automate the role of the operator, search engines stepped in to take the place of those who categorized the web by hand. And just as the Strowger switch allowed us to shape our attention, so too do search engines; they are "attention lenses; they bring the online world into focus. They can redirect, reveal, magnify, and distort" (Grimmelmann 2010).

No doubt, however, a modern Strowger would be equally frustrated with today's search engine. Searching Google for

"Kansas City mortician" yields nearly 90,000 hits. It seems unlikely that the bereaved would bother with more than the single mortuary that shows up on the first page of results. With billions and billions of webpages, and millions more being created daily, there is no way to present them all equally. Some are better, more useful, more interesting pages than others, and we need help finding those pages. The successful search engine does this: it is a technology as much of ignoring as it is of presenting. Who gets to affect that process of selection and who benefits from that process remain open questions.

Gaining attention has always been important to commerce, as well as to the advance of ideas, the formation of social groups, and indeed all social processes. The ways in which attention is concentrated and distributed are changing rapidly, and the search engine is today's equivalent of the post office or telephone exchange. In an attention economy, those hoping to capture the desires and interest of consumers have struggled with this new structure, and continue to try to understand how to profit from the ways search reconfigures our information ecology.

The web is not flat

The nineteenth and twentieth centuries saw a revolution in mass media, tied to what is often called "the second industrial revolution." The mechanized production of consumer goods extended to publishing, and the improvement of steam-driven presses and new kinds of paper and ink allowed for the creation of the penny press. Perhaps equally importantly, mass production of consumer goods necessitated a mass market, and mass advertising, something the penny press both allowed and needed (Schudson 1978). By the time electric media provided broadcast capability, the idea of a one-to-many model of communication had already become commonplace, and the power of the mass media to affect the economy well known. The advertising-supported media developed in the penny press were often adopted by the emerging broadcast media.

The penny press represented a major shift in control over the way in which information was distributed. No longer would the political elite have a stranglehold on public discourse; newspapers established a public sphere, a watchdog, a Fourth Estate. But in creating this counterweight, they established their own hold on discourse. Schudson notes James Fenimore Cooper's 1835 assessment of the new distribution of power: "If newspapers are useful in overthrowing tyrants, it is only to establish a tyranny of their own. The press tyrannizes over publick men, letters, the arts, the stage, and even over private life" (Cooper 2004, p. 118).

The internet and the web likewise have disrupted the way attention is aggregated and distributed, and so it is worth asking whether there is a similar "tyranny of the web." To many, the very idea seems strange. After all, the distributed, networked nature of the web suggests a radical lack of hierarchy, an idea expressed emphatically in John Perry Barlow's "Declaration of the independence of cyberspace" in 1996. That document declared the culture of the internet as independent from government intervention, because cyberspace was a world in which everyone could have an equal say: "We are creating a world that all may enter without privilege or prejudice accorded by race, economic power, military force, or station of birth. We are creating a world where anyone, anywhere may express his or her beliefs, no matter how singular, without fear of being coerced into silence or conformity." In overturning the Communications Decency Act, which outlawed indecent speech on the internet, the US Supreme Court echoed an earlier court's opinion that "the content on the Internet is as diverse as human thought" (*Reno* v. *ACLU* 1997), and as such should not be restricted in the way broadcast media had been. One of the justifications for regulating broadcast media is that, since only a limited number of voices may be heard, they naturally favor certain viewpoints over others. Implicit in the Supreme Court's argument is that the web gives a voice to everyone.

The assumption that computer networks are more democratic, and necessarily provide a greater voice to everyone, is probably misguided (Elmer 2006). As Ithiel de Sola Pool (1983) argued persuasively, while the distributed nature of computer networking may make it less inherently likely to become a medium controlled by a relatively small number of interests, equality can only occur if public policy is designed to maintain the balance of the medium. Any careful examination of the web today shows that it is anything but a level, unvariegated network. Some sites get more attention than others, and this is hardly by accident. Search engines both contribute to the selection of the more prominent sites, and in turn are more influenced by them.

One of the reasons why people assume that the internet is a technology that supports a diversity of content is that publishing material on the web is relatively effortless. Unlike broadcast television or radio – or even printing – it is easy for many people to publish to a large, potentially global, audience. In the early days of the web, it might have required learning a bit of HTML, and becoming familiar with FTP and web server technologies, but today the skills necessary to start a blog, create a Facebook page, tweet, or upload pictures or video to a cost-free sharing site are trivial. By 2016, nearly 80 percent of Americans used Facebook, and roughly a quarter used Twitter, LinkedIn, Pinterest, or Instagram (Greenwood, Perrin, & Duggan 2016). But it is entirely likely that any given contribution on the web will be lost in the flood of similar efforts. Of the millions of blogs in the blogosphere and videos on YouTube, most get viewed by only one or two people, while a small number get millions of hits – far from equal access to the greater web audience.

Even if we were to assume that attention to pages on the web was evenly distributed, it is hard to imagine that the hyperlinked structure of the web could be equally "flat." Assuming that every page on the web had eight hyperlinks leaving it, and that the targets of these links were picked at random from all the possible sites on the web, the structure would be entirely unnavigable. Unlike the telephone, the web is very malleable, able to take on the characteristics not just of a point-to-point network or of a broadcast network, but a multitude of shapes between the two (Agre 1998). Links are a valuable way of establishing meaning across pages, and they tend to make the web "chunky." Once cliques or clusters of websites are established, they tend to reinforce themselves. A reader might find site A by following a link from site B, and decide to link to both of them. This sort of linking can tend toward a process of Balkanization (Van Alstyne & Brynjolfsson 1996), which is particularly troubling when it comes to political discourse (Hindman 2008), but it is also a central feature of collective sense-making. Over the last several years, a number of researchers have written about the hyperlinked structure of the web and how it changes over time. It appears that the natural tendency of the web (and of many similar networks) is to link very heavily to a small number of sites: the web picks winners.

Or, to be more accurate, the collective nature of our browsing picks winners. As users forage for information, they tend to follow paths that are, in the aggregate, predictable (Huberman et al. 1998). Huberman (2001) notes that not only are these patterns for surfing the web regular, the resulting structure of the web itself exhibits a number of regularities, particularly in its distribution of features. The normal distribution of features found everywhere – the bell-shaped curve we are familiar with – is also found in places on the web, but, for a number of features, the web demonstrates a "power law distribution." George Kingsley Zipf (1949) described a similar sort of power law distribution ("Zipf's Law"[1]) among words in the English language, showing that the most frequently used English word ("the") appears about twice as often as the second most frequently used word ("of"), which appears about twice as often as the third-ranked word, and so on. This distribution – frequency inversely proportionate to rank – has shown up in a number of places, from the size and frequency of earthquakes to city populations.

The number of "backlinks," hyperlinks leading to a given page on the web, provides an example of such a distribution. If the number of backlinks were distributed normally, we would expect there to be a large number of sites that had an average number of backlinks, and a relatively small number of sites that had very many or very few backlinks. For example, if the average page on the web has 2.1 backlinks (Pandurangan, Raghavan, & Upfal 2002), we might expect that a very large number of pages have about 2 backlinks, and a somewhat smaller number have 1 or 3 backlinks. In practice, a very large number of pages have no backlinks at all, a much smaller number garner only a single backlink, and a smaller number still have 2 backlinks. The average is as high as 2.1 because of the handful of pages that attract many millions of backlinks each. Were human height distributed in a similar fashion, with an average height of, say, 2.1 meters, we would find most of the globe's population stood well under a meter tall, except for a handful of giants who looked down at us from thousands of kilometers in the sky.

Huberman notes that this distribution is "scale-free" – that is, the general nature of the distribution looks the same whether you are examining the entire World Wide Web, or just a small subset of pages, though there may be some web communities in which the effect is not as pronounced (Pennock et al. 2002).

I blogged for several years, and each blog entry ends up on its own page, often called a "permalink" among bloggers. I examined 1,500 of my posts, through the middle of 2007, to see how many backlinks each one received. Figure 4.1 shows a ranked distribution of incoming links, not including the first ranked posting. The vast majority (1,372) of these 1,500

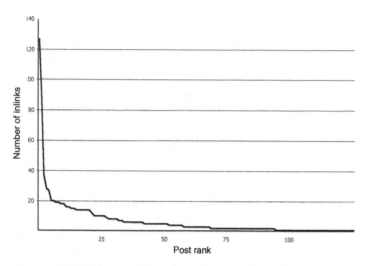

Figure 4.1 Total inbound links to a collection of individual posts on alex.halavais.net, ranked by popularity (first-ranked post omitted).

pages did not have any incoming links at all. Despite this, the average number of backlinks is 0.9, driven upward by the top-ranked posts. Incidentally, as figure 4.2 shows, the number of comments on each of these entries follows a similar distribution, with a very large number of posts (882) receiving either a single comment or none at all. In order to make these figures more legible, I have omitted the most popular post, entitled "How to cheat good," which was the target of 435 backlinks by August of 2007, and had collected 264 comments.[2]

One explanation of such a distribution assumes that there were a few pages at the beginning of the web, in the early 1990s, and each year these sites have grown in popularity by a certain percentage. Since the number of pages that were created has increased each year, we would assume that these older sites would have accumulated more hyperlinks over time. Such an explanation is as unlikely on the web as it is among humans. We do not grow more popular with every year that passes; indeed, youth often garners more attention than age. There are pages that are established and quickly

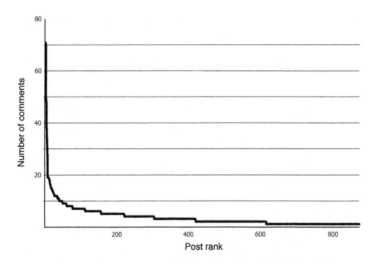

Figure 4.2 Total comments to a collection of individual posts on alex.halavais.net, ranked by popularity (first-ranked post omitted).

become successes, linked to from around the web. While it cannot explain the initial rise in popularity, many of these sites gain new backlinks because they have already received a large number of backlinks. Because of the structure of the web, and the normal browsing patterns (and, as we shall see, the construction of most search engines), highly linked pages are likely to attract ever more links, a characteristic Huberman refers to as "preferential attachment." Such preferential attachment is the mechanism responsible for how hits happen offline, as well, but the explicit nature of linking online, and the rapidity with which novelty can be endorsed, make the web a hot-house environment for "hits" (Farrell 1998).

Take, for example, my most popular posting. The earliest comments and links came from friends and others who might regularly browse my blog. Some of those people linked to the site in their own blogs, including law professor Michael Froomkin, on his blog, *Discourse.net*. From there, the site was eventually linked to from Bruce Schneier's popular *Schneier on Security*, and, having reached a wider audience, a link was posted to it from *Boing Boing*, a very popular site with millions of readers. Naturally, many people saw it on *Boing Boing* and linked to it as well, from their blogs and gradually from other websites. After several months, I received emails telling me that the page had been cited in a European newspaper, and that a printed version of the posting had been distributed to a university's faculty in Asia.

It is impossible for me or anyone else to guess why this particular posting became especially popular, but every page on the web that becomes popular relies at least in part on its initial popularity for this to happen. The exact mechanism is unclear, but after some level of success, it appears that popularity in networked environments becomes "catching" (or "glomming": Balkin 2004). The language of epidemiology is intentional. Just as social networks transmit diseases, they can also transmit ideas, and the structures that support that distribution seem to be in many ways homologous.

And just as diseases are often disproportionately spread by certain carriers (like Typhoid Mary), there are those sites and individuals that work to connect up these ideas with large audiences. Nahon and Hemsley describe "network gatekeepers," those who "have a tremendous impact on information flows: by choosing which information can or cannot pass, by connecting networks or clusters to one another, or in general by regulating the flow of information" (2013, p. 43). In one description of the web, it is envisioned as a bow tie, with an interconnected core, sites that link into that core, sites that link out of that core and "tendrils" that serve to connect otherwise unconnected sites (Broder et al. 2000).

Does this mean that this power law distribution of the web is an unavoidable social fact? The distribution certainly seems prevalent, not just in terms of popularity on the web, but in a host of distributions that are formed under similar conditions. More exactly, the power law distribution appears to encourage its own reproduction, by providing an easy and conventional path to the most interesting material. And when individuals decide to follow this path, they further reinforce this lopsided distribution. Individuals choose their destination based on popularity, a fully intentional choice, but this results in the winner-take-all distribution, an outcome none of the contributors desired to reinforce; it is, to borrow a phrase from Giddens, "everyone's doing and no one's" (1984, p. 10). This sort of distribution existed before search engines began mining linkage data, but has been further reinforced and accelerated by a system that automatically reproduces this winner-take-all structure.

In the end, the question is probably not whether the web and the engines that search it constitute an open, level, playing field, or even, as Cooper had it with newspapers, "whether a community derives most good or evil, from the institution" (Cooper 2004, p. 113). Both questions are fairly settled: some information on the web is more visible than other information. We may leave to others whether or not the web is, in sum, a good thing; the question has little practical merit as we can hardly expect the web to quietly disappear any time soon – though changes in search engines and filtering and discovery via social platforms may radically restructure it. What we may profitably investigate is how attention is guided *differently* on the web from how it has been in earlier information environments, and who benefits from this.

PageRank

By the end of the 1990s, search engines were being taken seriously by people who produced content for the web. This was particularly true of one of the most profitable segments of the early web: pornography. Like many advertising-driven industries, "free" pornography sites were often supported by memberships and ad placement, and in order to be successful they needed to attract as many viewers as possible. (An episode of the science-fiction television program *Black Mirror* takes the interest-grabbing nature of pornographic advertising to its logical extreme, with everyday users required to pay to *not* see such ads.) It did not really matter whether or not the viewer was actually looking for pornography – by attracting them to the webpages, the site would probably be paid by the advertiser for the "hit," or might be able to entice the visitor into making a purchase. The idea of the hawker standing on the street trying to entice people into a store is hardly a new one. Search engines made the process a bit more difficult for those hawkers. In fact, for many search engines, securing their own advertising profits required them to effectively silence the pornographers' hawkers.

Search engines were trying to avoid sending people to pornography sites, at least unless the searcher wanted that, which some significant proportion did. What they especially wanted to avoid was having a school-aged child search for information on horses for her school report and be sent – thanks to aggressive hawking by pornography producers – to an explicit site, especially since in the 1990s there was a significant amount of panic (particularly in the United States) about the immoral nature of the newly popular networks. Most advertisers have a vested interest in getting people to come to their site, and are willing to do whatever they can in order to encourage this. Google became the most popular search engine, a title it retains today, by recognizing that links could make it possible to understand how the webpage was regarded by other web authors. They were not the first to look to the hyperlinked structure of the web to improve their search results, but they managed to do so more effectively than other search engines had. Along with good coverage of the web, a simple user interface, and other design considerations, this attention to hyperlink structure served them well.

Google and others recognized that hyperlinks were more than just connections, they could be considered votes. When one page linked to another page, it was indicating that the content there was worth reading, worth discovering. After all, this is most likely how web surfers and the search engine's crawlers encountered the page: by following links on the web that led there. If a single hyperlink constituted an endorsement, a large number of links must suggest that a page was particularly interesting or worthy of attention. This logic, probably reflecting the logic of the day-to-day web user, was amplified by the search engine. Given the need to sort through thousands of hits on most searches, looking at the links proved to be helpful to sorting out which were worth showcasing.

Take, for example, a search for "staph infections." At the time of writing, Google reports "About 1,200,000" pages include those words, along with some other related questions that are often asked, and an article that describes the condition for the user. The latter feature, drawn from an authoritative source (the Mayo Clinic), is a response to the growing issue of what those in the health field often call "Doctor Google" (Escarrabill, Marti, & Torrente 2011): the tendency of people to try to self-diagnose with the help of a search engine.

The first 3 results – the ones most users will click, if they can filter out the ads – are from mainstream, relatively well-respected sites: MedicineNet, WebMD (which also owns MedicineNet), and the Mayo Clinic. They are also certified by the Health On the Net (HON) foundation, which seeks to promote better medical information on the web, and incidentally offers its own search engine as well. The 100th result is from a government-run public health site in the United States. The 234th and last result (despite the above count, Google only provides a fraction of that number) is from "TrustPharmacy: World Famous Pharmacy" which offers medications shipped discreetly to your home, without any mention of prescriptions. Gathering link data from search engines is not particularly reliable, but Google indicates that the median number of backlinks to the first 3 sites is 1,210, while the 100th site receives 61, and the last site receives none.[3]

Evaluating the number of backlinks alone can provide a useful indicator, but, on the web, not all links are equal. The earlier example of my blog is instructive: the most popular posts have been linked to from *Boing Boing*. Because *Boing Boing* has a large audience, those links are, in some way, "weightier" than a link from a less widely read site. I may value the link from a friend more highly, but, because *Boing Boing* itself is highly linked, it is safe to assume that a large number of people will become interested in a link from that site. Treating all links as an equal vote is a bit like treating all roads the same when some are dirt paths and others are multi-lane highways.

Sergey Brin and Larry Page turned to citation analysis for a guide on how to avoid the "junk" on the web and provide higher precision in the search results of the search engine they designed: Google (or "BackRub" as it was originally named). They assigned a PageRank to each page in the search engine's index, calculated by looking at the PageRanks of the sites pointing to it as well as the number of links from each of those pages to alternative sites, and an adjustable "damping factor" that added something like a transaction cost to the reputational boost given by each page (Page et al. 1998). Intuitively, PageRank represents the likelihood that a surfer who is engaging in information foraging will end up at a given page. Hyperlinks might be thought of, in this model, as a series of tubes, conveying what is sometimes called "Google juice." Those pages that collect more Google juice are also able to pass it along to other webpages. Perhaps ironically, this same approach is not taken to scholarly citations, so that a citation from an article in an obscure and rarely read journal generally "counts" in the same way that a citation from a highly regarded article in a top journal does.

PageRank tends to reinforce the mechanism of preferential attachment. Preferential attachment occurs in large part because those authors who create hyperlinks are assumed to locate the authoritative pages by surfing the web. Much of the browsing and searching process now occurs within search engines and social networking platforms, but since PageRank posits a "model surfer" within the PageRank algorithm, it tends to recreate and enforce the process of preferential attachment. In order for a website to make it onto the first page of results on Google, it first has to have a large number of links to it. However, without being on the first page of results, few website authors will know that it exists and be able to link to it. Every author is then faced with the question of how to draw enough attention to their pages to allow them to be seen by large audiences. PageRank and related esteem-enhancing search algorithms clearly increase the current imbalance, calcifying existing networks of popularity (J. Cho & Roy 2004).

A. J. Liebling famously quipped that "freedom of the press is limited to those who own one." He was wrong; owning the press is not enough, you must have people read what you have published. Perfect distribution of information is limited by our collective attention span. This is a problem for anyone who wants to persuade, from commercial producers to political activists.

An attention economy

In September of 2006, an online diamond retailer called Skyfacet.com was selling jewelry worth about $3 million each year, when a change in Google's ranking algorithms knocked the site off the first few pages of results for popular queries about jewelry. The result: sales dropped by 17 percent in three months (Greenberg 2007a). This is not at all a unique occurrence; each change to the Google algorithm ends up punishing someone: Answers.com saw its traffic drop 28 percent after such an algorithm change, with direct financial consequences (Answers Corporation 2007). And small businesses can find themselves going out of business if they fall foul of Google's ever-changing standards (Walter 2014). In real-life, bricks-and-mortar retail sales, much of a shop's success is determined by "location, location, location." It is not all that different in the online world. In both cases, where you are determines how often you get seen and by whom, and for commercial sites, that attention determines how many sales you are able to make.

The structure of the web and the demand for search engines are both, in large part, determined by a single factor: our limited span of attention. Or to put it another way, people wish to gain something with as little effort expended as possible. In information science, this is often referred to as the "principle of least effort," part of the title of a 1949 book by George Zipf. There is a relationship here between limits on individuals' capability to attend to something and the evolution of social networks. When faced with a search task, and most cognitive tasks are search tasks to some extent, people will generally "satisfice": attempt to use only the minimum amount of time and effort necessary to accomplish their information search to some satisfactory level (Simon 1956). It is tempting to see this lack of will to seek out optimal matches to their information-seeking goals as laziness or velleity, but it is a natural conservative function of human cognition. As George Miller (1956) maintained in his famous article on the "magic number seven," "The span of absolute judgment and the span of immediate memory impose severe limitations on the amount of information that we are able to receive, process, and remember." This limited processing, however, leads to efficient foraging, both for food in the original sense (Carmel & Ben-Haim 2005), and in the case of seeking information. Indeed, the kind of foraging other animals do can be replicated in the search space, and information about viewing aggregated across (human) users, perhaps even with better search outcomes than the automated scanning done by existing search engines (Longo, Barrett, & Dondio 2009). Of course, not all searches are equal, or all searchers. Some dig deeper for all their queries, and some dig deeper for those queries with particular salience (see Pass, Chowdhury, & Torgeson 2006). Understanding the variety of search approaches as well as the collective nature of search will probably lead to better search technologies.

The web increases the amount of information available to a person, but it does not increase the capacity for consuming that information. We are even less likely to read through the entire web than we would be to read through an entire library. The most important change the web brings us is not this increase of information of various sorts, from detailed astronomical observations to videos of grotesque skateboarding accidents, nor is it the fact that this information is accessible to a much more dispersed audience than ever before. The real change on the web is in the technologies of attention, the ways in which individuals come to attend to particular content.

Over a period of two centuries, the greatest challenge for mass media has been to improve distribution of a single message. As distribution became nearly ubiquitous, particularly with networked broadcasts of radio and television, attention could be concentrated to a greater degree than ever before. The term "broadcast" is perhaps misleading: the television program or major newspaper is instead a mechanism for collecting attention. The media famously tell us not what to think, but what to think about (Cohen 1963). They set the public agenda, and have been instrumental in drawing together common views of what is important. The most significant change brought about by the web is in how attention is distributed. Even if the web is far from flat, it provides a much larger number of options than does the television remote or newspaper stand. Advertisers, who rely on "eyeballs" for their messages, are on the front lines of these changes, and are looking for (and very often failing to find) new ways to aggregate attention.

Herbert Simon, who introduced the idea that information-seekers tend to satisfice rather than optimize, also foresaw the emergence of an attention economy as new sources of information were made available. In 1971, he wrote that "a wealth of information creates a poverty of attention and a need to allocate that attention efficiently among the overabundance of information sources that might consume it" (Simon 1971, pp. 40–1). Simon was before his time. The recent explosion of networked media, and particularly the participatory media that have boomed since the start of the century, means that attention is now a scarcer commodity than it has ever been before, and there is a renewed interest in the idea of an attention economy.

When we think of attention as something with tradable worth, it provides a new perspective on how media are consumed – or rather on how media audiences are consumed. The web surfer is not just a target of various persuasive messages, but rather someone who is providing attention in return for information. That attention is a valuable commodity. You are presently reading a book, and giving me your attention in the process. I can use that attention myself, to my own ends, or perhaps include advertising in the margins, selling your attention to eager buyers. The attention economy is attractive to advertisers and advertiser-supported media because it provides a model that allows for wealth and power to be measured not in terms of traditional currency, but in the ability to consistently attract attention (Goldhaber 1997). In an attention economy, the search engine is the ultimate aggregator of such wealth, and advertisers are the clearest source of revenue.

Spam, counter-spam

Ranking is inherent to the functioning of most (though not all) search engines, and, anywhere there is a ranking, there are those who wish to move upward. From early on, search engine designers and web producers have played a game of cat-and-mouse. Search engines have sought out results that made them competitive, while web producers found ways of doing the same. In the latter case, this has yielded an entire industry: "search engine optimization" (SEO). SEO practitioners range from the small-audience blogger seeking to draw fans to the "enhancement drugs" flogger, creating "link farms" to enhance its position on Google. Really, anyone who wants their message heard by a large audience must find a way onto the results pages of various search engines. What that means is that they need to consider the hyperlink not just as a navigational aid, but as an exchange of power (Walker 2005). If there is an emerging attention economy, the search engine has become its trading floor.

When the first spam message appeared, it was fairly easy to identify. Until lifted by the National Science Foundation in 1994, there was an unofficial ban on commercial activity on the internet, enforced by cultural pressures. When the Digital Equipment Corporation sent a broadcast email advertising the release of one of its new systems in 1978, it met a sharp rebuke from the recipients. The problem was not necessarily that the email had been sent to a large number of people, but that it contained a commercial message. Soon after the loosening of such restrictions, thousands of "Usenet" newsgroups received what would become a milestone in spam, an advertisement for immigration legal services from a pair of attorneys in Arizona. Not all spam was commercial in nature (some of the earliest spam consisted of chain letters, or accidentally duplicated messages), and as the 1990s wore on, not all commercial messages were spam. But all spam had one common attribute: it was forced on your attention unbidden (Specter 2007).

The idea, then, that spam could exist on the web is a bit confusing. Webpages do not arrive without being called up. At best, we might think of "clutter," advertisements on a page that are irritating or distract our attention (C.-H. Cho & Cheon 2004). Search engines, however, can become the unwitting host of spam, or what is sometimes called "spamdexing." The initial form of spamdexing involved inserting into a page keywords that were not directly related to the content. These could be inserted in a number of ways. Early search engines were likely to draw from the "keywords" metatag, trusting that the author was best able to determine the content of the page, but these quickly came to be ignored because they were so easily used to deceive. Content creators, however, could use other methods, like large amounts of text made invisible to everyone but the search engine (by making it the same color as the background, for example). They might also "stuff" keywords, by repeating them in a non-visible way over and over again. These keywords might include the names of competitors, or completely unrelated terms that are nonetheless popular at the time (e.g. "Taylor Swift"). These techniques were generally invisible to the user, but preyed on the indexing process of the search engine to subvert its function (Nathanson 1998). Other approaches included a bait and switch that allowed the search engine to index a legitimate page, but whisked the user off to an unrelated page if they visited. "Cloaking" can also be used: providing one page to visitors identified as crawlers, and a completely different page to human visitors (Chellapilla & Chickering 2006).

While redirection and keyword-based approaches to tricking their way to the top of results pages are still widely used by spamdexers, search engines do a good job of uncovering the most obvious examples, and rely more heavily on examining a given page within the larger context of the web. As already noted, Google shifted the way that search engines determine the focus of a site, and they no longer fully trust the creator of the page to tell the search engine what can be found there. PageRank provides a way for the web community to tacitly vote on the quality of a page, and Google also extracts keyword information from the text of those links (the "anchor text"), so that the pages pointing to a given page take on a greater role in describing it. Unfortunately, these approaches can also be compromised through "link spamming" and "Google bombs."

When spamdexers recognized that links mattered, they began looking for ways to increase their backlinks. One way of doing this was to establish a large number of pages, called a "link farm," to link to your target page. These supporting pages probably do not provide a great deal of Google juice because they remain relatively unlinked themselves, but in the process of trading out links, some amount of support is created.

Spamdexers are also able to exploit the fact that they can make links on some websites, and particularly on blogs and wikis. Large blogging platforms like Blogger, because they provide free hosting and an easy way to set up a website, have long been the target of spamdexers who used robots to automatically create "splogs" (spam blogs, or blogs set up as link farms). Blogs tend to be interlinked more than other parts of the web, and they have other attributes that seem attractive to several search engine algorithms: they are frequently updated and change their outbound links, for example. During the early 2000s, so many searches would produce blogs among the top results that it aggravated those who saw blogs as less useful (Orlowski 2003). These blogs also represented a wonderful target of opportunity for spamdexers. A link from a well-linked blog or wiki boosts the PageRank, and links from thousands of such sites can be very valuable. As the spamdexers began to take advantage of this, bloggers quickly found their comments inundated with spam messages linking back to the unrelated pages of spammers.

Comments on blogs, or any system that permits them, were doubly effective for the spammer. The messages are viewable by any visitor to the site, and are often automatically emailed to the blog author. But they are also an effective form of link spam, creating links from a high-reputation site, and misappropriating small slices of credibility, Google juice, from the host site. Since some blogs list other sites on the web that have linked to the blog, another approach has spamdexers tricking the blogs into recording reciprocal links. Cognizant of the negative effects these attacks were having, Google was a strong supporter of a tag that could be placed within links to nullify their effect on PageRank. By including the "nofollow" tag in links left by visitors, the thinking went, a major reason for leaving spam comments would be eliminated, and a significant source of noise in Google's search results could be removed. While this mitigated the problem somewhat, eventually many people restricted commenting to those with an account or removed commenting altogether. While blogs are still very popular, they have been displaced by new social and participatory platforms. The blogosphere is dead (Halavais 2016), and, along with it, the collective power to shape search results.

Changes to the Google algorithm have subsequently reduced the effectiveness of such link-based approaches. In the earlier discussion of PageRank, we encountered examples of results for a search for "staph infection." These examples are quite different from those a Google search revealed nearly a decade ago. At that time, the results beyond the first few pages were riddled with spam. At the time of writing, the first obvious spam site is an online pharmacy and appears as the 160th result. Over time, Google has managed to largely counter the tricks aimed at rising in the ranks of the search engine results pages. In particular, an algorithm update in 2012 labeled "Penguin" penalized sites that were drawing on link farms. As a result, many who had hired experts to help them rise through the ranks were effectively blacklisted from the index (Walter 2014). While Google provided a way to "disavow" such links, many web publishers didn't know why their site had disappeared. This, along with the "Panda" update that sought to de-list low-quality "content farms" (collections of sites that contain computer-generated or freelance-produced content of little value), has put a hole in attempts to manipulate ranking by buying links. Of course, these are just a few of the arrows in Google's quiver, which has recently moved from purely technological tools to an assertion that Google has the right under the First Amendment, which guarantees free speech, to de-list sites belonging to those who engage in "bad behavior" (Blacharski 2016).

Other approaches attempt to associate key terms in the index with otherwise unrelated terms. The paradigmatical example of a so-called "Google bomb" was the effort to associate the search term "miserable failure" with the biography of George W. Bush on the White House website. If enough links to that page included the text "miserable failure," Google would assume that this represented an important topic of the page, even though it did not appear on the page itself. Because of the distributed nature of Google bombs, they have been used most notably for political purposes, but commercial Google bombs were also employed, particularly to discredit competition (Glaser 2005). Updates in the semantic analysis of websites have largely made such efforts obsolete; the first hit on Google for "miserable failure" today leads to the Wikipedia article for Google bomb (as does a search for "Santorum," a former US senator).

This is not the only way to use search engines to make someone look bad. While Skyfacet's owner blamed his consultant, perhaps with just cause, the other possibility is that someone made him look like he was trying to game Google, when in fact he was not. Unscrupulous businesses may not be able to move themselves up in Google's rankings directly, but by making competitors appear to be spammers, they can bump them out of the running. This practice, called "Google bowling" by some (Pedone 2005), involves sabotaging competitors' sites by making them appear to be engaging in obvious link farming and other practices used by search spammers. Ironically, one of the remaining dirty tricks open to people hoping to do well in the search results is making your competition look like they are engaged in dirty tricks.

Changes in search, as well as in the wider web ecology, mean that "search engine optimization" sounds anachronistic. Despite many years of growth, by 2016 the number of SEO jobs began dropping (Southern 2016). Given the desire by both commercial and non-commercial web producers to have their work well represented by the search engines, it would be fair to suggest that everyone engages in some form of search engine optimization. This starts, as many search engines recommend, with good content and a well-organized website.[4] Almost all search engines make use of robot exclusion protocols so that authors have a way of indicating to crawlers what should be ignored, and the major search engines also use XML sitemaps to help crawlers discover and crawl all the important material on a website. All of this effort to be well regarded by the search engines is not just sensible, it is considered good design practice. Likewise, understanding that many visitors come from social media platforms and making sure your company or site is visible on those platforms is just common sense, whether that means setting up a personal Facebook page or hiring someone with expertise in social media marketing. Many of the approaches now used for site analytics and predictive modeling found their start in SEO practices, but those practices now sometimes seem to cost too much for too little in results.

There are millions of content creators all eager to have their work seen by people who want to see it and who will come away from the experience changed. There are millions of people who want nothing more than to be exposed to one of these pages that will help them to learn what they want to know, and to better control their own destinies. Between these huge collections of content producers and consumers is a relatively small number of search engines and social media platforms, switchboards of the internet generation, faced with the task of discovering how best to connect the content with the searchers. This is a complex process. Like a librarian, the search engine is a key to a resource that otherwise is far less useful. It adds significant value to the internet, and running a search engine requires significant capital and creative resources. Is there a mechanism that allows for that value to be expressed, and the work rewarded?

Who pays for search?

In a seminal article describing the Google search engine, S. Brin and Page (1998) include an appendix about advertising on search engines. They claim that Google demonstrated its worth by finding, in a search for mobile phones, an academic article on the dangers of driving while speaking on a mobile telephone, and that "a search engine which was taking money for showing cellular phone ads would have difficulty justifying the page that our system returned to its paying advertisers." They went on to suggest that advertising-driven search engines are "inherently biased" toward the advertisers and away from those who are using the search engine to find the most appropriate material. What a difference a decade makes. A posting on Google's "Health Advertising Blog," for example, suggested ways in which advertising through Google could counterbalance criticism of the health industry by Michael Moore's documentary *Sicko* (Greenberg 2007b). A number of commentators (e.g., Wiggins 2003) have become concerned with the potential for bias in Google's secret ranking algorithm. While Google's major product remains search, in its many varied forms, its main business is advertising.

It is difficult to remember a time when the web was not commercial, and when search was something people expected for free. Brin and Page attribute their thinking on the issue to Bagdikian's influential book *The media monopoly* (1983), which provides evidence that the concentration of the ownership of media leads to imbalances, especially in the news media. With the rapacious acquisitions of today's internet giants, especially the Google empire, it is appropriate that they would be interested in Bagdikian's critique. But given the trajectory of the company they founded, which became a publicly traded corporation in 2004, they might have drawn more heavily from the critique leveled by Robert McChesney. McChesney (1996) compared the state of the internet in the 1990s to radio in the

1930s. Radio thrived as an amateur medium in the United States until its commercialization, with the help of federal regulation that was friendly to industrial giants like RCA. McChesney suggested that in the 1990s the internet seemed to be following the same pattern, and although the nature of the technology might preclude its complete privatization, the dominance of profit-oriented enterprise could make the construction of an effective public sphere impossible. Radio was limited by the broadcast spectrum and only so many people could speak at once. On the internet, anyone can add to the web, but there is a limit on the amount of information that can be effectively attended to by any individual or group. For a while, it seemed as if commercial media producers would monopolize the attention span of web users.

Recent uses of the web to distribute user-created and participatory media suggest that commercial producers may not have an unassailable grip on the public's attention. Looking at a list of the most popular websites, it is easy to conclude that the web belongs to commercial interests. With the exception of Wikipedia, we find large internet businesses and especially portals and search engines dominating the top of the charts. But it may be fair to compare the search engine companies to internet service providers. In both cases, although the infrastructure may be privately held, a substantial part of content is not. The email messages on Yahoo! Mail, the vast majority of the videos on Google's YouTube, and the millions of photos that show up on Instagram or Snapchat each day are largely created by amateurs. On the other hand, as McChesney argues, without a political culture, even user-created work is unlikely to encourage an active public sphere. It has traditionally been relatively easy to associate mass media with industry, and amateur media was (by definition) non-commercial. Search engines have changed this calculus, by automating the identification of niches, and now, with aggregation of the attention paid to those niches, many individuals are able to advertise and sell goods to a global audience.

The argument has been made that Google's main source of income is selling advertising based on content that they do not own, whether or not that content is user-created (Bogatin & Sullivan 2007). People pay attention to ads on sites they trust, and that makes "user-generated media" a particularly good target for marketers (Fulgoni 2007). Like other search engines, Google now trades the attention of its users for revenue from advertisers who place ads on its site. But Google has gone beyond this, with AdSense, to place advertising across the web, where it competes with the ads fed by Facebook and other syndicated advertising networks. The relationship between search and advertising may seem strained, but, as Google has learned, there are certain affinities between the two.

When Brin and Page made their remarks, many of the successful search engines were seeking a path to profit. The "dot-com" era was under way, and many were certain that internet-related enterprises would be fabulously profitable, though at times it was not clear just how this would happen. It was apparent that search engines were a central feature of the exploding web, and, especially given that search was a relatively resource-intensive enterprise, search engine companies were eager to locate revenue streams. There were some experiments with subscription-based engines (e.g., Overture, which charged for search engine placements), but these generally gave way to freely available search engines. Advertising made sense from two perspectives. First, search engines were becoming one of the most visited kinds of sites on the web; traffic alone made them attractive. Second, when people went to a search engine, they were often in search of something, and that might make them more prepared to have their interest piqued by a banner ad, or, better yet, an appropriate advertisement right there next to the search results. Whether advertising on the search engine itself will survive the move to mobile and to social networking sites remains unclear. New revenue models will need to arise. But, for now, advertising to searchers is king.

What may at first appear to be an unholy union between search engines and advertising in fact hints at changes in the way advertisers are thinking about what they do. For some time now, expenditures on mass media advertising have indicated that the traditional view of advertising and marketing is dead (Rust & Oliver 1994; Gartner 2011). Much of this move was toward a broader view of communicating with customers, and understanding what they were looking for in a more personalized way. Both search engine designers and marketers are attempting to meet the practices and evolving needs of a diverse group of users. Online, this means they are focusing more heavily on web analytics and "behavioral targeting." By tracking how people search for and find information online, both search engine designers and marketers aim to present information in a more effective way. It should not be surprising that the two are converging, and there are opportunities for changing how people buy and sell things, and what role large corporations play in this process. Many see in these rapid changes an opportunity to counter a different kind of power law, one that favors large producers in the marketplace. As access to advertising is "democratized," they see new opportunities for small-scale producers.

While such a process may open the door to new producers, some argue it only serves to further commodify our social lives online. Ebay and Etsy may challenge other online sellers, but the (seeming) disintermediation it provides still encourages the continued commodification of online interaction. Likewise, although search engines may potentially provide access to minority opinions and amateur media, and even if those producers do not accept advertising directly, the process of producing and distributing media via advertising-based search engines requires the amateur producer to succumb to technological rationalization inherent to advertising-supported search engines, and to the new forms of "distributed capitalism" (Zuboff & Maxmin 2002) it supports. And the logic of the attention economy dictates

how successful our contributions might be, urging us to promote (and produce) novelty over depth or quality – a process
Marcuse (1964) referred to as "repressive desublimation."

The scarcity of attention is not artificial. There are real
limits to what we can attend to. But the market for attention
is a construct that allows for the ideology of the marketplace
to be granted access to new areas. This commodification of
attention occurs in a largely invisible way. Search engines
extract value through the freely given labor of millions of
people, and, by reconfiguring it, use it to draw attention to
themselves. That attention is then sold to producers who wish
to advertise their products. While the internet provides a platform for self-expression, that expression is constrained by the
values of the network. This does not remove the potential for
the creation of extraordinarily articulate work, demonstrated
by parts of Wikipedia, and, as Richard Sennett (2008) suggests, by those who work on the Linux operating system. But it
does tend to push such efforts to the margin, and requires that
they negotiate within a system of attention and exchange that
has become heavily commodified, and be aware of the tension
between truly liberating forms of online communication and
maintaining what Stewart Ewen (1976, p. 219) refers to as "an
unrelenting vigilance against and rejection of the corporation
mode of amelioration."

The culture of free exchange exemplified by the free software movement and prevalent on the internet from its earliest
days continues to win adherents. It suggests that software
and other content should be accessible to all, transparent, and
unburdened by restrictive licenses. The best bulwark against
bias and commodification in search would be a wide diversity of search engines (Mowshowitz & Kawaguchi 2002), but
it remains unlikely that markets will sustain multiple large
search engines. And if all of those search engines are supported by advertising, there is the potential that searches
will lean inexorably toward commercial enterprises. While
they remain at the earliest stages, and still face stubborn

challenges, there are several efforts being made to develop free alternatives to the search giants, but the current search engine industry is dominated by large, profit-seeking corporations, and this affects what we find when we search and how we evaluate it. Moreover, the practice of commodifying search has led many of those who work with and build search engines to adopt an ideology that identifies the practices of finding, of search, and indeed of knowledge itself as something of commercial value, and to build systems around that assumption (Mager 2012).

Curation and search

As has been noted throughout our discussions, the most marked shift in search over the last decade has been the rise of collaborative moderation systems. Jeffrey O'Brien already noted, in 2006, that the web "is leaving the era of search and entering one of discovery. What's the difference? Search is what you do when you're looking for something. Discovery is when something wonderful that you didn't know existed, or didn't know how to ask for, finds you." Search and social networking platforms are generally assumed to be different in kind, at least with the exception of some of the "social search" functions addressed in the previous chapter. They are closer than they might seem. Participatory social platforms are essentially designed to help users to find people and information that they might need or want, even when they do not know they need or want it. In the process, there has been a new recognition of the skill of curation (Mihailidis & Cohen 2013). We tend not to be very reflective of our activities online; if we were, we would think more about how we search, how we browse, and how closely the two are related.

Of course, curation processes on Facebook or Twitter or Pinterest are not entirely "human-powered," but instead mixed up with ranking and display algorithms. We might consider them a kind of "cyborg curation." The role of technology in curation is hardly new (Razlagova 2013), but the nature of the interaction here is deeper and in some ways less visible. As with other forms of social search, curation runs across a spectrum. In some cases, the user is faced with an automatic collection of things to attend to, and is probably aware that these are presented by an algorithm. Such recommenders are found in a growing number of systems: books are suggested on Amazon, movies on Netflix, Spotify constructs your "Discover Weekly" listening list, and Waze plans your driving route based on speedy previous drives by others who use the navigation app. And this has extended to an increasingly broad range of applications: recommending vacations, financial instruments, restaurants, cars, and candidates, among other choices. Naturally, as with search engines, human decisions are deeply present within the algorithmic processes, and it is often presumed that the algorithm aggregates these human decisions relatively accurately. The intent and assumption are that people who are like you (in terms of their previously expressed interests) can help you find other things you might be interested in.

Work on recommendation systems has grown continuously since the early 1990s (Adomavicius & Tuzhilin 2005), just as search engine development has, and often along parallel lines. Indeed, web search engines could easily be a subset of recommender systems more generally, differing largely in terms of their user interfaces – in the case of search engines, the recommendation is seeded with an explicit search query (Jack 2013).

The basis of recommender systems is pretty clear. Some recommenders draw chiefly from the content of the items being recommended – are the topics similar? – but most of the work done over the years has been based on collaborative filtering drawing on the decisions of a number of people. When *Howard the Duck* (1986) came out, my mother recommended it, saying that it was an entertaining film well worth watching. In the decades that have followed, I have discounted her opinions of movies – not because her opinion of the film was wrong (though I suspect many might agree that it was), but rather because it was less likely that we would find similar movies enjoyable. At the same time, my opinion on films differs from that of many film critics, so a site like Rotten Tomatoes, which aggregates the opinions of many critics, provides some indication, but isn't as useful to me in determining my next movie as is asking people who share my tastes. We are familiar enough with how this works within existing human social networks to expect the automated version to perform similarly.

And usually it does. But when it fails in an obvious way the flaws of recommender algorithms are laid bare. For a while I was doing research on white nationalism in the US, as well as on prison violence, and teaching a course on pornography. These were what I might consider temporary interests, but for some time led to the Amazon recommendation system providing flawed examples of things I would enjoy reading. Even when the recommender system is presented this way, it is hard to gauge where the error is introduced. My selection of books was guided by a scholarly interest in these areas, rather than a more personal interest, and Amazon's algorithm was unable to discern such a distinction. Mike Ananny, writing for *The Atlantic* (2011), noticed that when he downloaded Grindr, a gay and bi networking app, the Android Marketplace suggested he also download an app that allowed him to map nearby sex offenders. As he notes, the association between the two is at least offensive, and could lead to even worse assumptions and outcomes. Unfortunately, it is not at all clear how the two are linked. The only shared word between the descriptions is "sex," and he hypothesized that if this was the link, an app for marine biologists that also used the word would have made the recommendation list. Or was the recommendation made manually? As with search, recommendation systems provide no audit trail. Immediately after the article was published, the system (or its managers) ceased linking the two.

But this is not the first time that search-related algorithms have reproduced damaging stereotypes, and it will not be the last (Baker & Potts 2013).

When, as in the case of Facebook, Twitter, or Pinterest, the algorithm fades more easily into the background, understanding it drops even deeper into the black box, and its effects remain even further obscured from the user. Just as Google's PageRank is known, but other signals are obscured, Facebook's EdgeRank exists, but how it leads to the news feed remains secret. Like Soylent Green, my Facebook feed appears as if it is made *of* people – the question is to what extent it is made *by* people. Rader and Gray (2015) surveyed users of Facebook to determine how they thought about the algorithmic construction of the news feed. The majority (73 percent) recognized that not all their friends' posts appeared on their feed, and roughly half had thought a bit about the process and had some guesses about how the posts were ranked. As Tarleton Gillespie (2011) notes, although people may have an inkling that a social network is deliberately censoring their message, they are not as clear about whether an algorithm is doing this, or they are the victim of deliberate censorship. Of course, censorship by an algorithm is still censorship. Nonetheless, users of these social systems are less likely to recognize the degree to which ranking and display affect them, potentially with disastrous results.

In 2012, a group of researchers subtly adjusted the algorithm that organizes the Facebook news feed, eliminating either happier or sadder posts for a large group (689,003) of users' feeds. They then measured whether this affected the user's own posts through a process of "emotional contagion" (Kramer, Guillory, & Hancock 2014). Mostly this attracted the attention of research ethicists, who wondered whether this was an ethical form of experimentation on users who did not realize that they were subjects of a large-scale experiment. Such large-scale testing is not unusual, of course. Google, Facebook, Amazon, and most other social platforms on the web regularly engage in "A/B testing": serving multiple versions of a page or interface to users to determine which leads to their desired outcome (often a click or a purchase). These manipulations of the feed remain invisible precisely because *all* the manipulations of the feed are generally invisible.

The effects of losing the search ranking contest can, as in the case of sites that fall from grace with Google, result in economic losses for a company or for an individual using the platform to promote her services. But more than that, because of the essentially sociable nature of Facebook, disappearing from the feed represents a social shunning. Just as up-votes on sites with collaborative filtering lead to reputation boosts, Facebook users benefit from interaction, and are potentially acculturated to behave and interact in certain ways in order to maintain their visibility to the community (Bucher 2012). Failing to adhere to those standards, which are in some part dictated by the ideals inscribed in the sorting algorithm, can lead to a virtual shunning. There is some suggestion that, even more than social rewards, shunning can shape community and collective action, bringing people together, and shaping the way they work with one another (Fehr 2004). Especially as the search ecosystem comes to consist of ever more complex assemblies of social and machine-made attention attenuators, it is important that we better understand how individuals shape and are shaped by exposure to these "curated flows" (Thorson & Wells 2015).

The search ecosystem

All of these players, each with their own interests, interact within a larger information ecosystem. Users want to be able to find what they are seeking, no matter whether their goal is unfocused browsing, or a relatively narrow search. Familiarity means that searchers tend to be loyal to a particular general-purpose search engine, Google, and unlikely to switch to another search engine unless there is a significant advantage in doing so. Search engines, whose profits can be measured largely in terms of the attention they draw, must help to deliver on those search goals as quickly and as effortlessly as possible, for as many people as possible. To do that, they must constantly create new ways of keeping content creators in check. It's often suggested that Google uses about 200 "signals" to rank search results (Siu 2013), but with the increased use of deep learning, such a metric probably becomes meaningless.

As with any complex system, it is difficult to predict how the search ecosystem behaves, and how it might evolve over time. Attention will continue to be a scarce commodity, and we can expect that content creators, search engine developers, and social media platforms will continue to engage in a war of increasingly sophisticated means. As frustrating as the active efforts of spamdexers are, it is worth acknowledging the service they perform by exploiting the weaknesses of search algorithms. It would be nice to believe that mutual trust and assistance between content producers and search engines alone would yield a better and more equitable search environment, but it seems unlikely – now that attention has been so heavily commodified – that competition among content producers will diminish. That game has never been zero-sum, and there are benefits to the majority when the process is optimized, and when more people are able to find more of what they are looking for with less effort. It is a mistake to assume that network culture does away with the desires manufactured by mass culture. If anything, the ubiquity of advertising represents an increasingly flexible and accelerated extension of mass culture. Although it is difficult to get away from the macro-view, some of the most interesting changes brought about by the internet, and by search technologies in particular, are not at the peak end of attention, but in the long tail of interactions within niche information communities. It may be that developing more equitable search necessarily must occur at the margins.

Online advertising quantifies attention in new ways. The

internet and the web were developed within a culture of freedom, both in terms of access and speech, and in terms of cost to the user. In that environment, it is tempting to think of the web as flat, and without impediments to participation. When compared to earlier broadcast media, there can be little doubt that the internet provides at least the potential for more equitable access, but a paucity of attention, which drives the need for search technologies, precludes access to everyone by everyone. That means that, even absent the substantial biases that are created by economic forces, existing institutions attempt to use search to their own ends. The next chapter examines the ways in which these new structures change our processes for learning and governing, but it is worth remembering that the economic issues are never severable from those of power more broadly.

CHAPTER FIVE

Knowledge and Democracy

At the end of 2016, the United Kingdom and, to a greater degree, the United States saw the rise of nationalism. The battles leading up to the votes for the exit of Britain from the European Union and the election of Donald Trump were bitter, and rarely grounded in facts. While at the time of writing it remains unclear what effect these votes will have, there seems to be wide agreement that it represents the rise of a "post-fact society." Of course, that idea and the turns of phrase that accompany it are hardly new. It is part of the title of a book published in 2008 by Farhad Manjoo, and related to the term coined by comedian Stephen Colbert – "truthiness" – which Manjoo suggests is the essence of a new media environment, where "you're not just deciding a reality; you're also deciding to trust that reality – which means deciding to distrust the others" (p. 229). An informed public is essential to a functioning democracy, and with the emergence of a network that puts much of the world's knowledge in your pocket it is fair to assume that we would become a particularly informed public. The problem is, as we have seen, we can only drink so much from that firehose, and in response have become a set of fractured publics, informed by curated and self-reinforcing streams from that reservoir. As Karl Deutsch (1966) has argued, communication networks represent a sort of nervous system for the body politic, a means of information and control. The search engine, in this corporeal metaphor, is the spinal cord, and represents a nexus of feedback and control.

The idealized metaphor for the search engine may be a telescope, allowing us to pick out one star from millions and examine it in more detail. Such an optical metaphor suggests a certain degree of transparency; the search engine does not favor one page over another in this view, but simply selects the few pages among millions that most nearly meet a user's needs. Of course, this is not how search engines work. In the process of ranking results, search engines effectively create winners and losers on the web as a whole. Now that search engines are moving into other realms, this often opaque technology of ranking becomes kingmaker in new venues. Social media provide some form of access to what might otherwise be content on the fringe of society, but the most popular search engines tend to subvert this diversity. The investments required to show up on the front page of a search on Google tend "to favour large, institutionalized actors, who can link their websites with other, similarly important actors" (Gerhards & Schäfer 2010). This chapter engages the tension between the unifying force of the search engine and the diverse content of the web.

The default position of those in the search engine business has often been to claim that the search engine algorithms simply reflect the reality of the web (and of the world, by extension), and that any problems can be overcome by tweaking the technology. For some time, the top-ranked result for a search on Google for Martin Luther King was a site created by a white supremacist group, and, at the time of writing, that site still appears among the first ten search results returned. (At least it does in Brazil, Germany, Singapore, South Africa, and the United States. In Denmark it does not, for reasons that are unclear.[1]) The views presented by the group are abhorrent to mainstream society, and yet are ranked among those pages created by what many would consider "authorities" in the area, including biographical sites created by the King Center and by major newspapers. Then there is the first-ranked site on the page, Wikipedia, a user-editable encyclopedia that has become a controversial source of information on the web. None of these are "naturally" the best first choices (because there is no such thing), but they are the selections made by the ranking algorithm, the set of processes that aim to sort search results to make them more useful to the searcher.

The issue is two-fold. First, what is it about the technology of search that encourages the division between "winners" and "losers" in the contest for public attention? Second, to what degree do the winners of that game correspond with traditional authorities? Both of these questions are related to the flow of information in society, and the effect this has on discovery, learning, and self-governance.

Search engines represent a point of control in those flows of information. Those who use search engines well gain a certain advantage, but we are all used by the search engine to some degree, and come to conform to it. Current search engines, like communication technologies before them, contain both centralizing and diversifying potentials. These potentials affect the stories we tell ourselves as a society, and the way we produce knowledge and wisdom. Designers of search tools, as well as expert users of those tools, are structurally more capable of countering the centralizing and homogenizing effects of the new search technologies, and ethically obligated to act on behalf of those who will otherwise be drawn only to what they find on the top of a search results page.

Search inequality

In examining how adolescents search the web, one research study (Guinee, Eagleton, & Hall 2003) noted their reactions to failed searches. Searchers might try new keywords, or switch search engines, for example. One common reaction was to change the topic, to reframe the question in terms of what was more easily findable via the search engine. The models of search suggest that searchers satisfice: look for sufficiently good answers, rather than exhaustively seeking the best answer. Because of this, the filters of the search engine may do more than emphasize certain sources over others, they may affect what it is we are looking for in the first place. It is tempting simply to consider this to be poor research skills – or, worse, a form of technical illiteracy – but simple answers do not fit this complex problem.

First, we might focus on those doing the searches. A user-centric view places the search engine in the role of grand inquisitor, separating those who are able to search effectively from those who are not. The initial concerns over social inequality on the internet had to do with who could connect. This remains important – although there are many more opportunities to get online for many more people, the quality and frequency of the connection varies considerably – but, as we have seen, that physical access to a networked computer is not the same as access to the desired content on the World Wide Web. A divide between skilled and unskilled users of search engines represents a divide between those who can access the breadth of information on the net, and make an informed decision based on multiple sources, and those who are forced to depend on only the most easily found information. There is a relationship between income, race, and particularly education and the ability to find and access information on the web (DiMaggio et al. 2004). If the search engines serve to emphasize and increase already existing gaps in access to knowledge and communication, that represents a significant social challenge.

Differences in social class and education often map themselves onto geography as well. Since the end of the Second World War, the United States has become the central point in a global system of communication. Given the ways in which the United States (and not only the USA) has employed earlier electronic communication technologies to spread an American brand of consumer culture around the world (Schiller 1971), it is easy to mark search engines as a digital comprador, erasing national borders and the role of states in shaping policy. Many of the global media giants are based in the United States, to the extent that they are bound by nation at all. Not only do these transnational corporations distribute content into nearly every corner of the globe, the consumer culture they promote is now found in the alternative, domestically produced content they share the media space with (Sklair 1995, pp. 162–75). In the early days of the internet, there were reasons to be cautiously optimistic about the potential for disrupting the entrenched North–South flow of information and news, and there remain reasons to be hopeful (Hachten 1992, pp. 64–6). Nonetheless, because the United States dominates the search engine market, and because search engines present centralizing tendencies, this particular technology raises special concerns.

The search engine is not a totalizing technology. As noted in the previous chapter, it allows for work at the margins, and the more expert the user, the less influential its bias toward global consumer culture. Nonetheless, there is the distinct danger that, as more and more of our collective memories and culture moves online, the existing hegemony will crowd out global cultural diversity (Mattelart 2000). Jean-Noël Jeanneney, the former director of the Bibliothèque nationale de France, has seen Google's efforts to digitize major libraries as a challenge for just this reason. He notes, for example, that if Google comes to represent the most easily accessed and readily available source of knowledge on the planet, the ranking of various books in their collection will come to have far-reaching consequences:

> I want our children, as they discover the French Revolution, at least to read Victor Hugo's *Quatre-vingt treize*, or Jean Jaurès's *Histoire Socialiste De La Révolution*, as well as Charles Dickens's very hostile *Tale of Two Cities* or Baroness Orczy's *The Scarlet Pimpernel*, which I enjoyed as a child in the Nelson series (without harm, in my case, because I had antidotes): in the latter we saw ad nauseam those admirable British aristocrats tirelessly pulling their French peers from the bloody clutches of the Terrorists. (2007, p. 42)[2]

He ascribes no nefarious motives to Google in particular, but simply notes the natural tendency for an English-language resource to favor a version of the revolution that may not well represent the French perspective. He argues passionately for both book scanning efforts and search engines to be created and managed in Europe. This anglo-centrism is also Google-centrism (though it extends to other search engines, including those for scholarly texts: Fiormonte 2016).

This centralizing tendency remains, despite some early efforts at creating national search engines. The exception is China, whose Baidu rivals Google in terms of traffic, and which hosts 360 Search and Sogou, among others. Jiang (2014) looked at three metrics for Google, Baidu, and Jike, and examined the degree to which they tended toward concentration, bias, and parochialism (i.e., a lack of results outside the home country). She found, unsurprisingly, that each increased during her period of study, but by providing a comparison we are able to see a bit how they might differ, including slightly more bias in the case of Baidu, according to her metric of self-serving results. Unfortunately, comparisons with other engines are much more difficult not because they do not exist – there are dozens of national, linguistic, and religious search engines – but because there is such a large gap between "the" search engine and the also-rans. Though it is largely out of sight to many in the west, Baidu is an exception in terms of size and traffic. Part of that, no doubt, is due to a large user-base in a single language. Despite some indications that Google is improving its cross-lingual indexing and search (Zhang & Lin 2007), in most cases, difficulty with diacritic marks and non-Roman languages, as well as a relative lack of semantic analysis of non-English queries and sites, means that search engines developed for the local language generally work better for local queries (Lazazrinis et al. 2009). Because of these deficits, many choose to search in English rather than their first language. In a study of Arab students, nearly 75 percent preferred to complete their searches in English rather than Arabic (Gross 2014).

With particular exceptions, in which the companies may

be asked by the US government to behave in certain ways, we might assume that these companies follow an imperative that makes them uninterested in favoring their home nations. There are, however, national biases: US search engines tend to link to a larger proportion of the total US websites than they do to sites in other countries. As Vaughan and Thelwall (2004) explain, this does not appear to be an issue of linguistic differences, nor a disguised form of xenophobia. Rather, they argue, the difference is probably due to "natural" differences in authority, as determined by the hyperlink structure. In the language of PageRank, US sites simply have more authority: more links leading to them. They note that sites have existed longer in the United States, where much of the early growth of the internet occurred, and that this may give US sites an advantage. Add to this the idea that early winners have a continuing advantage in attracting new links and traffic, and that early on the US was by far the recipient of more international hyperlinks than any other country (Halavais 2000), and US dominance of search seems a foregone conclusion. Clearly, as argued above, the search engines do not merely reflect this authority, they help to reproduce it.

This assumption that a narrow attention market for sites, with clear winners and losers picked by market forces, is the "natural" configuration for a search engine is the very definition of ideology.[3] Even search engine creators who take a very inclusive view of participatory design are unlikely to be able to encode the cultural understandings of the diversity of global users into their search engines. When they judge relevance based on a model user, that model user is likely to resemble the designers themselves. It is difficult to overcome the variety of cultural understandings about how the world is organized. Metaphors of informational spaces and expectations about online social interactions ground our interaction with search engines, as they do in interactions with other milieux. For Bourdieu (2003), for example, the North African Berber home is a microcosm of the culturally constructed cognitive practices of the occupant, the arrangements of objects betraying an arrangement of thoughts. This difficulty of cultural translation is at the heart of anthropology, and despite the tendency toward a homogeneous "McWorld," particularly online, cultures assign authority and relationship in different ways. This accounts in large part for some of the popular nationally and linguistically based search engines, which feel a bit more like home to the user. But the need for broader coverage of a topic often drives users to global search engines, which are overwhelmingly oriented toward the American mainstream and the English language. Architects and designers of physical objects have learned to account for the social and political implications of the diversity of cultures that engage their products. For the designers of information spaces, understanding the cultural substrate that helps people to conceive of how to find things is equally important (Benyon 1998).

As the general-purpose search engines come to encompass ever-increasing portions of our media diet, the potential for such global inequities becomes even greater. A German is likely to draw her news from a major news search engine. But by visiting Google News or Yahoo! News, which are both popular options in Germany, she is likely to be exposed to news sources that are English-language-centric and oriented toward the United States. This becomes even more problematic when the precise selection process for the news search, like most search functions, is kept secret (Wiggins 2003).

There are arguments that this is exactly what should happen in a marketplace of ideas. If US news sources manage to attract more attention, that represents the utility of their product; people vote with their mouse-clicks. The problem is that people are not freely able to select a choice from the totality of options. While the system may not be intentionally biased, it acts to aggregate a range of views toward the most common interest. This structure, based on votes and aggregated opinion, may appear to represent a kind of democracy. But because it does not allow for deliberation and discussion at local levels, it makes us into a global mob, easily led by those at the center of attention (D. Johnson 1997).

As Jeanneney suggests, the "Googlization" of cultural artifacts also diminishes the role of the state in acting as a counter to consumer culture. Policies were put in place in France to protect small booksellers against the giant resellers, and restrictions placed on pricing remaindered books, precisely to preserve a diversity of sellers and content. Governments are charged with protecting the national culture and way of life, and managing the flow of information has traditionally been a part of this. The flow of new sources of information into a country is itself a significant threat to national ideas and ideals. What is worse is that it has the potential to exacerbate the loss of community and traditional institutions, leaving people with even fewer alternatives (Holderness 1998). One of the problems of global transparency is that it reduces the opportunity for nurturing new ideas within a community of like-minded people, without interference from the wider world.

Bursting bubbles

On the other hand, it may be that the real threat is not radical openness, but the formation of cliques in online communities. In its idealized form, the internet provides the powerful opportunity to communicate intersubjective knowledge, allowing people to experience the lives of others very unlike themselves (Warf & Grimes 1997). In particular, social and participatory media, from blogs to social networking sites to video sharing sites, provide an unprecedented view into the lives of others. In practice, this is a fairly rare occurrence. As Adamic and Glance (2005) found during the 2004 US elections, bloggers were far more likely to link to other like-minded writers than they were to those with differing views. And more recently on Facebook, algorithmic sorting and (to a greater extent) personal selection led to users exposing themselves moderately more often to information that supported their existing beliefs (Bakshy, Messing, & Adamic 2015).

The hallmark of the 2016 presidential election was an even more extreme division between supporters of the two candidates, who seemed only able to talk past one another; as Bruno Latour (2016) explained, "We thus find ourselves with our countries split in two, each half becoming ever less capable of grasping its own reality, let alone the other side's." A visualization called "Red Feed / Blue Feed" was created by the *Wall Street Journal*, which showed what many people getting their news from Facebook were missing.[4] The *Guardian* went a step farther, picking out conservative and liberal voters and having them log in exclusively to the opposing Facebook feed for a month (Wong, Levin, & Solon 2016). Some were not swayed but all were surprised. The two feeds not only provided very different opinions of the candidates and the issues, they also provided an entirely different set of facts, invalidating Senator Patrick Moynihan's dictum: "You are entitled to your own opinion. But you are not entitled to your own facts."

This was often driven by what has come to be called "fake news." Several years ago, that term might have been used to refer to satirical or humorous programs and sites, like *The Daily Show* or *The Onion* (Marchi 2012), but during the 2016 election, it generally was a label for "clickbait" headlines of news items and conspiracy theories. The BuzzFeed website, itself no stranger to clickbait, found that the hyperpartisan political Facebook pages that were widely shared contained significant false information: 38 percent of all the posts on the right, and 19 percent of the posts on the left (Silverman et al. 2016). The idea, for example, that Hillary Clinton had a double who was attending events in her stead was passed around as news. Some of this, of course, had to do with the unusual Republican candidate in the race, who had been a part of "reality" shows and had a special relationship with the media, but many argued that the "bubbles" and "echo chambers" encouraged by Facebook and (to a much lesser extent) Twitter drove the spread of fake news and conspiracy theories. The idea that networked technologies lead to this kind of segmentation is longstanding. As noted earlier, arguments about the decentering nature of networked communication stretch to before the internet emerged. But a number of books and articles over the last decade have pointedly taken on the self-reinforcing communities of thought that seemed to be emerging online, not least Eli Pariser's book entitled *The filter bubble* (2011). There's no disputing that the kinds of algorithmic and human-tuned filtering that Facebook and others encourage can lead to closed communities of discourse. It is surprising the degree to which arguments about the narrowing of viewpoints place Google squarely in the crosshairs.

Pariser's main argument is particularly aimed at the personalization features of Google, which alter search relevance based on previous searches. There are many reasons why search personalization can be helpful in finding and re-finding: if I have demonstrated an interest in construction in the past, a search for "cranes" that yields largely resources about waterfowl will be of limited use. But this does tend to constrain our world to our previous interests rather than acting as a cosmopolitan force for discovery. It limits serendipity. And even if personalized search is not nearly as constraining as Pariser makes it out to be, Hindman (2008) suggests that search makes it much easier to re-find our most familiar sources, rather than explore new ones.

There is also a secondary level of search: whatever your specific interest is, you will find documents and people through search that support you. Once you have found the material, the responsibility to evaluate it is the searcher's – often alone. The ranking algorithms that search engines use are essentially voting systems, so particularly popular delusions tend to be well represented in search results. Someone searching for "vaccination" on Google in 2001 would find all 10 sites on the first page of results leading to anti-vaccination sites (Davies,

Chapman, & Leask 2002). This particular case has since been rectified, but a search in late 2016 for "Is climate change a hoax?," "Was the moon landing fake?," and "Is the earth flat?" all yield a mix of answers in the affirmative and the negative among the first 10 results. Others have found similar results for information on health issues like the human papillomavirus vaccine (Fu et al. 2016), and common conspiracy theories (Ballatore 2015). Conspiracy theories have always existed, but they floated at the fringe – on the web there is no center and there is no fringe, or perhaps it only feels that way to users.

While these sorts of extreme delusions represent the outside cases, reinforcing one's own position is made much easier with the help of a search engine that does not resort to traditional forms of authority to rank salient results. Rather than rely on experts – even local experts whom we know – to help us to evaluate the veracity of a claim, we seek the information directly and make up our own mind. Bennett and Manheim (2006) labeled this the "one-step flow of communication," a flow unaffected by opinion leaders of the kind Katz and Lazarsfeld (1955) identified decades earlier. Wojcieszak and Rojas (2011) similarly described "egocentric publics" – those publics not defined by place, community, or topic, but by the individual and her own networked connections. In practice, this is much more complex, and networked flows of information inevitably make use of intermediaries (see Hilbert et al. 2016), both human and non-human.

Of course, Google is also blamed for the opposite. Nicholas Carr titles his 2008 article in *The Atlantic* "Is Google making us stupid?" (or "stoopid" in the original print edition), though the actual connection to Google or search is tenuous – much of the article is pointed more broadly at "the Net." Nonetheless, the central idea he presents is that because search engines make such a very large amount of information available to us so easily, we no longer read in depth (as you are hopefully doing right now), but instead skim through materials we find on the web, then quickly move on to the next distraction. In the book that followed, he suggested that "Google is, quite literally, in the business of distraction" (2010, p. 157), the argument being that Google's business model is search, and the more of it we do the better. In other words, instead of deep reading of the literary canon, search pushes us to gather from wide sources, but in far less depth.

How can Google be exposing us to too narrow and too broad a set of items at the same time? It seems that the two positions are contradictory. But that is not the only option – it may be that both arguments are correct at the same time. Despite the bubbles in the US election, Dvir-Gvirsman, Tsfati, and Menchen-Trevino (2014) found that selective exposure to ideological sources of news and information was relatively rare, or counterbalanced by more mainstream sources, during an Israeli election, so perhaps the US and UK cases were anomalous. Bozdag (2013) examines much of the recent research and theorization of the filter bubble hypothesis and suggests "extensive empirical research is needed to determine the extent of so-called 'echo chambers' in social networks." The conclusion we have to draw for now is one familiar to Facebook users: it's complicated.

Knowledge glocalization

An article published in 2001 by DiMaggio et al. asked what effect the web would have on the culture of its users. Would it lead to "bountiful diversity, hypersegmentation, or massification?" Six years later, it appears that it leads in all three of these directions at once. One explanation is that it sits somewhere between centralized and segmented, which Yochai Benkler reveals as a configuration that "if not 'just right,' at least structures a networked public sphere more attractive than the mass-media-dominated public sphere" (2006, p. 239). Rather than a balance, the current structure is a complex combination of a high degree of centralization at the macro-level, with a broad set of diverse divisions at the micro-level. Barber (1996) refers to two forces driving shifts in global politics and business. There is a tendency toward rationalization and standardization of business practices, and a coming-together of the world under the yoke of global capitalism, moving toward "McWorld." At the same time, local culture is re-asserting its uniqueness and desire to remain apart: "Jihad." Barber attributes these changes, in large part, to global communication technologies. James Carey (1969), writing about another communication technology – the newspaper – notes a similar tendency: centripetal and centrifugal forces unleashed by the penny press. On one side, a geographically dispersed nation like the United States could be bound together when it was reading the same newspaper. At the same time, the rise of newspapers that united the voice of distributed groups – gays, African Americans, and women, for example – allowed for the creation of new communities that were kept connected through this publishing medium. These two forces in combination led to a newly complex media environment. In the end, many people would probably agree that the unifying forces of mass media have won out. The same is true of search engines: the general-purpose search engines like Google and Baidu tend to draw global attention to a relatively narrow portion of the web at large. And as we have seen, when it comes to search engines, the rich are likely to get richer. Ideas with current purchase attract more links, and therefore more attention, leading to these ideas prevailing even as large minorities are being gradually silenced.

The rule of the many even extends to spelling. Until recently, a search for "colours" on google.com led to the suggestion that you may have intended "colors," since more searches occur with this spelling. There is reason in this: if more people search using the Americanized spelling, it may also be that more results are available with that spelling. Of course, given that the search engine already does some synonym checking (a search for the plural "colours," for example, will also include the word "colour"), it seems odd that the engine would not consider the alternate spellings of the word to also be synonymous. And it is worth noting that a search for "colour" at google.co.uk does not lead to a suggestion of the American spelling. It would be wrong to condemn Google entirely for this tendency toward dominant spelling. After all, difficulty with standard spelling can represent a significant obstacle for those who are less educated, or speakers of English as a second language, and spell-checking represents a way to provide these groups with a chance to access material more effectively (Hargittai 2006). But, like other filtering processes, the biases introduced – for perfectly rational reasons – may have pernicious effects on the diversity of information accessible.

Beyond a biased set of results, searchers may be encountering a bias in inquiry. As noted earlier, those who are unable to obtain satisfactory results from a search engine often decide to change their topic and look for something more easily found. More disturbing, and more difficult to measure, is the possibility that search engines encourage us to frame our thinking in terms of search. Over time, search users seem to become more skilled in determining search terms and working with search engines (Howard & Massanari 2007), but it is possible that in doing so they are favoring the search orientation over other ways of thinking about discovery. For all the inaccuracy of the major search engines, there is something appealing in the idea that a few words can generate the information wanted. If someone wants to know more about making carbonated beverages at home, they could pick up a book or magazine article on the topic. But a quick web search will yield the information, often without context, but also without having to wade through that context. Does this mean that we treat inquiry as a kind of fast food: not very nutritious, but quickly delivered and satisfying? As with the "slow food" movement, is it time for a "slow search" movement (Teevan et al. 2014)?

At the same time, we should not ignore the rich diversity

of content that is available on the web, and at least potentially available on search engines. In 2004, *Wired* editor Chris Anderson introduced the "long tail" phenomenon, drawing on an article the previous year by Brynjolfsson, Hu, and Smith (2003) that described the success of online booksellers and other online retailers who provided a very large variety of products. A substantial part of the sales for these companies were obscure titles that a physical store would not bother to stock. No bookstore can afford to keep something on their shelves that may sit there indefinitely, but the volume of shoppers on, for example, Amazon.com ensures that even the most obscure titles are likely to sell eventually. Because they are able to warehouse many of their items, or have them drop-shipped from the publisher, they can provide a limitless selection with very little additional investment.

Obscure books, of course, have always been available. Any small bookstore is generally pleased to order a volume specially from even an unheard-of publisher. Amazon and other online retailers, however, also make these titles findable, and the result has been a shift in the market toward producing more for the tail. We might consider two counterweights. On one hand, there is the *New York Times* Best-Sellers List and Oprah's Book Club, acting as filters and providing consumers with guidance on what titles are likely to appeal to them, since they seem to appeal to so many other consumers. On the other, there are the search and recommender functions of the online bookseller. Amazon.com might provide similar lists of bestsellers, but rather than pushing everyone to buy the same set of best-selling books, it also has mechanisms that push buyers into the long tail. A recommendation system matches buyers to other buyers with similar tastes, and suggests books they may have missed. Individual reviews by readers also provide opinions that can quickly identify a niche product that has broader appeal. Unlike online bookstores, the web at large does not have strong counterbalances to the centralizing forces of search engine rankings. There are portents that such a counterbalance may arrive via the social platforms, but at present the largest search engines, and especially Google, continue to push toward the center.

There can be little doubt that, at one level, search engines are contributing to a process that calls on us to understand the world in particular ways. This is especially true of a transnational elite who are heavy users of information technology. During the 1990s, there was a growing feeling that the internet would create a new virtual culture, a cosmopolitan deterritorialized community that shared a new form of global knowledge. Not surprisingly, the creation of new space adds complexity to the issues of culture and local knowledge, rather than providing a ready-made solution (Robins & Webster 1999).

Cass Sunstein shares a story about visiting China and finding that his assessment of Genghis Khan was diametrically opposed to that of his host, mainly because of the differences in their education (2006, p. 217). The promise of a globalized, universal core of knowledge is that there is the potential for greater global cooperation when we share common ground on which to build. At the same time, there can be little doubt that search engines and related technologies of findability allow people to unite over fairly small interests and domains of knowledge. Young people who become obsessively knowledgeable about very narrow domains – often fanatical followers of sub-segments of popular culture – have taken on the Japanese label of *otaku* (Tobin 1998). The idea that there exists local knowledge in tension with universal understanding is not a new one. We will encounter this tension in other parts of the discussion of search engines, from interface design to public policy, but the nature of this tension is not easily discovered. Coming to an understanding of it requires us "to navigate the plural/unific, product/process paradox by regarding the community as the shop in which thoughts are constructed and deconstructed, history the terrain they seize and surrender, and to attend therefore to such muscular matters as the representation of authority, the marking of boundaries, the rhetoric of persuasion, the expression of commitment, and the registering of dissent" (Geertz 1983, p. 153). For now, it is enough to note that knowledge is at once universalizable and particular – that is, we are able to share, but not completely. Search engines promise to make that already complicated relationship even more complex, as they break through the friction of geography and affinity, forcing collisions between local and global knowledge.

Search and traditional knowledge institutions

The prototypical web search is often that of the scholar, academic, or student seeking authoritative knowledge on the web. The reasons for this prototype are varied. Many search engines, including Google, have been developed by those working in academic settings. Moreover, the history of information retrieval has until more recently been closely tied to traditional libraries as authoritative repositories of knowledge. Libraries can be used to discover a wide range of information, both practical and scholarly, but do not reflect the full breadth of queries found on the web. The world of scholarship is not the sole source of knowledge for a society – far from it. Scholars have, however, for many centuries, been primarily involved in creating, storing, finding, indexing, and evaluating recorded work. It makes sense, then, when seeking out an understanding of search engines, to examine how these technologies are related to changes in academic research.

It is difficult to draw a clean line between the technologies that drive internet search engines and those used for library search, as they frequently draw upon one another. Some evidence can be found in citations of online materials in formal academic publishing, but even here, the fact that many scholarly resources are now available online, though not necessarily openly accessible, means that it is difficult to discern an online citation from a citation to a printed journal. A number of factors affect the decision to draw from online materials when doing research, including the availability of work online, and its accessibility by a given researcher. As long as a scholar has physical access to the internet, their self-perceived online skills are the most salient factor in determining the use of online resources (Y. Zhang 2001). Even once the more traditional barriers to using online work – access and skill – are overcome, it seems that there remain institutional and organizational impediments.

Search engines are derived from systems that have been used for many years to perform electronic searches of the literature from within libraries, or through paid services. Two of the largest and most complete indexes are the Web of Science and Scopus. These two indexes have a well-earned reputation for the reach of their indexes, the quality of the work they index, and the reliability of their citation data. Some universities base academic advancement on the citations found in the Web of Science, an indication of both its status in the academic community and the relationship of search technology to the institutionalized power of the academy. Until recently, it would have been hard to imagine that metrics built on open search engines like Google Scholar could rival these established search systems (Delgado López-Cózar & Cabezas-Clavijo 2012), and yet those exploring "altmetrics" often turn to social media mentions as better indicators of impact (Thelwall et al. 2013). There is something enchanting about the ease with which a search may be accomplished on Google Scholar, and its ability to quickly identify the most frequently cited articles on a topic. On the other hand, it is difficult to know just how extensive the Google Scholar record is, and what might be missing. As with Google's search engine more generally, the ranking algorithm is closed from public scrutiny. Finally, because it is drawing together a heterogeneous set of references, Google Scholar tends to be plagued by repeated references, link rot, and layers of access protection. These flaws are enough to damn Google Scholar for many of those more familiar with citation indexing (Jasco 2005), but there can be little doubt that it has been widely embraced by many users who see it from the perspective of general-purpose search engines, rather than from positive experiences with traditional literature and citation indexes. At the same time, if the literature itself changes in ways that make it more easily crawled and accessible via open channels, it may be that open search tools gain more of an advantage (see Tatum & Jankowski 2012). As with search engines more generally, the question becomes whether commercial scholarly indexing services can survive when many of their clients are deserting them for the bigger, quicker, easier Google Scholar (Gorman 2006).

Siva Vaidhyanathan (2012) warns against adopting a techno-logical determinist position when it comes to knowledge and search, but the profession of researcher, teacher, or scholar is more closely tied to technology than just about any other. Putting professors in front of their computer screens instead of in the physical library hints at a larger shift, just as the move to the printed word did. Scholarship, as we understand it today, owes a great deal to the rise of the printing press and the libraries distributed around the globe (Eisenstein 1979). Victor Hugo haunts us: will the internet kill the university, at least as we know it? He had the advantage of hindsight when he wrote that "human thought was going to change its mode of expression, that the most important idea of each generation would no longer be written in the same material and in the same way, that the book of stone, so solid and durable, would give way to the book of paper, even more solid and durable" (Hugo 1999, p. 192). The university has traditionally served three functions: transmitting knowledge, storing knowledge, and creating new knowledge, all of which are quickly moving into the online world (Abeles 2002). Just as the library was the heart of the traditional university campus, the search engine has become central to the scholarly processes that occur online. What is now considered the physical university will, over time, be disassembled and distributed, with connections reaching out over the internet to draw learners into collaborative virtual and physical engagements (Halavais 2006). While some institutions are sure to survive relatively unscathed – Vaidhyanathan suggests the University of Virginia will be one – many have already felt the tectonic shift toward online and hybrid education. Such a far-reaching disruption of technological, social, and physical infrastructure cannot occur without some significant stress on existing institutions.

Chief among the challenges to existing hierarchies of the academy is the new demand for transparency and open access online. There is nothing about the internet that necessitates open access, and most universities continue to provide internet access to their paid, secure databases. However, there is a cultural imperative found on much of the internet that encourages the open sharing of information, and that imperative finds fertile ground among university faculties. Despite early efforts by universities to control access to scholarly materials on their servers (Snyder & Rosenbaum 1997), most large universities now provide open indexing of their public websites. Many retain intranets in order to protect their intellectual property and private information, but like other professions that communicate ideas, universities recognize the importance of gaining and accruing attention, and eschew gates and boundaries. Increasingly, universities mandate that their research faculty keep openly accessible archives of their publications, offer open versions of their course materials, or allow free enrolment in MOOCs ("Massive Open Online Courses") and other online programs. Completion of open courses may not lead to a degree, but as they begin to yield their own searchable microcredentials, they may not need to.

Material that is on the web has the opportunity to be integrated more widely into the larger flow of writing and ideas. The early growth is centered squarely on scholar-centric sites that often represent a combination of search engine and archive. ArXiv, for example, has revolutionized publishing in physics, changing the way in which physicists approach scholarly communication (Ginsparg 1997). CiteSeer has done the same for literature related to computing and information science, Social Science Research network to the range of social sciences and humanities, and now sites like Academia.edu and ResearchGate have spread author self-archiving to a broad range of fields. While these sites may fall under the label of "archive," they represent something more lively, something more akin to "professional working spaces" (Galin & Latchaw 1998). There was some early resistance to the transparency of the internet, and the open-access model of publishing, but there has been a sea change among faculty who are aware of open-access publications and willing to publish in them (Rowlands & Nicholas 2005). Scholars are exploring online in ways that move beyond publishing and accessing those publications, and in fields that might not be expected. It is hardly surprising, in some ways, that information science and physics have established themselves quickly on the internet, since the work of each already necessitates heavy use of computing. But these fields are being joined quickly by the social sciences, arts, and humanities. Patrick Leary (2005) writes about how historians of the Victorian era find their scholarly practices changing: "the eureka moments in the life of today's questing scholar-adventurer are much more likely to take place in front of a computer screen" than in the bowels of an Irish castle or over boxes in an attic. Open-access publishing becomes even more open, and visible, as search engines extract the contents of open-access journals and present them to a wider audience than closed journals could ever hope for (Suber 2007). Scholarly verticals like Google Scholar are particularly important here, since otherwise the academic literature, as a whole, would find it difficult to make its way into the public eye.

The ability to easily access and search the literature online is important, but each of these systems also provides the opportunity to explore scholarly literature in ways that have not until now been possible. There are certain affinities between citations and hyperlinks, and both undergird the distributed conversation that is at the heart of scholarship (Halavais 2008). Researchers have always made use of citations to explore backward through time to understand the development of a literature, but sites that collect citation data provide the opportunity for a scholar to move forward or sideways through that literature. Some of the information provided on a detail page for a Google Book Search – including key phrases, passages frequently used in other books, citations, and even a map of locations extracted from the text – presents us with a glimpse of ways in which scholars in the future might work their way through the literature. While it is still far from commonplace, automated conceptual analysis of the literature has led to medical breakthroughs, and has the potential of being expanded to other fields (Gordon, Lindsay, & Fan 2002).

The opening of this material onto the web also means that the walls and ivory towers of the university are far more permeable. Google Scholar provides no way of filtering results according to the traditional gold-standard of academic publishing, peer-reviewed journals, and does not (yet) rank the authors of these works. Of course, one could argue that the Google algorithms, as obscured as they are, represent a kind of peer review. Unfortunately, it seems unlikely that they are rigorous enough to stand alone as a filter, and they miss the beneficial impact good peer review has on revisions of an article before it is published. Nonetheless, the opening of material onto the internet has had a felicitous effect on the discussion of the efficacy of peer review, and a number of well-established journals are experimenting with various ways of opening up their peer-review process.

The opening of the academy represents an opportunity for new kinds of balances between authoritative information. Traditionally, the institutionalization of knowledge has allowed for the creation of paradigms, the policing of truth, and agreements over commonly held beliefs. This practice – like that of the search engine – is exclusionary by design.

Also like the search engine, academic institutions sometimes conflate authority over how we understand the world with other forms of political and economic authority. The diminishing power of the academic sphere does not, however, mean an end to that process of filtering knowledge. Search engines are taking on greater parts of that role, perhaps without some of the safeguards that have traditionally permitted a diversity of ideas in the academy. In practice, the structures of knowledge that were once the purview chiefly of professors are now shifting to technologies of knowledge, just as trust in journalism has shifted to trust in Google. The presentation of search results projects an aura of completeness and balance that many feel the news media, universities, and governments have lost. So when, for example, Google presents curated facts – such as the fact that Taipei is the capital of the "small island nation of Taiwan" (C. Dewey 2016)[5] – it is likely to be met with far less skepticism than similar claims found elsewhere on the web. And since Google tends to favor the popular and commercial over the traditionally detailed and authoritative (Diaz 2008), there is reason to be concerned.

Academic institutions are perhaps the most important group undergoing these changes, from the perspective of accumulating and distributing knowledge. But all institutions work with knowledge and information, and all institutions are faced with similar demands for transparency and access. The kinds of questions that search engines force universities, libraries, and academic publishers to ask are also being taken up by businesses and government organizations.

Addressing the imbalances

Umberto Eco's protagonist in *Foucault's pendulum* writes: "I had a strict rule, which I think the secret services follow, too: No piece of information is superior to any other. Power lies in having them all on file and then finding the connections. There are always connections; you have only to want to find them" (1989, p. 225). We would not want an entirely flat set of search results. Search engine ranking exists because there is a demand for it. Nonetheless, the rankings provided inherently reflect the status quo, and may not serve the interests of individuals or marginalized groups well. Relevance is an intrinsically subjective notion, and the "generalized" relevance revealed in search engine rankings may have little to do with the relevance of an individual query situated within a very particular context and with a particular aim (Blanke 2005). As we have seen, most searchers are not sufficiently motivated to find the connections to relevant material if it is not provided to them at little cost to their attention. There are both reasons to counteract the role of the search engine as a technology that reproduces existing orders of authority, and ways in which this may be accomplished.

The problem of global monoculture is often assumed to be obvious, and it may be, but it is worth noting why it is something worth fighting against. Groupthink, at a massive scale, is only successful if it is always right. As a group, humans are fault-prone, and placing all of our bets on one cultural understanding or one course of action introduces a significant degree of risk. A lack of biodiversity allows for catastrophes like the Great Potato Famine, and a global monoculture risks the same kind of problems: there is no one right path for culture. On the other hand, there are real dangers in cultures unable to collaborate or exchange ideas. The difficult project of balancing cultural integrity with integration is central to the political project of multiculturalism (Parekh 2000). Likewise, for the larger issue of findability to be effective, we must recognize the rights of local culture not just to be represented, but to thrive, and those local groups must recognize that there are substantial global benefits for those who can translate their local practices into global practices.

Search tools are not innately homogenizing or authoritarian. However, ranking implementations that directly measure and reinforce authority are conservative in nature. It is not a question of whose power they conserve, but rather that they tend to enforce a winner-take-all structure that is difficult to break free from. As such, they comprise what Lewis Mumford (1964) called "authoritarian technics," those systemic tools that centralized power and control, "not limited by village custom or human sentiment." He went on to argue that these systems now constituted authority in and of themselves, without recourse to a human directing things from the top of the hierarchy. He argued not for an overturning of authoritarian technics, but to "cut the whole system back to a point at which it will permit human alternatives, human interventions, and human destinations for entirely different purposes from those of the system itself."

Although some have questioned the secrecy surrounding many search engines' ranking algorithms, it is not necessary to infer that the system is intentionally serving one group and not another. But, in a fitting metaphor, we might borrow from Langdon Winner (1980), who suggested that sometimes the technological deck was simply unintentionally stacked in favor of one constituency. For search engines, that constituency is generally those who have traditionally been able to command the attention of the mass media. There were complaints, both from journalists and from bloggers, about the amount of attention heiress Paris Hilton received in the United States during her brief incarceration for driving while intoxicated. Nonetheless, mass media and the networked media of the web seemed to give it equal weight. Broadcast media and search engines go hand-in-hand as powerful concentrators not of the collective will, but of the will of the largest block, and those who have traditionally shaped attention.

The seeming coincidence between the agenda online and that offline may be somewhat misleading. There are millions of people around the world who had no interest at all in the scandal, but general-purpose search engines over-represent the central tendency. Just about anyone can create content for the web, but, as Introna and Nissenbaum (2000) tell us, "to exist is to be indexed by a search engine." That indexing alone is not enough. To return to the long tail of the bookstore, Google contains links to a reasonably large proportion of the web, but only a very tiny percentage of those links are made easily accessible to users. Accessing the deeper content of Google is as unlikely as accessing the deeper content of the web itself.

Like Nicholas Carr, Gideon Haigh (2006) provides a compelling argument that Google is making us stupid by lulling us into complacency, providing a comfortable, convenient, and familiar service that we think we can depend on. That trust is a legacy of teachers and journalists who took their jobs as gatekeepers seriously, and we assume that Google is fulfilling a similar role. Edelman (2016) has tracked trust in media outlets over time; while others have remained relatively stable, search engines are now trusted more than any other medium, including traditional news media. Especially young people may be willing to accept a top-ranked result on Google as representing an endorsement of the accuracy of the information on the page, quite apart from traditional metrics of credibility (see Pan et al. 2007; Hargittai et al. 2010). This level of trust directly affects important decisions like what to buy, or who to vote for. Epstein and Robertson (2015) found that shifting search results could swing undecided voters 20 percent or more. Google dismisses the search engine's biases as natural outcomes of the ranking algorithm, but Haigh argues we would never accept such an explanation from a human charged with providing accurate information. Whether these systems are actually making it easier to be uncritical, or whether they simply remain too difficult to use effectively (Brown 2004), the fact remains that the average searcher is probably finding less information, and less accurate information, than they should be, and they probably remain blissfully unaware that this is the case (Graham & Metaxas 2003). Search engines are a tool of unprecedented power when used appropriately, and a regressive system when the users become the used.

There are those who are "at home" on the web and within the technological milieux of the internet – who are, as Prensky (2001) terms them, "digital natives." He uses that term to describe a generation of children who have grown up online, but in practice those children do not all have the same process of inculcation of navigation skills in that online world. For some, search engines represent a part of their everyday experience, and work to connect them with a world that seems familiar. This feeling of belonging in a search-enhanced world is a result of, as Bourdieu suggests, "the quasi-perfect coincidence of habitus and habitat" (2000, p. 147). This coincidence applies particularly to a group of people, of various generations, who have been among the first to make heavy use of searching technologies, and who have become skilled at finding and evaluating information online. Those who are particularly able users of search have a special responsibility to find ways of restoring the balance of knowledge.

There are several paths of resistance to the homogenizing process of major search engines. One alternative is to encourage competition among the top providers of search, moving from a handful of general-purpose search engines to scores. Unfortunately, the process of creating a general-purpose search resource is highly scalable and lends itself naturally to monopoly: one search to rule them all. In addition to the technology that initially brought the search engine to the top, Google has a particular set of advantages. Its visibility, verging on ubiquity, as well as its familiarity and financial resources mean that it continues to win ever more adherents (Sokullu 2007). Much of the discussion surrounding Google's supremacy does not ask whether the marketplace of search engines will expand, but rather who will usurp Google's position as search hegemon. The search engine that accomplishes this coup would need to not only deliver a superior search experience, but overcome the entrenched mindshare that Google enjoys, and would create its own entrenchments.

Rather than competing with the search oligarchy, one possibility is encouraging change from within the search giants. After all, the prototypical examples of companies opening up the long tail are not small organizations, but large corporations like Amazon.com, Wal-Mart, and Netflix. Indeed, very little encouragement is necessary, as some of the largest search engines have already recognized the need to draw links from the long tail and are providing structural access to it. Forays into non-commercial and scholarly search represent one example of this. Yahoo! Research, for example, offered an experimental engine called Mindset that allowed the user to filter the level of commercial results on the fly by sliding an indicator more toward "shopping" or more toward "research." In fact, most of the niche vertical search engines provide access to results that may be pooled closer to the long tail. Taking this a step farther, and drawing on the influence of a broader public, is Google Custom Search, which allows users to create their own vertical search engines and share them with others. Within a narrow area, this provides sites in the long tail a little "boost" onto the results pages, and with some fine tuning, and tagging by individual or group editors, it is possible to introduce even more differentiation (Biundo & Enge 2006). At least one group of researchers has suggested that random boosting of certain pages would act as a counter to the entrenchment of PageRank, and "reshuffle" the stacked deck (Pandey et al. 2005).

Jakob Nielsen (2003) has suggested that one way of bypassing the power of established websites on search engines is by buying advertising or sponsored placement. Unfortunately, those who have money to buy their visibility on search engines are often the ones who have the least need. The commercialization of SEO means that, while almost anyone can publish a webpage, that page is likely to be relegated to the end of a list of search results. New forms of search literacy can help here, in order to offset the disadvantage of those who cannot afford the expertise of search consultants, but this may have only a limited effect on the disparity, since the SEO industry remains in place by keeping its practices esoteric and providing them only to the highest bidders.

Creating room for diversity, for conversation not smothered by the homogenizing force of a global index, is the ethical responsibility of the networked organic intellectual: the journalist, the librarian, the scholar, and the technologist, among others. They are charged, as William Blake had it, with the task of "Striving with Systems to deliver Individuals from those Systems" (1982, p. 154). As media have converged, these social roles have converged, and take on similar kinds of tasks. In each case, they are charged with communicating with the public, and, increasingly, with helping individuals in the public communicate with each other.

The search intellectual

What is needed is a level of information literacy that allows for effective use of search. Being an informed user of digital media means more than being a critical evaluator; it means that the person is a producer of media, a willing interlocutor in the distributed conversation of the web. Recreating search as a democratic technology requires a "leap towards digital authorship" (Vadén & Suoranta 2004), an authorship that understands the role of search and recognizes findability and making connections as central to what it means to create in a hyperlinked world. What is needed is a group of educators who have the skills necessary to understand search, and the ability to pass that understanding on to others.

A combination of technical skill, area knowledge, and conceptual acumen make up the searching elite. The best searchers understand what search engines are available, how each of them works, and what the strengths and weaknesses of each might be. They are equally aware of how to structure an effective query on a general-purpose search engine, how to use various forms of vertical search to mine the deep web, and how to find the people with appropriate area knowledge to help them when they are stuck. They may be able to locate expertise because of an extensive personal network, or by using social forums online. They are able not only to research a particular question as a single project, but to engage in continuous, real-time search, drawing in data on a topic automatically, fitting newly minted information into an emerging picture, and synthesizing a larger picture from the whole (Calishain 2007). Some of the most skilled users of search engines might even use them as tools to infiltrate computer systems, or to uncover military secrets (Long, Skoudis, & van Eikelenborg 2004). This set of skills is held by a relatively broad group, from intelligence analysts and private investigators to stock analysts and venture capitalists.

Some individuals are particularly capable of translating what they have found, and the means of finding it, to a broader group. This act of translation requires that they speak the language of the group they are serving, that they understand the cultural biases, and the metaphors that make search work for a particular group. This combination of skills and knowledge exists in what we might broadly call the "informing professions": journalists, librarians, teachers, scholars, computer professionals, marketers, public relations professionals, attorneys, and others. All of these groups are generally ethically obligated to help others to find information, though the professional codes may not directly address search engines. All searches provide some form of information that can become the basis for action. Less savvy and less educated searchers fail to understand the factors that influence the creation of hyperlinks, and the ways in which search engines exploit and are exploited by those hyperlinks (Hargittai 2008). It is the responsibility of more able searchers to help to inform their fellow citizens.

Knowledge is a vital part of democratic self-rule. Thomas Jefferson declared that "whenever the people are well-informed, they can be trusted with their own government; that whenever things get so far wrong as to attract their notice, they may be relied on to set them to rights" (Jefferson 1903, vol. VII, p. 253). Wikipedia reminds us that there is value in the broad creation of knowledge by non-experts, but there is still room for experts. Although Jefferson was highly critical of the practice of journalism in his own day, calling newspapers "polluted vehicles" of information, journalists have a long history as agents of social change (McChesney 1996). John Dewey is often remembered for his work on newspapers and the "organized intelligence" of the nation. He believed the right kind of journalism, written by experts, could provide for informed discussion among citizens (Czitrom 1982). For Dewey, newspapers were eroding community ties and social capital (though he did not use that term), and so were the obvious target for reform. At the time, technology was blamed for the changes at hand, but Dewey suggested that instead it was a lack of understanding of how those technologies work:

> Only geographically did Columbus discover a new world. The actual new world has been generated in the last hundred years. Steam and electricity have done more to alter the conditions under which men associate together than all the agencies which affected human relationships before our time. There are those who lay the blame for all the evils of our lives on steam, electricity, and machinery. It is always convenient to have a devil as well as a savior to bear the responsibilities of humanity. In reality, the trouble springs rather from the ideas and absence of ideas on connection with which technological factors operate. Mental and moral beliefs and ideals change more slowly than outward conditions. (1927, p. 141)

That was then, this is now, and not very much has changed. Once again, the technology that informs the public has changed more quickly than our conceptual or moral order.

James Carey argued that the changes in newspaper technology during the last century created the "new social role" of professional communicator: "one who controls a specific skill in the manipulation of symbols and utilizes this skill to forge a link between distinct persons or differentiated groups" (1969, p. 27). These brokers would work "vertically and horizontally," linking across social classes as well as those who were at the same "level" in the social structure. Carey goes on to suggest that this means the journalist takes on the role of an intellectual, translating discourse between communities. This calls to mind another description of the role of another intellectual of the people, Antonio Gramsci's "organic intellectual." The role of the intellectual for Gramsci (1957) is as a builder: someone who creates the scaffolding for collaboration and discussion, who translates between divergent "grammars" and unites groups. This organic intellectual diverges from the stereotype of the scholar in an ivory tower. Today's intellectual must "develop strategies that will use these technologies to attack domination and promote empowerment, education, democracy, and political struggle" (Kellner 1997). Further, she must recognize the ways in which the moral basis of search engines, and that of the engineers who build them, are embedded in the technologies and the corporations that control search and social platforms on the web, and that their solution for avoiding "evil" may differ substantially from that of many of the users (see Fuchs 2011).

Journalists are not the only professional communicators to take on this new intellectual charge – librarians also have a special role in helping people to understand the limits of search engines, and suggesting ways to overcome these limits (Brophy & Bawden 2005). Many have suggested that the internet fundamentally changes the role of the librarian, but nothing could be further from the truth. The core role of a librarian is connecting people with the information that they need, and fostering the effective use of information resources (Noruzi 2004). The idea of the librarian is rapidly shifting from that of a person who collects and archives materials, to that of a person responsible for connecting people with information they can act on (Kane 1997). With good reason, many librarians have been critical of new technologies, and see search engines as threats. They are threats, but to libraries of the traditional mold, and not to librarians. The idea that knowledge is no longer bound by ancient walls, wooden shelves and bound volumes may be an aesthetic challenge, but the capabilities of librarians to organize, sort, discover, and disseminate knowledge are more important now than they have ever been. Librarians who are determined to fight against search engines, seeing them as a force for disintermediated access to knowledge, are fighting an unwinnable battle (Kenney 2004). Pandora's box is open, and the dominance of search engines today is likely to continue even as new approaches are taken.

Those who design search systems also have an ethical obligation to the communities in which they work. Computer professionals have the capacity to "be key agents in the redirection of computer technology to democratic ends" (Schuler 2001), and are in a position to encourage healthy debate, "helping a democratic populace explore new identities and the horizons of a good society" (Winner 1995). The stereotype of the computer programmer is that of a social recluse, someone without a clear social consciousness, a person who has taken on the characteristics of the machines she works with, and someone who has no interest in tackling social problems. There are many exceptions to this stereotype, but perhaps not as many as there should be. As Herbert Simon (1969) demonstrated in his classic *The sciences of the artificial*, there are close ties between the synthetic worlds inside the computer and the synthesis of policy "programs" that seek to solve a social problem. And this is hardly the first time we find computer systems that are reproducing existing social inequities, or that computer professionals are faced with confronting that ethical dilemma (Boguslaw 1971).

An earlier chapter addressed the importance of drawing users into the design process. Any designer hoping to have a popular service is likely to test the system on potential users and look for the features that are likely to attract new users.

For the general-purpose search engines, this may mean a user model that is very broad indeed. While the company may find addressing the most general cases most profitable, there is also profit to be extracted by including the less common users from the long tail in the design process. Doing so may not just provide a new source of users, it may fulfill the ethical responsibility of an information professional to provide universal access. Universal access not only provides for the most common type of user with the most common kinds of skills, but recognizes the broad diversity of people who make use of a system (Shneiderman 2000). If a search engine works well for the average user, but systematically excludes, for example, older computer neophytes, it is important to understand the potential needs of this less numerous group and design alternatives for them (Dickinson et al. 2007).

Many of the problems with search can be addressed by search engines themselves, but doing so would require designers to recognize the shortcomings of their own systems and adopt a proactive ethical agenda. Engineers are notoriously unskilled at detecting the assumptions built into the technologies they design, and search engine builders are no different in this regard (Van Couvering 2007). John Law (1989) has argued that there is a need for "heterogeneous engineers" capable of considering the social, political, and economic dimensions of their work, in addition to the material outcomes. Some of the experiments general-purpose search engines are presently engaging in suggest, however, that they are aware of the problem of self-reinforcing hierarchies of ranking, and interested in mining the long tail of the web. There are technological solutions to the problem, particularly solutions that draw on social networks, and recommender systems like those used by the retailers who have exploited the variety found in the long tail (Gori & Numerico 2003), but technological solutions alone will not provide a more useful bias to a search engine. Although Google is responsible for the algorithm that represents the strongest example of such self-reinforcing hierarchies, in other ways it has demonstrated an affinity for some of the traditional values of librarians, at least relative to earlier search engines (Caufield 2005). We cannot rely on search companies as a whole to enact these changes. The long tail does not promise profits for search companies in the same way it does for retailers. Instead, what is required is an ethical commitment by the professionals working for these companies that goes beyond doing no evil. That is merely the first step.

The second step may be keeping fewer secrets. The competitive nature of the search engine business and the social platforms business means that most advances have been either kept under wraps, or patented, which results in power being further consolidated with heavily resourced corporations. The recent advancement of open source search engine technologies provides some opportunity for search to be provided outside the commercial framework. Some of these systems rely on peer-to-peer crawling and indexing, reducing the resources needed even further. Those companies that open up greater parts of their search engines to public participation in design, public scrutiny in ranking, and public re-use of the resource are most likely to thrive in the new search environment. There are proposals in some countries to require search engines to open up the algorithms, and make clear how they rank results. There is value in such required disclosures, but it should be part of a larger embrace of access to knowledge and information.

From problems to issues

Search engines are our window onto the web world, and, without alternative views, it is not obvious when we see through that window darkly. It is extraordinarily difficult to gauge the social changes search engines have brought about, and what the shifting search ecology means to social interaction. Early indications are that it is changing how we acquire knowledge, and what knowledge means. Self-government requires that citizens are able to find relevant information, to actively seek out information from a variety of sources, and to engage in informed discussion. Search engines make it easier to find answers to specific questions, but can do so at the expense of the larger, diverse world of information and opinions. Unless countered with new kinds of search technologies, and new uses of the current technologies, we risk the internet becoming another anti-democratic, centralized medium, just the "latest blind alley" for those who hope communication technologies can be emancipating (Schiller 1996, p. 75).

Those who are skilled searchers command a particular amount of power in that they are able to locate and evaluate their information environment better than the average person. That power provides them with a competitive advantage in the marketplace, as well as in the marketplace of ideas. Those with the ability to connect to a broader discussion have the responsibility to help others to do the same. "Search intellectuals" need not give up their own advantages, and need not abandon the capabilities of search engines that reinforce existing disparities, but they have a special responsibility to provide a counterweight, opening up discourses, and making sure that alternative voices are heard.

It is important that these search intellectuals are able to see the problems of searchers as more than merely individual problems. C. Wright Mills (1959) wrote about the relationship of individual problems to larger social issues, and the need to develop a "sociological imagination" that allowed for an interpretation of those social issues. The informing professions have a responsibility to develop that same sociological imagination, and to look beyond their narrow interests and help others to do the same. The problems of the individual are not the only indicator of social issues relating to search engines. As we have seen in this chapter, existing educational institutions and practices have had to evolve quickly in order to meet the challenge of a search-centric society. They have rapidly made changes in the way students learn and the way scholars do research. Likewise, we have seen significant changes to electoral politics that are closely related to technologies of discovery and search. The institutions that most clearly come into conflict with search, however, are those that have traditionally exercised control over the way in which discussions unfolded in the public sphere. Governments, and particularly national governments, have found managing search engines to be a challenge. What happens when the putatively natural, rational exercise of power by search technologies comes into conflict with the equally naturalized power of the state?

CHAPTER SIX

Control

Google has found its informal corporate slogan – "Don't be evil" – to be more of a stumbling block than it had anticipated. Because it is, at present, the most visible and most utilized general-purpose search engine, its efforts to shape access to information have led to criticisms. Leaving aside complaints over its corporate structure, including issues of antitrust and tax evasion, the company has weathered censure for bowing to pressure from the Chinese government to filter search results, for bowing to requests by the US government to produce records of searches by users, and for presenting content to users (news stories, books, and images) without licensing it, among other actions that led to loud complaints. The core social question for a search engine is "Who sees what under what circumstances and in what context?" and in answering this question, political and economic battles are inevitable.

The argument over search engines is in some ways a recapitulation of the broader arguments of cyber-libertarians during the early 1990s. Riding on the profits of the dot-com bubble, there were suggestions that technology would usher in a new era of affluence, freedom, and leisure (Schwartz & Leyden 1997). By 1997, Eli Noam was already making clear that such utopian visions ignored the very real challenges that national governments were unlikely to overlook. "Thai child pornography, Albanian tele-doctors, Cayman Island tax dodges, Monaco gambling, Nigerian blue sky stock schemes, Cuban mail order catalogs," among other content objectionable to other countries around the globe, were not only inevitable, but would inevitably draw regulators of national governments onto the net.

Governments are most familiar with national borders, and so there was an early focus on ways of enforcing borders on the flow of traffic. Even if the internet is largely a distributed network, search engines are a common gateway for most users, and, as a locus of control (much like the Domain Name System is), they quickly became a target of national police forces around the world. In the previous chapters, we considered how this control structure affects the commercial distribution of content on the web, and how it shapes exposure to balanced opinions. As it happens, these two forms of control come into very open confrontation in the case of search engine policy.

This chapter begins with a discussion of the most visible policy issue for search engines, and the one with the longest history: government censorship of ideas and discussion, imposed through search engines. That is followed by an examination of the shift to search engines and related technologies as global systems of governance. After briefly exploring a particular subset of this challenge – relating to the search and discovery of protected intellectual property – the chapter concludes with some suggestions of ways governments might ameliorate the opaque and unbalancing influences of search.

Containing search

As noted in previous chapters, at their base, search engines perform as a global index. That word, "index," was first used in the modern sense in the sixteenth century (indexes required the technologies of consistent printing and pagination), as an "indication" of where to find key terms in a book. The word had been used before this period also as a list of items that "indicated" something – most commonly, works that were not permitted to be disseminated.[1] Search engines perform a function analogous to switches in rail networks: they select and route information to the user. As such, they represent the latest in a long line of gatekeepers.

Gatekeepers were once closely related to national governments. National public and private broadcasters often had cozy relationships with national governments, and, as a result, what the population was exposed to was shaped by media companies to conform to the ideals of the government. With technological changes, interactions around the globe are no longer routed through official channels. International relations now has little resemblance to billiard balls bouncing off one another, and more an affinity to spiders' webs, as individual actors, government representatives, and a criminal underclass all interact directly, without mediation from the national government or the national media (Burton 1972). This person-to-person global communication is facilitated by the internet.

Countries face a difficult choice when regulating content on the internet. If they are too open, it represents a challenge to the nation's ability to enforce moral or political order; if they are too restrictive, lack of access to the global knowledge market means a national economy that is unable to compete as effectively on a global scale (Benkler 2006). A number of countries have faced this dilemma, but perhaps none so acutely as Singapore. Singapore has had a history, since gaining independence in 1965, of strong police authority, particularly in matters of the press. Both printing in Singapore and distributing publications printed elsewhere generally required licenses, and had been carefully regulated for some time. At the same time, Singapore traded on its reputation for having an open market and its history as a global entrepôt to drive its success in a global information economy. Seriously restricting access, as Burma and others had, would have meant economic suicide.

Instead, Singapore crafted a policy in the 1990s that let some things in, but carefully watched to see whether users violated administrative policy. They accomplished this, in large part, by only allowing licensed internet service providers. The Minister of Communication at the time, George Yeo, likened Singapore's media policy to a cellular organism (1995). Cells have a semi-porous wall that lets in material important to its functioning, but shields it from threats. Rather than opening Singapore up to the net as a whole, he argued that there was a role for the government to play in controlling access. The hope was to balance internet access with the kinds of governmental control Singapore had exercised for decades. In this approach, Singapore differed from other national governments mainly in its degree of control. Many countries have attempted national filters of one kind or another to stop material as it "crosses the border" on the internet,[2] and others control the content by punishing those who create or distribute certain kinds of materials.

The web provides a way of accessing documents, but search engines provide awareness. A filter can be counter-productive if a person knows that a page exists on the other side. In many cases, the search engine can actually provide a cached copy of the site, but even if this is not available, an enterprising internet user can often find ways around the filters if they know a document exists and want to see it. Creating a national filter but allowing access to search engines is a bit like building a giant wall to keep things out, but leaving an unlocked door in the middle of it. Unless there is national control over that door, the wall itself has only a limited effect on the exchange of information. As the importance of search engines to web access has increased, national governments have become more interested in influencing how they work.

The most frequently cited example of such control is China's so-called "Great Firewall," though as Lokman Tsui (2007) argues, that term tends to obscure the complexity of internet control in China. In practice, China's system of filtering and control is a complex combination of technologies that include IP blocking, keyword filtering, DNS re-routing, and a range of other "hard" technologies, along with "soft" technologies that restrict what everyday Chinese *should* be doing online. At the same time, millions of Chinese students and young people (just like grade schoolers in the US) use Virtual Private Networks and other technologies to check Facebook or interact with friends. An essential piece of that question of control has long been that of search engine access. The government, ultimately, has had great success in fostering domestic search engines, much more so than many of the other countries that have attempted the same. But from early on, Google and the Chinese government sparred over questions of access: Google to the Chinese market, and Chinese citizens to an index free from governmental censorship.

The tension started with Google's entry into China. Google.cn was established under an agreement that certain topics would be absent from the search engine's results. It quickly became a popular search engine within the country, but there is some indication that Google felt that the controls on the content would slowly be loosened as Google demonstrated its utility. It bridled at the continued insistence on censorship, indicating on its search page that the results had been censored by the government, and when things came to a head in early 2010 (with Google insisting on removing restrictions and then being hacked), they shuttered the Chinese portal (Stevens, Xie, & Peng 2015). Yahoo! took a more conciliatory approach, and while both drew criticism by US legislators for their willingness to aid the Chinese government in censoring search results, Yahoo! bore the brunt of the scorn.

After several years of absence, Google re-entered the Chinese market in 2016, and it could be argued that Google has evolved more than the Chinese government has (Waddell 2016). The Chinese censorship issue is not the only case in which Google has faced criticism for adjusting (or not adjusting) results in order to comply with local wishes. In 2004, it came to the attention of American Steven Weinstock that a search for the word "Jew" on Google resulted in links to sites run by anti-Semitic groups, and he started a petition requesting that Google ban those sites from appearing (Becker 2004), though Google again argued that they appeared there as a result of a "neutral" algorithm. At the same time, Google had quietly removed the results in countries where hate speech is not permitted – the site did not appear as a search result in France or Germany, for example. In short, Google was willing to interfere with its own technology when the linked material violated the law in a given jurisdiction, and has said as much in another case (Finkelstein 2003). The problem with such an approach is that, without transparency in either the ranking algorithm or the more human process of deciding what is excluded and where, there is always the potential for abuse and mistrust (Hinman 2005). Moreover, it seriously calls into question Google's hard line against "fine tuning" results in the US, and raises questions of whether Google should censor in support of governments' political objectives, in cases where the censorship is more social (e.g., pornography), and in cases where they are protecting intellectual property (Rees-Mogg 2006). By creating local versions of their engine, Google is effectively providing a venue in which governments are able to regain their traditional role as censor.

Such censorship can have substantial public value. A number of countries, for example, have investigated search engines for inadequately distinguishing between sponsored links and organic results. As of the early 2000s, the US Federal Trade Commission indicated that search engines needed to make clear which results were the outcome of payment. The Australian Competition and Consumer Commission has pursued court action to compel changes in Google's ad placements, and the Federation of Consumers in Action in Spain has requested that the government pursue the same issue with Google, Yahoo!, and Microsoft ("Google y Yahoo" 2007; Scardamaglia & Daly 2016). Though search engines do generally provide some indication of which results are "organic" and which are "sponsored," one study suggests that a simple change to tagging paid results – changing the words "sponsored" or "ads" to "Paid Advertisement" – significantly reduces the number of people who click on these ads (Edelman & Gilchrist 2012). Given the ways in which paid ads support search engines, they must walk a thin design line between encouraging users to be affected by ads and clearly distinguishing between the ads and the "organic" results (White 2013).

And restrictions are not limited to the traditional search products. Take, for instance, Google's response to government requests not to display certain areas on their mapping products. At present, Google Earth and Google Maps have pixilated the US Vice President's official residence and its environs, as well as blurring military sites at the request of the Indian government (Anderson 2007), and everything from private homes and palaces to ecological preserves and oil refineries around the world. Here, Google has abandoned the question of legality, and suggests that sites might be obscured under "exceptional" circumstances, which seems a bit too tautological to be a useful explanation. There are rational explanations for such exclusions; a plot was uncovered to plant bombs at New York's John F. Kennedy airport in 2007, for example, that had relied on Google Earth maps for planning (Buckley & Rashbaum 2007). In the aftermath, many have argued that expurgating potential targets on Google's mapping services has very little effect since the information is easily obtainable elsewhere (Bar-Zeev 2007; Harper 2007). But such a debate is moot, since there are no public criteria under which such exclusions take place, nor any easy or systematic way for observers to engage search engines to determine why exclusions have occurred, or to request that they be reconsidered. If we accept that some things should not be indexed, and other things may not belong at the top of the rankings, there should be some way for the public to learn that these decisions are being made and how they are made, at the very least. Better yet, search engine companies should engage in conversations with their users about what should and should not be excluded.

Naturally, for many national governments, a compliant Google is not enough. Why should they accede to a company based in the US "organizing" the knowledge in their own countries? Rather than constraining foreign companies, they seek to displace them by encouraging local efforts to build search capacity; as Jacques Chirac put it, "Our power is at stake" (Meyer 2006). The Chinese government has both protected and promoted a burgeoning search industry in that country. Others leverage particular linguistic and cultural groups. In South Korea, Naver controls nearly half the market due in no small part to better searching the Korean-language web and appealing to Korean sensibilities (*Economist* 2014). Yandex has garnered more than half the Russian market, no doubt in some part due to an effort to engineer a particularly effective search engine, but also because it is better able to search the Russian-language web. At times, particularly in the case of Yandex, local government has attempted to exert more pressure on the search engine. In several countries, national search companies are attempting to argue that Google's Android phones give the company an unfair advantage in the market (Bershidsky 2015).

But in Europe, as in the United States, Google dominates. A number of countries have tried to foster their own search tools, either through encouraging research or through direct investment. Like Yandex, Naver, and Baidu, some of these have had relative success because they have tuned their indexing process to address languages and character sets that Google has ignored, though most have lost out to Google over time. Walla! (Israel), Goo (Japan), Nadji (Macedonia), Onet (Poland), Sapo (Portugal), Search.ch (Switzerland), and Cốc Cốc (Vietnam) all continue to draw small amounts of mostly local traffic to their sites, many of which are as much cultural and news portals as they are search engines. But linguistic and cultural boundaries alone are not enough to pull people away from Google. In most national markets, Google commands at least 90 percent of the search traffic (Return on

Now 2015), and many of the efforts at national search engines have shuttered. Guruji.com, for example, launched in India in 2007 to provide a national search engine in the vein of Baidu and, given the large and growing online population in India, it seemed reasonable to expect a strong showing for a national search service. But without the political support (in fact, the CEO was eventually arrested), it had little chance of surviving (Sinha 2007).

On the other hand, even substantial political backing does not guarantee success. Quaero was a French effort (initially with significant German partners) to design a Google-killer for Europe. Despite France's early advances in national networking, notably with the pre-internet Minitel system, many saw the effort as doomed from the start: an under-resourced, prestige project to overtake what was already a well-developed and widely known search engine (Ross 2007). The choice to focus on multimedia search prompted the exit of the German collaborators, who saw a traditional text search as a vital first step and created their own project, the Theseus program, which likewise failed to come to fruition. Both programs actively engaged in search engine technology research and development (particularly in voice recognition and image search – e.g., Moise et al. 2013), but the goal of a Google-killer remained – and remains – elusive. Instead, governments have sought to shape Google's actions, with somewhat more success.

Algorithmic governance

Governments constrain search engines, but sometimes search engines constrain society in ways that resemble state actors. Search engines and related technologies now actively shape the information environment, and make decisions – either directly or through the algorithms they design and deploy – that have far-reaching effects on society. Particularly over the last few years, the effects of what Gillespie (2014) terms "public relevance algorithms" have grown, as has recognition of their influence. Search engines are essential to the functioning of the web, and living socially in the modern world without access to the web represents a substantial challenge. The web is used to connect us to each other, to help to find opportunities, and to interact with institutions in education, in finance, in government, in health, and in every other area of our lives. As such, the policies and the algorithms that shape search, on search engines and on other social platforms, have at least as much influence on our daily lives as the state does.

Direct policy is particularly obvious in cases where Google has inflicted the "death penalty" and de-listed sites, or has restricted the availability of AdWords or AdSense (i.e., placing or showing advertisements via Google's platform). Examples of such censorship abound. In some cases, they do so for reasons that seem to be related to protecting its users. In 2016, for example, Google announced it had rejected ads from nearly 800 million weight-loss scams (Kulp). Later that year, it announced that it would no longer accept advertising for "pay day loans," an industry that has long been criticized as predatory (Graff 2016).

By far the most common reason for removing sites from the Google index is the decision that they tried to raise their rankings in ways Google doesn't like. In 2002, a search optimization company called SearchKing created the "PR Ad Network," an attempt to build the PageRank of several companies by linking them to one another. Those who create websites knew then, as they know now, that achieving a high rank on Google's results pages was accomplished in large part by encouraging incoming links. Although the sites may not have been related, interlinking helped their position on the charts – for a time. Then both SearchKing's ranking and that of its clients began to drop precipitously. SearchKing sued Google, and refused to drop the suit when its ranking was restored. Google successfully defended against the suit, arguing that they had the right to determine their own rankings, including blacklisting companies like SearchKing. An article in *Slate* summarized it thus: "More than anything, the suit proves that when you pit the questionable virtue of an Internet parasite against the dubious integrity of an Internet monopolist, you're left with a case that makes everyone just a little bit nauseous" (Lithwick 2003).

Other sites have also been hit with penalties when Google felt they had sought to manipulate ranking. The search engine blacklisted the German websites for BMW and Ricoh for that reason (Miles 2006). More recently, the *New York Times* discovered that the US department store J. C. Penney had managed, thanks to some link farming, to rise to the top of the search pile (Segal 2011). When alerted, Google took "manual action" against the retailer, dropping it to the bottom of the results for a number of keywords. In 2013, Google estimated that it "quarantined" as many as 10,000 pages every day, often because they were seen to be infected by malware (Kavilanz).

In each case, Google alone made the decision, and though there are avenues for appeal, not everyone knows where to find them, or how those appeals are handled. Google makes clear that it disapproves of search engine optimization, but, as we have seen in a previous chapter, the line between spamdexing and simply creating effective information design is not always as clear as we might hope. If I change the titles on my blog to list the subject before the blog name in the title, is that unfair manipulation, or just making clear what the topic of the posting is? If I leave my website address in the comments of blog posts on other blogs, is that a form of linkspamming, or am I just an active commenter? Google knows well that a high ranking on its search engine commands a certain value (it is, after all, value that also accrues to Google itself), but at the same time forbids website creators from actively pursuing that value. When a Google "death sentence" can mean the end of a company in the most extreme cases, it is no wonder that Google is seen as holding a disproportionate amount of power. As the CEO of Springer (a German publisher) wrote in an open letter to Google's Eric Schmidt: "We are afraid of

Google. I must state this very clearly and frankly, because few of my colleagues dare do so publicly" (Döpfner 2014).

Google has wielded its black pen for some time, deeming certain searches too controversial to allow – at least in Google Instant. The autocomplete service on the search engine will suggest your search for "Chinese are" might be best completed with "Chinese are subhuman," if you try "Mexicans are" it will suggest "rapists," but if you type "white people are" it doesn't seem to have a clue. Indeed, there are a number of autocomplete "stop words" that seem to catch in Google's throat (2600 2010).

Facebook also has an increasing role in search, and its often opaque policies create a structure of censorship that rivals some of the most oppressive state actors, all while insisting that it is a neutral platform. I taught a course with a significant discussion within a Facebook group. Near the end of the semester, Facebook summarily removed the entire group, with thousands of comments and discussions among students, for unspecified violations of its terms of service. That sort of capricious and offhanded censorship is hardly uncommon. In 2011, Facebook removed a picture of two men kissing, and indicated that it violated their community standards, despite the lack of any clear connection to those standards (Zimmer). For years, the site has faced continuous controversy thanks to takedowns of pictures of mothers breastfeeding (C. Dewey 2015a). Creating a set of "community standards" for a platform that has members from around the world is a challenge, but it is made much more of a challenge when those standards are vague or unevenly applied. In the wake of the 2016 US presidential election, both Google and Facebook have taken steps to limit the spread of "fake news" by blocking sites that spread it from their advertising networks (Wingfield, Isaac, & Benner 2016). This was after it was revealed that, during the election, members of the Facebook editorial team routinely manipulated the "Trending Stories" list and "injected" stories that they felt should have been getting more attention (Nunez 2016). The combination of claims that algorithms of relevance are "natural" and the periodic manual tweaking of results leaves many users and regulators uneasy.

While Facebook is by far the most dominant social networking platform, many people find their ways to stories through Twitter, Reddit, or any number of other platforms. Traditionally, censorship has been employed to silence unpopular or marginal ideas. Both in search and on social platforms, censorship is often intended to mitigate the tyranny of those who are already in power. Reddit has continuously faced issues around where to draw the line. Is it acceptable to ban groups ("subreddits") that encourage fat shaming, as it did in 2015 (C. Dewey 2015b)? With millions of users, and a history of being very permissive, when Reddit decides some topics are beyond the pale, the community has rarely embraced such decisions. Adrienne Massanari (2015) describes two incidences in which what she calls "toxic technocultures" were confronted by the Reddit administrators to some degree, including harassment related to #gamergate. While the "manual action" in both cases could be seen as a form of censorship, in fact they were fairly minor checks on what otherwise is the more common disciplining of non-dominant voices. In other words, the algorithmically enabled community filtering that occurs on Reddit tends to land conservative, patriarchal, and regressive content that serves existing power structures on the front page ("/r/all") and at the top of the comments in many subreddits.

Focusing on individual cases of censorship distracts us from some of the large-scale incidental bias that the concept of relevance produces. This ordering of information easily becomes a social ordering, and reinscribes existing differences in power and control. In the summer of 2016, a high school student named Kaber Alli uploaded a video on Twitter showing the Google Images search results for "three white teenagers" and for "three black teenagers"; the former generally showed models on stock-images sites, the latter mainly mugshots.[3] The tweet has been shared more than 80,000 times, and sparked a discussion around whether Google was racially biased. Alli, in a subsequent tweet, indicated he did not feel this was the case. Google insisted that its search engine was neutral and reflected society's existing biases, rather than introducing any of its own, and generally the consensus was that the neutral algorithms simply highlighted the existing bias in images of black people online.

And that is true: Google's search results do reflect social power imbalances. And when they do, they amplify them, justify them, naturalize them, and entrench them. So an image search for "dreadlocks" results mainly in images of white people with dreadlocks. A search for "hands" results in mostly the hands of white people. (The worldwhiteweb.net seeks to rectify this handily, by posting pictures of non-white hands – so far with little success.) A search for "Asian teens" is likely to lead to pornographic images and links. A search for "C.E.O." turns up a disproportionately small number of female images (Kay, Matuszek, & Munson 2015), and women tend to be served ads for lower-paying jobs than men (Datta, Tschantz, & Datta 2015). Despite the Google Instant blacklist noted above, Baker and Potts (2013) found that the search engine tended to suggest stereotypical racial and gender traits. Search engines reflect the central tendencies of a population, and in so doing reproduce them. Safiya Noble (2013) concludes that "under the current rhetoric of search fairness and objectivity, the seemingly neutral algorithms by Google cannot be held responsible, nor can the authors of the mathematical language of the web search tool."

And these are just some of the ways in which the search engine may not be "biased" in the sense that it is deliberately manipulating results to allow for a winner, but nonetheless creates winners and losers. That Amazon.com or the Democratic Party (Trielli, Mussenden, & Diakopoulos 2016) are the "natural" and "neutral" winners of the search engine lottery likely does little to assuage those choices relegated to dark corners of the web. These search interfaces shape our experience of the world, "from how to find a particular plumber to what type of news to read" (Nahon 2016). The cloak of neutrality allows for Google, Facebook, and others to reproduce hegemonic injustices as a service, a bias that serves existing centers of power – not least those platforms themselves (Mullins, Winkler, & Kendall 2015).

Intellectual property

Search engines provide more than just search – they provide access to the intellectual labor of the world. Google's mission is "to make the world's information universally accessible and useful." Intellectual property laws around the world provide some degree of that power over access to the creators of intellectual goods. Given that search engines "indicate" the location of items that may be of interest to searchers, one might easily assume that the strictures of intellectual property are of little concern to search engines. In fact, the interests of major search engines are sometimes at cross-purposes with those of copyright holders.

Most search engines provide some form of a preview of the results for a search: Microsoft Academic provides citation data for search results in a separate pane; Yahoo! and Google, among others, provide a "cached" version of results pages and thumbnails of images found on the web; and many newer search engines provide everything from audio snippets to "RSS" feeds. Each of these has caused trouble for search engines. The largest search engines contain a repository of a large portion of the web that they usually have copied without the explicit permission of the creators, and without payment. In some cases, these collections are available to the public, though search engines are generally responsive to requests to have items deleted from their caches, as are sites like the Internet Archive, which stores copies of websites for the use of future historians and other investigators.

The question is whether and under what conditions a search engine can make use of some piece of the original work in creating an index of the web, and how much of that work they can present to a user as a guide to the content. As we have seen, search engines routinely retrieve and process the content of the web and other sources of information in order to try to provide an indication of what is available there. While there have been some attempts to legally restrict search engines from accessing information in order to index it – particularly in the case of Google's book-scanning projects – most of the issues that courts have addressed were related to how much information search engines could reveal about the material they had indexed, and in what form. In the United States, much of this focus has been on the reproduction of images.

The defunct Arriba Vista Image provided users with the ability to easily search for and save images found on the web. When it found an image it copied it temporarily, made a small, thumbnail version, and added it to its index. It also allowed users optionally to view a full-size version of the image, linked directly ("inline linked") from the original site, and, at a later date, presented the resulting page in a frame. One of the sites the search engine indexed hosted photographs of the American West sold online by photographer Leslie Kelly, who sued Arriba for infringement. The decision by appellate court in 2003 on one hand established the use of materials for indexing as a fair use, but also put limits on that use. Thumbnail images, linked directly to the original work, were deemed to be a fair use of the material. The court found that the nature of the use, as well as the likelihood that it would help rather than hurt Kelly's photography sales, provided the grounds for considering it to be an accepted fair use. The inline linking of images from the original site, pulling them from their original context and providing for easy downloading, was not seen as protected by the fair use exemption, and Arriba eventually paid damages to Kelly, based on this infringement.

The Kelly case established that, at least for the time being, the initial copying of materials in order to make an index did not represent an infringing use of the material. *Field* v. *Google* extended this further in 2006, suggesting that text in Google's cache, which was made available to the user, was also subject to the fair use exception, since it provided a new kind of use of the material and, again, was unlikely to affect the potential revenues of the copyright holder. Later cases, including one pressed by a pornographic magazine called *Perfect 10*, made clear that such thumbnails were permitted.

Despite increasing alignment of copyright law around the world, the fair use doctrine, which provides statutory exclusions limiting the power of copyright, is not common in many legal systems, and search engines have encountered difficulty in working within various copyright regimes. Some have characterized copyright law, as it is currently enforced, as being antithetical to the operation of a search engine. Google, after a 2006 decision in favor of news service Copipresse in a Belgian court (Gibson 2006), noted that the suit "goes to the heart of how search engines work: showing snippets of text and linking to the websites is what makes them so useful" (Whetstone 2006). While producers of materials in the United States worry that search engines have too much freedom to make use of their materials, the relationship appears to be reversed in Europe.

The successful suit against Google in Belgium followed a similar Danish suit. In cases that appeared very similar to the Kelly case, German courts – while noting the finding in Kelly – reaffirmed the lack of any such clear protection under German law. German courts made different findings in two cases: in one, finding Google guilty of copyright infringement, and, in another, finding that sites had given implied consent by not restricting access to their images using the robot exclusion protocol. The question of implied consent, as a defense, has come up in many of these cases, and some have argued that an effective solution may be to create a clear indication that copyright on the web is an "opt-in" sort of protection, requiring appropriate use of robot exclusion protocols and the like (see Allgrove 2007).

One of *Perfect 10's* other claims, and a claim that seems to come up repeatedly, is that search engines are linking to other instances of infringement, and thereby contributing to the pirating of their images. Indeed, the combination of Google's ads and search capability drives a number of attempts to capture attention in order to profit from it, including the hosting of pirated materials and the creation of "fake news." Again, search engines argue that, because they process millions of links each day, there is no way of effectively knowing whether the content on any of these sites is infringing. In 1998, the United States enacted the Digital Millennium Copyright Act (DMCA), intended to update copyright so that it would be more easily applied to digital communications, and to enact agreements reached within the World Intellectual Property Organization. It included a "safe harbor" provision for "information location tools," which would shield a website from lawsuits as long as they took down any material that infringed on a copyright or trademark after being notified of the infringement by the owner of that intellectual property. Although this may seem counterintuitive, linking to copyrighted work hosted else-where has been considered by the court several times to be a form of contributory infringement. Because taking down a link frees them from legal liability, search engines are very likely to comply immediately with a DMCA "takedown notice," even where there is little evidence of actual infringement (C. W. Walker 2004).

DMCA takedown notices are now a matter of course. The Chilling Effects Clearinghouse (now known as Lumen[4]), a project supported by the Electronic Frontier Foundation and a number of law schools in the United States, attempts to track DMCA takedown notices, copyright suits, and other legal actions that may cause a chilling effect on free speech. At the time of writing, it lists nearly 4 million takedown notices to Google. Google is not only the most popular search engine for web search; many of its properties support user-created media. Google began providing data about the takedown notices to the Chilling Effects Clearinghouse after what has come to be seen as an iconic use of the DMCA to quell criticism. In 2002, Google received a takedown notice from the Church of Scientology, requesting that they remove links to sites critical of Scientology. Despite wide criticism, Google complied with the request and removed links to the individual pages containing what the Church of Scientology claimed were infringements, but not links to the entire site. A search today on Google for "Scientology" yields a link to the protest site Operation Clambake on the first page of results.

The DMCA, of course, is a local law, and applies in theory only to the United States. Filtering, as a form of censorship, in France, China, or Belgium mainly affects the citizens of those countries, and there is room to argue that the citizens of a country, not search engines, are responsible for changing or maintaining the laws that encourage such censorship. But if the provisions of the DMCA are affecting users in other countries, search engines become another instrument of international power. Those who run a torrent tracker (a sort of search engine for distributed files) based in Sweden called "The Pirate Bay" routinely poked fun at DMCA takedown letters sent to them, as in a response to DreamWorks that read in part, "As you may or may not be aware, Sweden is not a state in the United States of America. Sweden is a country in northern Europe. Unless you figured it out by now, US law does not apply here" (Anakata 2004). While a takedown notice may have little direct effect when delivered to a foreign website, if a site does not appear in global search engines it is effectively invisible. The ability to have local filters installed in China or France avoids the problem of the most restrictive speech laws holding sway over the globe (Spaink & Hardy 2002), but it is equally disturbing if the concentration of the search industry in the United States means that US law predominates globally when it comes to search.

Search engines often fall back on the idea that the web is a new medium, and that the rules for that medium have yet to be fully written. When Google's efforts to digitize the world's books got underway in 2002, it is hardly surprising many publishers and authors saw such copying and indexing as an infringement on their copyright. After all, "scanning" a book certainly appears to be akin to copying. Google saw it as directly analogous to the process used to build an index of the web. After over a decade and a failed settlement, the US courts generally agreed with Google that scanning the books and presenting snippets of text represented a fair use of the copyrighted material. (Cases in Germany, France, and China did not turn out as well for Google. "Fair use" is a distinctly American concept.) After all of that, the actual project has largely flagged. Tim Wu, writing in the *New Yorker* (2015), suggests that there is plenty of blame to go around. Despite claims that the effort was meant to promote the spread of knowledge, Google never spun off a non-profit corporation to manage the process, which might have reduced concerns of Google profiting from the monopoly it had created around scanned books. Ultimately, the real outcome of the case may be less on Google Books, and more on the clarification of fair use in a digital era (Peet 2015).

The ranking of search engine results presented by the largest search engines is shaped by three types of policy: the algorithms built by the search engine companies, the policies of national governments, and the enforcement of intellectual property rights (or threats of such enforcement) enabled by new copyright laws. Censorship is just another word for filtering, and we rely on search engines to filter our results. It is important to understand that these filters, while they are generally not manipulable by individuals, remain subject to those who have traditionally wielded social power.

Promoting search diversity

The interventions by governments mentioned thus far are intended to restrict the flow of particular classes of information, but there is at least the potential for governments to play a different role. Given the importance of an informed citizenry to effective government, there may be an interest in countering the hegemonic tendencies of search engines, and encouraging more open discourse. For much of the last century, media outlets in the United States were required to provide equal access to opposing positions. The idea was that because newspapers and television broadcasters had special access to the living rooms of Americans, they should be responsible for providing a balance of ideas. This justification for interference in privately owned media was largely removed when in 1974 the US Supreme Court ruled that the *Miami Herald* had the constitutional right to publish the political opinions of its choice and that a Florida law demanding equal time for alternate views violated the newspaper's speech rights (*Miami Herald Publishing Co. v. Tornillo* 1974). The tradition of state management of the airways, and of the cultural heritage of the nation, remains far stronger in Europe and in many other parts of the world. Unfortunately, the tools we used for encouraging diversity in the broadcast model are no longer suitable for diversifying the networked search environment (Burri 2016).

Given the even greater ability to distribute ideas online – just about anyone can create a website – it would appear that there is even less need for government intervention. But the ability to create media matters little when the ability to find those publications rests with a very small number of search engines. The vast majority of searches around the world occur on just four search engines. Under those conditions, it certainly seems like there is something approaching monopoly or cartel control of search. If the companies that are handling the searches were open about how they ranked results, that might not be a concern, but because they control the vast majority of search functionality on the web, they deserve to be carefully scrutinized.

Some suggest that the most damaging biases, the retrenchment of current inequities and "winner-take-all" search, are best met with technological solutions. After all, the issue of "local maxima," favoring a solution that is the best among nearby solutions but not necessarily the optimal across the board, has long been a problem across search domains, not just on the web. The special case of image searching is one area in which this has been pursued. The last thing you want is for a search for "African animals" to result in a page full of elephants, or indeed the same image of the same elephant, perhaps in different resolutions. So there have been efforts at diversifying the results of image searches by making sure there are well-ranked results of different sorts (M. Wang et al. 2010). This approach of clustering a set of search results to present different relevant examples from each cluster can be used in other contexts. In fact, researchers from Microsoft and Google, as well as academic researchers, have shown that such results can prove helpful to the researcher (Agrawal et al. 2009; Rafiei, Bharat, & Shukla 2010; Küçüktunç et al. 2015). A great deal of additional research has suggested ways of providing more diverse search results by personalizing the search process to present results that are related to previous searches by the user and similar connections (Radlinski & Dumais 2006).

Engineers generally support the idea that these kinds of bias are a sort of "bug" and something that will be changed with the natural progression of technology: that, as Eric Goldman (2005) has it, "technological evolution will moot search engine bias." Goldman's rosy assessment is that, as personalized search becomes more capable, it will break up the unitary nature of global search, and there will be as many winners as there are people searching. The only problem with this, he suggests, is that it may lead to intellectual isolation of the sort described by Sunstein (who, ironically, sees the serendipity of search engines as a counterweight to the atomization caused by personalized filtering: 2001, p. 206). If history is any guide, there is a tendency for just the opposite to occur, and for communications technologies – particularly those controlled by monopolies and oligopolies – to become more centralized. Political and economic forces both favor such centralization, though recent changes in niche marketing may diminish some of the economic desirability of the "one size fits all" service.

Goldman is right, however, in his core argument: that search engines are biased because that is their intended function. Rather than personalized search, sociable search aims to provide a middle ground for avoiding either centralization or atomization, and the direction of the industry suggests that there is an economic impetus to move toward sociable solutions. But it is unlikely that this will occur at the expense of continued domination of search by a handful of companies. Even as search becomes more complex, there will always be the need for general-purpose global search engines, and, with them, the need for social and political checks on their power.

Pasquale and Bracha (2007) have proposed a solution that relies on federal oversight of the industry. The early utopian thinking about the internet as a place where anyone could become a pamphleteer has given way slowly to a reality that – while still supporting an amazingly diverse assortment of content – it seems to be gradually converging toward points of control. After reviewing some of the common arguments on both sides, the authors suggest that in order to protect democratic discourse, ensure economic competition, promote basic fairness, and avoid deception, the search engines need oversight. They endorse a "Federal Search Commission" that is able to investigate claims of bias. They acknowledge that there are legitimate reasons for maintaining secrecy, in order to thwart SEO efforts, and that it might be possible to create something similar to the US court charged with secretly hearing national security surveillance matters, the Federal Intelligence Surveillance Act (FISA) court.

There are less extreme solutions that still do not require an entirely laissez-faire approach to governing search engines. A more palatable solution might be a quasi-judicial agency like the Securities and Exchange Commission which, particularly with the addition of the Sarbanes–Oxley Act in 2002, routinely deals with balancing corporate desires for secrecy with the public's right to know. Perhaps a small nod to earlier fairness approaches would require a "right of reply" so that those who dispute the results of a search have a space to present their case and perhaps discuss it (Weinstein 2007). Google has already taken interesting steps in this direction, by allowing the subjects of news articles that appear on Google News to reply to stories that include their name. Google's contribution to the Chilling Effects Clearinghouse also suggests a move toward opening up a discussion over the forces that shape the results it produces. At a minimum, there needs to be a concerted effort to make users aware of the sources of bias in search engines so that they can account for this bias when they search. Other countries' approaches to regulation at this point provide little guidance. The heavy-handed censorship of China and dozens of other countries does not provide a model that allows for equality or access. In practice, because a number of the most popular search engines in the world are owned by American companies, the solutions taken in the United States will inevitably have global repercussions.

Don't be secretive

In 2012, a curious document was leaked. It detailed the *actual* conditions under which materials would be removed from Facebook, replacing the rather ambiguous guidelines published in various places on the site with something a bit more concrete for guiding the temporary workers tasked with deleting objectionable content (Gillespie). What was remarkable about this document was not as much its contents as the idea that the explicit rules that shape Facebook content exist, but are not known to those who choose to post material on the platform. Google similarly keeps its exact ranking algorithm a secret, and an entire industry has built up around reading the tea leaves of the search engine results pages and seeking out hints in the elliptical comments of current and ex-Googlers in an attempt to reverse-engineer the process.

Google has been perhaps unjustly criticized for its unofficial motto "Don't be evil," but the phrasing of that motto is telling, particularly in light of its recent difficulties in interacting with governments globally. Some have criticized the lack of sophistication in that motto, and no doubt Google is finding that it is not always clear how to avoid being evil (Argenti, MacLeod, & Capozzi 2007). It is important for a search engine that is the gatekeeper for much of the world's communications to understand that it is not necessary to be evil in order to do evil. Sometimes structural inequities and technocratic decisions that may be perfectly rational and lacking any harmful intent can nonetheless lead to problems in the human systems that make up the web. The safest way to avoid doing evil is to be as open as possible about the decisions you make as an organization, and why. That means being clear about when material or people are being censored, whether those manipulations of the system's flows of data are based on the actions of an algorithm or of a human decision-maker, and how those decisions were guided by particular corporate policies or intercession by governments (MacKinnon et al. 2014). Google, Facebook, and the other platforms for search and discovery need to raise the bar beyond avoiding malevolence, and take on the ethical responsibility of the global mission they are seeking. While the fact that they are answerable to their stockholders and demands for an ever-increasing share price may place an upper limit on how much trust they can accumulate, they can do far better than they have in crafting a social contract with their users. That will not end the scrutiny, nor should it. Google, which has embraced the long tail and open transparency of blogging and of user-created media, has to demonstrate its trust of the public if it hopes to retain trust from the public.

The first step is understanding what is obscured when search platforms present the web to us. As it stands, most people do not think about the ways in which algorithms shape what they see during a search or what appears in their Facebook feed. It may be that there are tools and interfaces that would allow them to see how their searching and browsing is shaped by these processes (Hamilton et al. 2014), opening up what Zimmer (2008a) refers to as "one of the critical junctures for society to re-negotiate its Faustian bargain with Search 2.0." Transparency comes with its own dangers and potential costs (Grimmelmann 2008), but just as we seek transparency and openness from our governments, we should expect something similar from the search and social media industries. As technology advances, such transparency will be ever harder to achieve. Increasingly, algorithms that determine what information and communication is "relevant" to the average user are driven by evolutionary learning processes that are difficult even for their programmers to adequately understand or explain. And, as Adrienne LaFrance (2015) has recently written, "it's going to get more convoluted before it gets clearer. In fact, for a few reasons, it probably won't get clearer *ever*." Ian Bogost (2015) rails against the new mysticism of algorithmic culture, rejecting it in so far as it "euphemizes a corporate, computational theocracy."

Although the specific nature of an individual decision made by an algorithm may be complex and difficult (though certainly not impossible) to trace and audit, the idea that it is a black box of necessity is tinged by a certain amount of ideology, a belief in the nature of machine learning. Moreover, even if the specifics of a single assessment by an algorithm remain difficult to trace, the structures and assumptions of the engineers who made the algorithm and the organizations in which they work remain potentially open to user-controlled tools of observation and assessment (Neyland 2016). By moving beyond the idea of algorithms as inscrutable technologies and toward both the ways in which they are embedded in institutions, and the ways in which they are structured as institutions (Napoli 2014), we can escape the kind of technological sublime that renders political action powerless.

As systems that help to shape our attention and bias our flows of knowledge increasingly rely on algorithmic processes, they become darker and darker black boxes. This is by design. It seems that systems that best do what the designers want them to do often do so in ways that are not easily described. And while we shudder at the idea of our communication being censored by the megalomania of a despot, is the "gut feeling" of an algorithm drawing together billions of individual pieces of data much better, or far worse? The concentration of informational and cultural power into the "hands" of companies and the algorithms they produce reaches its epitome in the platforms for search, and suggests a world very different from the anarchistic, distributed, revolutionary hacker often associated with the cutting edge of computing (Golumbia 2009). These platforms engage in "ideological engineering of neutrality and objectivity" (Bilić 2016), which is essential to their business model. But there is something intensely conservative and institutional about the rise of the algorithm. While we may not be able to audit exhaustively the processes by which such systems arrive at decisions, it is essential that we demand to know at least as much as the engineers do about how they operate, that we seek to discover what their bias obscures, and that we learn how to resist the inertia of the algorithm.

CHAPTER SEVEN

Privacy

Search engines' mission may be as a finding tool, but their business is personal information, and that is a profitable business. As we saw in the first chapter, Google owes its success, and much of its operating budget, to efficiently extracting surplus value from the information it collects from its users (Mager 2012). And in this, it has created a model that other social platforms have sought to emulate. First you get the users, then you can sell them to advertisers, or use their data to sell them products directly. Twitter was the poster child for social media enterprises seemingly without a business model, and the company was valued at more than $18 billion when it made its Initial Public Offering in 2012, despite having operated at a loss throughout its existence (Gadkari 2013). The market bet (wrongly, as it turned out) that Twitter would be able to monetize its nearly quarter of a billion users; the income Twitter generates is drawn mostly from advertising, along with reselling large collections of tweets to marketers, but this has ended up being far less than is needed to break even.

While many consider their privacy to be a fundamental right, the social platforms, and especially search platforms, see it as a product. Even before the search engine and social networking site made such a commodification painfully obvious, many saw the coming age of buying and selling personal information. Oscar Gandy wrote in 1993:

> An individual is defined, in part by what she does, or does not do. Personal information is produced by an observer in

the apprehension and interpretation of another's behavior. We might consider behavior as generating raw data, and the interpretation of that behavior as a value-added process, where additional information is produced as the behavior is assessed. This assessment, like other productive activities, may include the use of other information that has been stored from past experience or has been acquired from other sources. (p. 75)

As much as 3 years before Google was created, and 11 years before Facebook launched, Gandy had described their business models. And these two companies alone collect nearly two-thirds of digital advertising revenues, with Google pulling in $30 billion in 2015 and Facebook $8 billion (Gjorgievska 2016). For many users, the collection of this information seems incidental, and perhaps in the earliest days of these services it was. Most are aware that the platforms observe and record their behavior (Hoy & Milne 2010). As Zimmer (2008b) noted, Google suggested that such collection was really an extension of the kinds of logs that were already being kept by internet service providers, and therefore no more of an intrusion than already exists. Elsewhere, Zimmer (2008a) writes that the collection and concentration of this data represents an externality of Search 2.0. Historically, this is probably right, but the current situation is probably reversed: Google continues to offer search as a way to cull both attention and personal information, which it can then sell to a global network of interested parties. Like Gmail (the most popular webmail provider), Google Docs, Google Maps and Waze, and even the Android mobile operating system, web search is another incidental service designed to draw in users and their personal information.

In the last few years, Google has been ascendant, but a few small search engines have gained increasing shares of search visits. DuckDuckGo has made inroads, especially among those who think seriously about their data and how it is used. And there have been occasions over the last few years (for example, disclosures of the breadth of surveillance activities by the US National Security Agency) that have led to people thinking more about what information is collected about them online. While DuckDuckGo does serve advertisements based on a user's search terms, by default it does not retain searches or create search histories. This attracts both those interested in privacy and those concerned with the potential for personalized search putting them in a filter bubble. It also serves those who are searching via Tor and makes use of encryption and other technologies to attempt to make searching more secure. Of the new privacy-enhancing search engines, DuckDuckGo is the most popular at the time of writing, though there are a range of others, including Ixquick and blekko, both of which make similarly open promises about not retaining or sharing data and taking measures to protect users from "search leakage." Despite broad coverage by news organizations and continuous gains in the number of searches, the share of the search market DuckDuckGo retains is still tiny. DuckDuckGo reports that it averages a little over 10 million queries per day (duckduckgo.com/traffic.html), and while Google is a bit more cagey about its number of queries, many estimate that it is probably somewhere over 3 billion per minute. For now, this is, rather, a reminder to Google and its users that there is a more private option available. Something similar has happened with Facebook (with Diaspora, among others) and with Twitter (with Izmy, among others), but these have not had the same kind of luck in prying users away from the social media giants.

Taking your behavior to a platform where it will not be tracked is only one response to the commodification of your personal data. The capacity for accumulating personal profiles encourages platforms to make use of them, and goes hand-in-hand with a shift in what we consider private information. Gandy noted that the fact personal information has been commodified by marketers does not mean that this is its only use, and the creation of new kinds of publics owes much of its impetus to the ability to more easily discover people online. Yochai Benkler (2006) draws on several examples of this new watchdog function, including the distributed investigation of the Diebold voting machines. These new conceptions of how privacy works are reflected in the language that is used to discuss it: "dataveillance," "sousveillance," and "reciprocal transparency" all suggest that privacy is far from a unidimensional concept (D. Brin 1998; Clarke 1988; Mann, Nolan, & Wellman 2003). Search engines and social platforms will continue to play a role in determining the future of privacy, but also in the creation of public identities, self-conception, and new public records of the "webs of group affiliation," as Simmel (1964) termed them.

Mark Poster (2006) links the rise of identity theft to the new transparency of the internet, a transparency encouraged by search technologies. Identity, from the perspective of such thefts, is "not one's consciousness but one's self as it is embedded in (increasingly digital) databases. The self constituted in these databases, beyond the ken of individuals, may be considered the digital unconscious" (p. 92).

Finding and forgetting the individual

In the film *The Jerk* (1979), the title character, played by Steve Martin, is excited when he finds his name in the telephone directory: "Page 73, Johnson, Navin R. I'm somebody now. Millions of people look at this book every day. This is the kind of spontaneous publicity – your name in print – that makes people." No doubt many people had the same reaction when they first searched for their own name on a search engine, and it generated a link to a site that was actually relevant. These days, it is rare for someone not to appear by name somewhere on the web, but appearance on a search engine seems to put a person on the global stage.

Self-Googling, personal brand management, ego-surfing – all describe the act of monitoring one's own image as reflected by the major search engines. Excessive self-Googling may reflect a certain vanity, but finding out how others perceive you is a natural impulse, as is the temptation to shape that image. In 1956, Erving Goffman (1997) described this activity as "impression management," a term that is still often used among psychologists. Some find the overt concern over managing one's impression unseemly, and others think it is vital. In either case, it seems that, from fairly early on, the web was seen as a place for creating and distributing that impression (Erickson 1996). Tom Peters (1997) argues that "our most important job is to be head marketer" for our personal brand. There are a number of companies that specialize in protecting our online reputations (Adams 2013). Checking for one's name in a search engine provides a glimpse of what others might see and, since search engines often influence others' opinions of us, or even provide a first impression, it is important to know what kind of picture a search portrays. That image is inevitably incomplete and disjointed, emphasizing certain features while ignoring others.

The cultural currency of using Google to find out about someone is reflected in the neologisms that surround the practice (McFedries 2003). The relationship of Google to identity is also reflected in online games built to reflect the information found on the search engine. Googlism is a site that simply collects information from websites found on Google using the "is" pattern to describe people, places and things. Entering a name like "David Bowie" results in phrases like "david bowie is god" and "david bowie is to release an album consisting entirely of instrumentals," along with several dozen others. Google Fight graphically depicts the number of hits for each of two terms, so that you can determine the winner between, for example, "pen" and "sword" ("pen" wins). There is a natural assumption that the number of Google hits a name receives corresponds in some way to the popularity of that person (Bagrow & ben-Avraham 2005).[1]

A serious strain underlies this playfulness. In many hiring

situations, the employer will search social networks for more information (Acquisti & Fong 2015). That means that the way in which you present yourself online can have negative effects on your hiring prospects. Of course, the opposite is also true: given the importance of social capital and "weak ties" in obtaining employment, developing a good social media presence can help pave the road to a career (Ellison, Steinfield, & Lampe 2007). The recruiting process, and any other process that involves trust and potential partnership, requires a reduction of uncertainty. Rituals have evolved around the process of uncertainty reduction, the process by which we gradually reveal ourselves to strangers. Search engines change those rituals, providing a way of finding out about someone without engaging in the ritual dance of conversation (Ramirez et al. 2002). It remains to be seen how exactly this affects the way people establish and maintain friendships. However, there are problems with what we reveal to others online.

First, names are very rarely unique, and it can be easy to mistakenly assume that the pages called up by a search engine are all about the same person. Even a search for the very common name "John Smith" on Google yields information about the founder of Jamestown, Virginia, a researcher at IBM, and a British folk singer. Someone looking for information on one of these Smiths would probably be wary, because the name is so common, but it is all too easy to conflate the people returned as results. Since people are far less likely to encounter other identifiers in the text along with the name (say, birthdates, telephone numbers, or other forms of personally identifying information), it can be difficult to disaggregate the results, particularly for someone you do not already know.

This has led to the phenomenon of "Google twins," people who become obsessed over others who share their name on search engines (Heyamoto 2007). It is sometimes amusing to see what you "might have been," or what others are likely to find (erroneously) when they try to learn more about you. It is also sometimes awkward. Many of my graduate students have encountered difficulties with what employers discover on the web when they go out onto the job market. One of my graduate students discovered that she shares her name with an adult films actress. Although she has never been questioned about this, she worries that people may search for her name and be confused. Since there is no easy way to bring up the fact that one is not a porn star, without raising even more concerns, she is left with the possibility that her "twin" leads to others prejudging her, for better or worse. Something similar happened to one of the founders of BrandYourself.com, who discovered during his first job search out of college that he shared a name with a drug dealer (Weber 2012).

The other possibility is that search engines may reveal material that is related to you, but does not put you in the best light. There have been several highly publicized cases of people writing things on public blogs that reflected poorly on their employer. Once the employer discovers the writing, the employee is "dooced," or loses her job because of the post, a term named after a particular case (Twist 2005). This bad publicity might never have been discovered if not for the ability to search by a person's or company's name. Sometimes someone's past can come back to haunt them through a search engine, bringing to the fore youthful indiscretions, or choices that seem particularly bad only in retrospect (Swidey 2003). One former student emailed me requesting that I help him to remove a blog he had created while a graduate student – in the hiring process, a company he was hoping to join had discovered that he had criticized one of their major clients. However, once material is out on the web, it can be extraordinarily difficult to remove, particularly if it is interesting enough to save. It may be cached or archived in various places around the web, so removing it from the original site may not be enough. Increasingly, the problem material may not be anything you posted. It is now common to post photographs publicly, and often to identify the people in the photographs. After a wild party, you may find images of you are available online. That need not be a problem until someone "tags" the photograph with your name, helpfully making it findable by anyone searching for your name on the web. Someone may have less than flattering things to say about your talk at a local library, about the quality of what you sell on eBay, or about your fitness as a mate. As amateur genealogists move online, they may connect you in familial webs that you may not have wanted the rest of the world to know about, or that may not be accurate. And sometimes it is material that existed before in other forms, but that has become digitized and searchable. When the *New York Times* opened their archive to the web they received daily complaints about embarrassing articles that were suddenly far more accessible than they had been in decades (Hoyt 2007).

Identity theft is much easier when so much information can be discovered from a few web searches. The kinds of questions that have traditionally been used to ascertain identity – things like your mother's maiden name, or the name of your pet – are now often found on search engines. If they are not available there, searches of public records and private databases also contain this previously "private" information. When individuals assemble a dossier of this kind of personal information and share it without consent, it is often referred to as "doxing," and is the tool of both the internet harasser and the vigilante (Douglas 2016). When corporations do the same, it is called "marketing."

Searchable digital identity is a two-edged sword. For all of these dangers, there are still good reasons to be easily findable online. By making it easier for people to meet you and by making clear what your interests and desires are, you have the potential of finding people who share similar interests. One of the reasons recruiters search the web is that a search engine can collect documents from a range of sources, which provides a more trustworthy picture of the individual. The credit bureaus, which collect a dossier of your credit worthiness, are illustrative here. While they have been opaque and discriminatory, as they draw on past experience that may not be available to everyone, they provide some indication that a person can be trusted to pay their debts. They find their history in a kind of corporate doxing: keeping track of those who do not pay their bills. In the United States, the three major credit bureaus all have roots going back many decades. Experian, for example, got part of its start as the Manchester Guardian Society in 1826, when London merchants established a blacklist of non-paying customers. (This followed along the lines of the much more colorfully named precursor, the "Guardians or Society for the Protection of Trade against Swindlers and Sharpers": Bennett 2012).

Today, being offered a credit card or a home mortgage is dependent on what is found in that credit file. Many of the discussions around privacy and sharing data, as well as what little privacy regulation exists in the United States, surround – along with medical records – the rise of the credit bureau. The 1970s in the US saw a small industry of books and seminars on how to protect your privacy in the face of these large collections of records. The questions around the sharing of data are hardly new. The credit bureaus are regulated, and are required by the Fair Credit Reporting Act (FCRA) in the United States to allow individuals to see and correct their contents, something generally not available to the user of social media and search. Or at least it should allow for that. As Frank Pasquale (2015) writes, in practice the credit bureaus exercise almost complete control over those records, and the FICO score, which is often used to determine whether you qualify for a home mortgage, is almost entirely opaque: the original "black box" in our emerging "black box society."

But, like credit ratings, what appears in those social media and search dossiers affects what opportunities you are exposed to: are you enticed by a free gift for test-driving the new Maserati, or are you served ads for prepaid credit cards? Credit reports generally are focused on your bills and how you have paid them over time, but as we have moved to digital systems, the ability to record and assemble details of our everyday lives has led to a new, quantitative reputation. We not only rate people's comments on Reddit or "like" the photos of their children on Facebook, and get rated on eBay by the quality of our used goods, our professional and personal activities are often rated. If you drive for Uber, that rating (for both customer and provider) is built in. It is for professors too, who have been rated by students for years but now see that follow their careers on public sites like RateMyProfessors.com. And when you open your home to strangers on AirBnB, you also allow your house and your skill as a host or guest to be rated. Even your attractiveness and your personality can be rated by those on dating sites. At present, the number of miles you have flown, the number of times you slam on the brakes in your car, and the number of times you have searched for pictures of Beyoncé are all recorded and maintained separately, but they are unlikely to be separated for long. And what is the trajectory of our growing online ghosts? Perhaps the Chinese "Social Credit System," an effort to expand credit ratings to professional conduct, driving, and citizenship activities to arrive at a single score, is one portent (Hodson 2015). And while this definitely moves into the "creepy," there are advantages to knowing you can trust a person you have never met (Hendrikx, Bubendorfer, & Chard 2015).

There are also advantages to being able to move past your own history. Many people encounter points when they are ready to leave the past in the past, make a clean break, and start over. Some of these changes are so common that they are almost ritualized. When many people make the transition from high school to university, they deliberately leave behind the personality and personal histories they had in high school. With a new set of peers, and often a new city, university provides people with a chance to reinvent themselves. Already, with Facebook and other social networking sites, this process has become more difficult. As search engines pervade most of our lives, it will be difficult to leave personal histories behind.

All of this has led to the recognition in various jurisdictions of a new "right to be forgotten."

The right has a slightly longer history in Europe, where several nations put rules around how long criminal or employment records may be shared or retained. The new data protection rules in Europe ("General Data Protection Regulation") included a provision that would allow individuals to request that a search engine remove links to materials that concerned them. After a decision in Spain enforced this new rule against Google, the site has received requests to remove nearly 2 million links, and other organizations are wondering how far this might extend in the future, and what kinds of limitations can legally be put on such requests. In the United States, California has been at the forefront of laws intending to limit the long-term effects of information shared online. In 2013, they established a new law (SB 568) that required social media platforms to allow minors to remove photos and posts. The broader idea of a right to remove private information from public view seems to be gaining ground, though a similar restriction on retaining private information privately has not seen as much demand yet.

Many suggest such laws are attempting to put the genie back into the bottle, and point to what is often called the "Barbra Streisand Effect," so-named when the efforts of Streisand to hide photos of her California estate instead led to their wider distribution. The case establishing the right to be forgotten as a human right immortalizes the name of the Spaniard who lodged the initial complaint: Mario Costeja González. Now Google may not link to the original newspaper article, or presumably another new article in the *New York Times* that describes what it was he was hoping would be forgotten, along with his name and photo. Ironically, the case has made Costeja a "public figure," and thus perhaps unable to assert the right to be forgotten (Arthur 2014). This prompted comedian John Oliver to suggest that Brin's suggestion of "reciprocal transparency" was the only sensible response, encouraging people to leak their own most embarrassing material under the hashtag #mutuallyassuredhumiliation (Oliver 2014).

It seems likely that we will see an ongoing discussion of the idea that at least public records should be erasable (or, more accurately, de-indexed). Google has struggled to implement the kind of index removal that many people want to see happen. The current solution seems unsupportable, and does not look much like the solution Viktor Mayer-Schönberger described in his book *Delete: the virtue of forgetting in the digital age* (2011), in which he argues that public information on the internet should have an expiration date, just as browser cookies often do today. Another proposed framework seeks to provide a clear linkage between users and their private data, allowing for automated "forgetting" of personal data on the internet (Simeonovski et al. 2015). Systems that provide various forms of permissions, however, are complex even in non-distributed networks – the solution here is not a simple one.

The degree to which this right extends to knowledge about, and control over, private records is another question. Does it really matter if a search of Costeja yields nothing from the Google search engine (at least European versions of that engine), but continues to produce results in databases that are less publicly accessible, including those of credit bureaus and newspaper indexes? Will this give rise to sites that seek to retain deleted materials, as has happened for tweets and YouTube videos that have been removed? The devil here is in the details, which remain ambiguous.

The largest search engines and social media platforms are headquartered in the United States and China, neither of which has a history of robust privacy protection. Crawford & Schultz (2014) propose a model of "data due process" that finds support and analogs in the US context, and it is possible that the internet-enabled vigilantism in China (the "human flesh search") will result in new privacy controls. But, more generally, Europe is likely to continue to be the lever pressing forward recognition of privacy rights, and platforms that hope to keep a footing in the European Union are likely to have to adapt to these new demands. Whether compliance with European laws will lead to greater protection outside Europe and for non-Europeans is a separate question. If past experience is a guide, these platforms will see an advantage in handling European and non-European users differently, and continuing to profit from the collection of personal information about the latter.

Your search is showing

In August of 2006, AOL publicly released data from a three-month period so that researchers could make use of it (Arrington 2006). It contained the search history of over 650,000 users, collected at random. The intent was a good one: by providing a massive database of queries, it was possible to gather how and why people searched for items. Usernames had been stripped from the data and replaced with numbers. Under immediate and heavy criticism, the data were removed from the site three days later, but the archive had already been downloaded and made available on other sites. The scandal eventually led to the resignation of AOL's Chief Technology Officer and the researcher responsible for the release of the data (Zeller 2006).

The release provided a great opportunity to ask the question: how much is revealed by what we search? Particularly when the names of the searchers were concealed, could it even be claimed that there was a violation of privacy? Within hours, people around the web were picking out patterns. Within days, individuals had been identified and intriguing examples of search streams had been extracted. Some of these were disturbing. For example (as quoted in McCullagh 2006):

replica loius vuitton bag
how to stop bingeing
how to secretly poison your ex
how to color hair with clairol professional
girdontdatehim.com
websites that ask for payment by checks
south beach diet
nausea in the first two weeks of pregnancy
breast reduction
how to starve yourself
rikers island inmate info number
inmatelookup.gov
www.tuportal.temple.edu
how to care for natural black hair
scarless breast reduction
pregnancy on birth control
temple.edu
diet pills

Copies of the database ("mirrors") are still available, and some allow for the rating, tagging, and discussion of interesting search histories.[2] An article in the *New York Times* detailed how it tracked down one user, a 62-year-old widow from Lilburn, Georgia, based on what she searched for. When alerted to the trail of searches that had been recorded, she said "My goodness, it's my whole personal life. I had no idea somebody was looking over my shoulder" (Barbaro & Zellner 2006). The article notes that, like other search histories, this one was a "catalog of intentions, curiosity, anxieties and quotidian questions."

John Battelle (2005) refers to Google as a "database of intentions." We search for things we are hoping to know, hoping to do, and hoping to become. It is the most powerful unobtrusive measure of collective and individual desires that society has ever known. Google has capitalized, to a certain extent, on the aggregation of that data. By watching what searches are becoming more popular, Google is able to gauge the global consciousness directly. If tens of thousands of people are suddenly searching Google for the same person or issue, it is a pretty good indicator that there is a consensus that the keywords describe something interesting. It does not tell you why they are interested, but mapping the attention alone is powerful. Google first provided summaries of this aggregated data in a report called the Google Zeitgeist, ranking the searches in various thematic ways. Zeitgeist has given way to "Top Charts" on the Trends site, a list of the fastest-gaining searches, but without the minimal level of analysis Zeitgeist provided. Google Trends itself allows you to chart attention over time, and compare politicians, products, or ideas. To draw on an earlier example, it is possible to plot "pen" against "sword" to see what people are searching for. "Pen" wins here as well, with the five-year trend increasing that gap over time.

Google maintains a list of previous searches by a user, basing this on either a cookie on the user's machine or a log-in on a Google product. Users can delete their own history, but it is not clear whether this deletes it only from the user's view or from all of Google's records. Google has the capability of tracking users even further than search. Because Google advertising appears on many websites, and many websites make use of Google Analytics (a free tool for analyzing traffic to a site), there exists the potential to track users as they move around the web. DoubleClick, one of the first web advertisers that placed ads across multiple sites, did just this. Naturally, each could only detect user activity on sites where they had placed advertisements, but as more and more websites hosted DoubleClick ads, it was possible to map users' moves across these sites. These data were valuable enough for Google to acquire the company in 2008. And it does not stop with web search: as Google either innovates into new areas or acquires existing services, new sources of behavioral information are created, from location data to mobile use data, and even into things like health logging and daily schedules. The list of applications and services offered by Google today is staggering and nearly all-encompassing. It would be entirely possible to communicate and conduct all of your business without ever leaving the warm embrace of Google, and this is just what Google wants: its product is you.

Given this concentration of private information, it is natural to question Google's actions and policies. In the past, Google has been criticized for using cookies that did not expire to track user activities, for tracking email content in a way that was not transparent to the user, and for a number of other transgressions. Efforts to personalize individuals' experiences with the search engine and Google's other services mean creating an electronic dossier that is exceptionally detailed. Indeed, Google's CEO, Eric Schmidt, has suggested that a more complete profile of users is at the heart of the company's rapid expansion, just as many other search engines have sought similar enhanced portraits of the people who visit their sites (Daniel & Palmer 2007). More recently, Google has attempted to become more transparent, and has taken steps to limit the collection and retention of certain private information, but as much of our lives moves online, and we increasingly find ourselves among suites of applications from one of the search oligarchs, we see a concentration of private information like no other. Although Google says that they have no intention of combining data from all of these sources (including DoubleClick) into a single profile, the concern is that nothing outside this intent would stop them from doing just that (Edwards 2007). If we continue down this path, Google will know more about you than anyone else does, including yourself.

Even if Google does not collect those data into a single profile, there is the added concern that the US government might. A decade ago, there was a great deal of concern over a project that went under the name of "Total Information Awareness," and sought to combine multiple sources of data to track and predict domestic threats. The project was scuttled under public scrutiny, but the elements that make up information awareness were actively pursued (Harris 2006).

The degree to which such cooperation can be damaging has already been seen in the Chinese case. The major social and search platforms only gained access to the Chinese market under the condition that they both censor certain topics and allow the Chinese government access to user data. Yahoo! provided information to a Chinese court that allowed a dissident, Shi Tao, to be sentenced to prison for ten years (Zeller 2006). These acts have led many to question whether privacy is appropriately placed in the hands of national policy. Google has responded by urging the creation of coherent and coordinated international policy on privacy (Ljunggren 2007). While certainly a laudable goal, handing the problem over to national governments is irresponsible; these companies should abide by a set of ethics that rises above national policy (Fry 2006). Though it is, as Google's Elliot Schrage told the US House of Representatives in 2006, an "imperfect world" that requires "imperfect choice," Google and other search engines should be as prepared to fight for their customers as they are to fight for approval of their corporate acquisitions.

Edward Snowden's revelations have since shed some light on the extent of the monitoring by the US government's own intelligence agencies (and sharing among governments' intelligence bodies), as well as the complicity of many of the major social platforms and search providers in the US. Although the existence of such records and a willingness to provide them to the government is troubling, it is not entirely surprising, and fits with the history of close ties between US communications companies and the US government. Government monitoring programs like Shamrock and Echelon worked largely through the collusion of communication companies (Bamford 1983; Singel 2006).[3] The availability of applications and records provided by Google, Facebook, Twitter, and others has opened up a whole new world for intelligence services, who now have easy access to the surveillance we perform on ourselves and our friends as part of our online social lives (Lyon 2015). Executives from these companies deny any willing collaboration with government officials (Levy 2014), but given both history and continuing revelations, along with a background of secrecy about how they do what they do, it is difficult to trust them. In 2016, Reuters revealed that Yahoo! had built a backdoor into their mail services to make it easier for federal agencies to monitor private email (Menn 2016). And when Barack Obama signed the Cybersecurity Information Sharing Act of 2014, an Act that (despite its name) provided a structure for directly connecting social platforms' databases with government data collections (Fulton 2014), it made such claims even harder to believe. The task of protecting Google and Facebook from attackers is closely bound up with the task of monitoring and profiling its users, all part of a growing "military-internet complex" in which it is growing more difficult to discern where the policies of the corporately owned platforms end and government actions begin (Harris 2014).

If Google and the other social platforms are already at the center of global flows of information, they represent the ultimate targets: treasure troves of private information. The threats to that information are varied. They might, through some unforeseeable error, accidentally leak that data to the public. Identity thieves may find a way through their security. The profiles would be amazingly valuable to anyone who wished to be able to match a set of intentions to a group of people. Anyone who has anything to sell would love to have access to such data, as would many governments. And given the potential of this compiled set of dossiers, it seems unlikely that Google will choose not to take advantage, someday. Even if they are not sharing these profiles with the US government on a regular basis, they are still collecting these data and each year they collect a greater amount. And while we can consider hypothetical situations in which such collections can be used by governments to sort us into those with privileges and those without – something along the lines of the TSA (Transportation Security Administration) Precheck line that privileges some citizens over others, but applied more broadly

– the truth is that search engines and social platforms *already* have dossiers on us, and these are *already* being used to decide who is worthy of more attention and benefits (Marwick 2014). That concentration of informational power is dangerous whether it is in the hands of the government, of hackers, or of the companies themselves. And once they are in the hands of one, they are likely to fall into the hands of the others. These companies are simply too big to trust (Gruman 2014).

Search, surveillance, and transparency

In 2007, science-fiction author Cory Doctorow penned a short story that puts all of this into dystopic relief. In the story, a man returns to the United States after some time abroad, to find that the Department of Homeland Security has partnered with Google, and that they had used behavioral targeting to assess him as a risk. The story goes on to explain that, once he was on a watchlist, Google would allow the government to watch his every move. It appears to be the worst-case scenario of a distant future, but it is not.

In 2005, a Canadian citizen was turned away at the Buffalo, New York, border crossing after border guards used Google to locate his blog and interrogate him about its contents (Vaas 2005). The same happened to a Canadian psychotherapist, whose identity as it appeared on Google included a description of drug use when he was younger (Solomon 2007). As if using the story as a plan of action, the Department of Homeland Security (DHS) began actively seeking out mentions of a set of keywords on social media. In 2012, the Electronic Privacy Information Center successfully won a Freedom of Information Act case that allowed them to see the contents of a manual instructing those working at the DHS how to search various platforms and which keywords should raise suspicion. There was further speculation that the DHS was both manipulating conversations online and had been provided special access by the platforms (Charette 2012). As of late 2016, immigration agents are piloting a new program that would have them requesting that visitors provide their social media accounts for further screening (Nixon 2016). While the idea that terrorists might use Facebook to plan criminal acts is not one that most people would find far-fetched (and a DHS study of Facebook found it being used in that way: Department of Homeland Security 2010), few people would assume that they would be caught up in a search merely because they fit a particular profile. Michael Zimmer (2008a) has argued that the rise of a more sociable web ("Web 2.0") has created new sources of rich data about how people live their everyday lives, and, as a result, the kinds of things the border patrol, advertisers, and employers have access to is expanding rapidly. The problem in this case is really one of expectations. Since we expect our blog to be used only in particular contexts – and assessing our fitness to travel in a foreign country is not one of those contexts – this particular use of Google, Facebook, or Twitter is surprising and unsettling.

Several countries have used specialized search engines in order to locate illegal content within their own borders. An early Singaporean effort merely searched for files with image-related extensions, in order to find potential pornography (Ang & Nadarajan 1996). In 1999, the government-supported ISP SingNet faced popular dissent for putative "virus scanning" of computers on their network that led to the arrest of one network user when the search uncovered illegal materials. Although the World Wide Web represents a very large database to search, various forms of "policeware" – programs that allow for intrusion and the collection of large amounts of data – and signals intelligence programs also create huge databases that must be searched and sifted.

There are really two types of intrusions on our privacy. The first is the actual physical recording of an image or a piece of data. This extraction of information from our control need not be a serious breach. When we enter a convenience store, we do not generally glance at a security camera and assume that the images it is showing will appear on a video sharing site because the owner is auctioning the video. At least, that is not what we expect today; those expectations will probably be changing in the coming years. Already, the Insecam website streams images from 73,000 unsecured cameras to the web (Zhang 2014). But when it is merely the owner recording the activities in her store we are not particularly bothered, because we trust, to some degree at least, that the images and data gathered will be handled appropriately – that the camera's tapes are not archived or shared, that our credit card number and shopping habits are not being sold to the highest bidder.

It is really that second step, the decontextualization of our personal information, that is particularly invasive. When the information that is collected by a security camera, or by a hotel's maid, or by a search engine is then used in a context that we did not expect or approve of, this can be disquieting. As a former New Yorker, pizza makes up a substantial part of my diet, and the pizzeria down the block recognizes my voice, knows where I live, and knows how I like my "pie." I know that they know these things about me, and, far from bothering me, I enjoy the convenience of that personalized trusted relationship. If, while traveling in London, I ordered room service only to find that the hotel knew what my favorite pizza toppings were, I would find this disturbing. It is true that it would still be an added value, but it would make me feel that I had less control over my environment than it had over me. Both my pizzeria and the hotel would have violated my confidence. This sort of unexpected leakage, or a mismatch between what I feel is reasonable use of my data and what engineers and marketers think, is often considered "creepy" (Tene & Polonetsky 2013). The most oft-cited example of this kind of creepiness is one described in an article by Charles Duhigg (2012) in a *New York Times Magazine* article entitled "How companies learn your secrets." It describes how the US discount retailer Target managed to figure out that a man's teenage daughter was pregnant before he did, and began sending her coupons for diapers and other baby supplies, leading to his discovery. The idea that a major retailer knows you are pregnant before your family does is creepy. Target did not stop targeting pregnant women, but now they camouflage the baby coupons by surrounding them by other less relevant ones so customers do not feel watched. And when I call for a pizza, and my number provides the shop's ordering system with my home address and last order, the person taking the call still asks for it, so that I am not creeped out.

Both sides of this equation – the increased number of digital sensors and the increased ability of those sensors to be linked into complete models – are accelerating exponentially. As it is, each activity you perform online leads to a data stream, and those data streams are combined and classified using analytics to predict how you might behave in hypothetical situations. Especially with the explosion of the Internet of Things, your digital footprint will now extend more clearly into the real world. These metrics seem to be naturally more invasive and the potential for violations of expected context is high. Consider, for example, when someone noticed that the Fitbit personal activity tracker could reveal when users were having sexual intercourse. The company noted that they "certainly did not intend or expect the sharing of intimate information," and neither, I suspect, did most of the users (Hill 2011). Likewise, some have suggested that the Pokémon GO game, and the Ingress game it was modeled on, were in fact a way of convincing users to provide map data to Google (Goggin 2017). And while at one point the major privacy threat may have been surveillance cameras mounted on buildings, now they are just as likely to be flying overhead (McKelvey, Diver, & Curran 2015) or on people's faces (Hong 2013). Naturally, this kind of visual and spatial intrusion is already creepy, but when combined to create personal filters (Koene et al. 2015), or to learn and predict probable future actions (Liebelson

2014), the levels of intrusion into what we have traditionally considered private matters reach extreme heights.

It is all too easy for the personalization services and predictive analytics of search engines and social platforms to do the same thing: allow my relationship with the site to bleed over into my relationships with other companies and with the government. Yet these platforms are in business to do exactly that. In other words, it is creepy business, and if they want to be able to remain profitable, they have to do creepy things without antagonizing their users enough to lose them. I do not want Google to know how I like my pie any more than I want the pizzeria to know how I like my search results.

The move toward more surveillance in society is not inevitable, and, likewise, there is no inherent necessity for search engines to collect and make use of information about us. There was a time when search engine developers paid very little attention to the transaction logs produced, and as DuckDuckGo shows us, there is nothing that says that a return to that point is impossible. Although about three-quarters of American users say they do not want search engines to track what they are searching for (Purcell, Brenner, & Rainie 2012), and the majority would like to do more to protect their privacy (Madden 2014), so far that has not meant a large desertion from Google or Facebook. That is fine as long as users are aware of what is happening to their information and make an informed choice. Many will decide that free email is worth having Google's algorithms read and learn more about them and about the people they correspond with. Many are willing to have Google or Facebook predict their needs and desires if it means reducing the time they spend searching the web (or maps, or mail, or health data, or learning opportunities). They may make that choice even when presented with an alternative that does not collect, package, and sell their personal information. But they should know enough about how that information is being used to be able to make an informed choice.

This extends equally to government surveillance. The idea that the police and intelligence communities should open their doors so that targets of their surveillance – the "bad guys" – can better understand the way they work is likely to be treated with more than a little suspicion. The police and intelligence communities have cultivated a culture of secrecy that has served them well in the past. Clearly, some sources of data cannot be openly accessible to the public. But there is value in knowing the kinds of data collected and the ways in which they are processed. Knowing more about how the government works allows us to balance the power of police authority with the need for public autonomy. Generally, people are more wary about how governments might be using their information. That is sensible: while a company may deny you a credit card, a government has the ability to take away your freedom. Most do not realize that when their personal information is captured by private businesses, some of the consumers of that information are likely to be the government agencies they are more concerned about.

The global village and new legends

Wired Magazine at one point considered Marshall McLuhan to be its patron saint. His polysemous aphorisms appealed to the popular idea that technology changes everything. One of the memes that continues to survive is the idea of a "global village," and like so much of what McLuhan (1962) wrote, it is often interpreted quite differently by different people. The original conception saw a retribalization brought about by electronic mass media, and the potential for homogenization. The digerati appropriated the term, and suggested a global forum, a meeting of minds.

Early sociology drew heavily on Ferdinand Tönnies' (1957) distinction between people who are organized primarily as communities (*Gemeinschaft*), bound by familial and tribal expectations, and those who are organized as societies

(*Gesellschaft*), bound together by a shared goal. Simmel (1964) noted that the major difference between these groups was whether individuals could choose their own social ties. Particularly within cities, it was likely that a person would choose ties with others who might exist in completely separate communities. For example, I have social ties to many of my colleagues in the field of internet research (who also have ties to one another), and ties to members of my extended family (who also have ties to one another), ties to those who share my interests in tinkering or judo, ties to parents of the children in my kids' classes, as well as ties to people in my neighborhood, in previous neighborhoods, and in earlier workplaces. These connections are to groups that are not particularly interconnected. If I were to draw circles around the members of each of these groups, they would certainly intersect – since I am in each – but they would intersect very little. This differs from a traditional community, in which one might go to school with the same people one works with, one goes to church with, one plays sports with, one vacations with, and one marries.

The internet is thought to encourage an even more extreme level of *Gesellschaft*, as we gain close relationships with those we might never meet in person (Walther 1996). Sherry Turkle (1996) has argued that this is the distinctive feature of identity online: just as we flip through applications on our computers, shifting our attention from context to context, we switch identities online to suit our needs. The reason for this is that our interactions, say, in a multi-user game can be easily walled off from our behavior in other social contexts, online and off. But social technologies like blogs and other social networking platforms, along with search engines, make such walls very thin. The mark of *Gesellschaft* society is that we do not really know what our grown children are doing: they move off to a new city, and, except for the infrequent telephone call, they are strangers. Likewise, they know little of our private lives. A combination of social media and search engines changes that, leading to connections that can be maintained much more easily over time and space. There is a danger that search engines can conflate more than one person's life into an impression of one person, but at the very least they draw together pieces of our lives that otherwise would not intersect. Students are surprised when they discover that recruiters are looking at pictures of them drunk and wild at a college party on Facebook. In some ways, though, this is a return to small-town life, where everyone knows everything about you. Under those constraints, it is more difficult to live a "double life."

As time goes on, we are witnessing a reversal of the nature of online networking, with those groups that were once segregated – family, friends, work, school – being integrated through the power of technologies that aggregate identifying information. The work of social media and search engines is being enhanced by community policies that insist on positively identifying members of the community as "real" individuals. Paypal, the online payment company, requires users to tie their account back to a bank account in order to root identities in the real world; Amazon attempts to certify real names for their reviews; and increasingly even news discussions online seek to remove anonymity in the hope of restoring civility. The idea is that trust is only possible when a real identity stands behind it.

There are ways to resist this. Readers of spy novels are familiar with the idea of a "legend," a cover story constructed to give the spy a believable background (Mahle 2006, p. 366). Those who spend a great deal of time online are probably equally aware of the usefulness of multiple identities. Sometimes, these are throwaway identities used to gain access to free resources that, nonetheless, require a user name. Gaining access to *Los Angeles Times* stories, for example, requires people to log in. Reluctant to share private information, many people simply invent a false login identity, or turn to a site like Bugmenot.com to use one of their proven identities. Sometimes people create false identities for fraudulent reasons: in order to steal money or services. Sometimes they create identities to do what they do not want to be associated with, "sockpuppets" that support them in public venues, or play the antagonist. Finally, many people keep a blog or social media account under the cover of a pseudonym in the hope that a search engine will not connect it with their "main" identity. Sometimes these identities are tied to a character played in a multiplayer online game. At present, the only viable way of defending privacy while still maintaining a public life is the creation of masks and false identities. If the use of surveillance cameras in public spaces is any indication, it is likely that there will soon be increasing numbers of rules against contributing pseudonymously to discussions, and possibly new legal structures that restrict our ability to play a character rather than our "real" identity. It is important that we recognize that, despite the dangers of allowing pseudonymous interactions, they are the best way of mitigating the loss of our personal privacy in a world where search engines peer into every part of our lives. As the integrating technologies of the search engine and social media bring down the walls between social contexts, people will take one of two paths: either give in to the integrating force, or, for a few determined souls, develop far more intricate legends or create new ways of obfuscating their identity or their intentions (Aonghusa & Leith 2016).

Many people are not alarmed by the idea that they might be observed by a machine. Few enter the local convenience store and feel oppressed by the eye of the camera above them. The collection of data does not seem intrusive until it is networked, findable, and available to a wide group of people. Search engines will provide the technology to aggregate each of these small intrusions into a wholesale removal of distance between our public and private lives. It seems unlikely that this will change. The most promising solution is perhaps counterintuitive: we must learn more about those systems that seek to learn more about us. While technologies of surveillance continue to expand, those same technologies can be employed to reduce the secrecy of corporations and governments as well as individuals. Many individuals have chosen an exhibitionist path, tweeting their everyday interactions, hopes, dreams, workouts, and lunches. But in exchange for this disclosure, they should expect institutions to reciprocate. If they watch us, we should be able to watch them.

Mann, Nolan, and Wellman (2003) term this "sousveillance," watching from below, and see it as a way of confronting organizations by using their tools against them. Their work is grounded in the assumption that surveillance is a technology of social power, and that by confronting those who are engaging in surveillance with an inversion of the technology, an opportunity for discussion is presented. An alternative approach suggests not so much "watching from below" as "watching from beside." Observation is not the problem – the problem is an unequal distribution of the observing and the observed. As Amitai Etzioni (1999) argues, the right kinds of transparency reduce, rather than increase, the necessity for government control and intrusion, and scrutiny is the antidote to control. Many take issue with Etzioni's communitarian approach to privacy and transparency – the idea that, in a global village, the villagers should be watching one another.[4] The putative needs for camera surveillance in a shop – to stop shoplifting and prevent criminal acts in the store – are better met by a culture of mutual respect, along with peer-to-peer reciprocal observation. The degree to which search engines allow us to watch each other, and to watch the search engine, will determine the degree to which it is performing as an ethical member of the global community. David Brin (1998) suggests that this kind of reciprocal transparency is our last, best chance of creating an open and creative society. He acknowledges that there are dangers – for example, that we will become obsessed with each other's lives in the same way we seem to be obsessed with celebrities today – and it is clear that this alone will do little more than partially mitigate the present imbalances, but it is worth taking those risks if there is the potential it will lead to a sustained open society.

At present, it is impossible for us to know who sees the information search engines collect and under what conditions that occurs. In 2002, a cartoon appeared in the *New Yorker* in which a person tells his friend, "I can't explain it – it's just a funny feeling that I'm being Googled." Many people have that funny feeling, and when they take into consideration the often immediate rewards of disclosure, the less tangible risks entailed in that disclosure, and the sometimes complicated processes necessary to mitigate that risk, they often are left with little more than an uncomfortable feeling that their privacy is already gone (see Hargittai & Marwick 2016). If only we had a kind of search engine radar that told us who was looking for information about us and why – the equivalent of the red light on a camera that lets us know we are being recorded. More than just a dot on a screen, this would inform us of when, for example, Google was combining data from Google Mail with our search histories or medical histories.[5] The first rule for search when it comes to privacy and transparency should be: take only what you are willing to give. The clickstreams and other data generated by individuals using the web are valuable, and when the trade is transparent, many people will be willing to exchange it for services. But when search engines and social platforms collect data without clearly explaining how they will make use of it, and to whom they will release it, it represents an unjust imbalance of power.

CHAPTER EIGHT

Future Finding

Predicting the future is always a dangerous game. But if you have a grasp of the current environment, and the current trajectory of the cultural understandings, institutions, and technologies in that environment, you should be in a good position to at least map out a range of possible futures. If you have arrived here after reading the chapters that come before, you have probably already projected out a similar set of futures.

The fading of the search engine

It seems a daring prediction to imagine that the search engine, as we know it, will no longer exist. After all, the title of this book is predicated on not only the existence of search engines but their centrality to social organization in the Internet Age. Perhaps a better title would have been *The Search Society*.

Search and discovery remain central to the process of moving from mass-mediated society to network society. Our attention is shaped no longer by the evening news, but by networks of friends and machines that tell us what is worthy of our time and energy. We have directed much of that attention to the oracle of the last two decades, Google, and the other search engines that help to make the mess of the web comprehensible. Indeed, Google has had to fight to make sure that it remains capitalized, and does not become a synonym for "to find." Can you google that for me? No, it is ungoogleable.[1]

It is not clear how much googling we will be doing. We will certainly be asking questions. We will need to know things.

And we will be typing things into boxes until well after this book is out of print. But, ever so gradually, the interface of search and discovery will further occlude the engines that are building the results. This is already happening, of course. Few have a good idea of how search works or how their feeds are ordered. There are a few reasons for this.

First, it is complicated. Even people who think they know how search works will admit that they do not know exactly. Like Coca-Cola's secret recipe, nobody really knows all of it. And it is becoming ever more complicated, thanks to systems that evolve on their own and reach conclusions that are difficult to model. Second, it is in the interests of most of those driving search and discovery for you not to know. There are the obvious reasons for this: they worry that you may create your own Google or Baidu. Then there is the question of what we might find when we lift the hood. While it is clear the emperor has some clothes, they may not be what we expect. And finally, most of us don't know because we don't need to know – at least in detail. There was a time in the evolution of the automobile when anyone with a basic mechanical sense could do maintenance and repair of their own vehicle. Now it requires specialized tools and knowledge that most shade-tree mechanics do not possess. Likewise, anyone with a basic grounding in coding can create a small search engine, but the major players in search and discovery have built engines that are more complex than any single person can comprehend. It is good for those who search to understand the basics of how results are delivered, but they do not need to know the details in order to effectively use search.

We do not know exactly what goes into search, and for these reasons we will know less as time goes on. We will not recognize that our grocery shelves are organized in such a way as to nudge us toward certain purchases. We will not recognize that our car is navigating us past a donut shop that is sponsoring navigation that week. We will accept the recommendations of our phone, our car, our virtual assistant and the other pieces of machinery that make up our lives because they are right more often than wrong, and because it is so much easier to follow their advice on the minor things so that we can be freed up to make the major decisions.

The rise of the findable ecosystem

Eric Brewer (2001) dreams of a search engine that will let him find things in his chaotic office. Because we have learned to turn to search, it can be frustrating when something is not indexed, but every day more of the world is becoming findable, because even as search becomes less *visible* it becomes more *attached* to our everyday lives. How we search and what we find are no longer trapped exclusively in a window on our desktop.

Search ventured out in our mobile devices. If over dinner we could not remember who played Léon's patron in the Luc Besson movie, we no longer have to wait until we get home. We just search it on our phone. Or I can ask Siri, Google, or Alexa. Voice recognition is not perfect yet – in fact, Siri has difficulty recognizing Luc Besson's name – but it would have been difficult to imagine a decade ago that the sort of voice interface found on the Starship *Enterprise* was going to be found on the devices in our pockets (as Google's Hal Varian has noted: Smith & Anderson 2014). Consumer dictation has been around in working form for nearly three decades, and even longer in hobbyist form. But the ability to recognize the variety of spoken language, often in noisy environments, is new, and improving every day. This means that for the first time the years of voice conversations the National Security Agency collects every second can be converted to text and searched in the same way any other digital document can (Froomkin 2015). One interface that is a mainstay of science fiction is the conversational agent, ready to make sense of your needs and reply verbally. Despite advances in speech recognition and production, we do not yet have our HAL 9000, though Mark Zuckerberg of Facebook is said to be seeking his own Jarvis from Iron Man (Seetharaman 2016).

How long will it be before my phone, my watch, or the dinner table is listening in to the conversation at the table and predicting the kinds of searches I might do in real time, ready to step in when I stumble on Danny Aiello's name? That sort of predictive discovery already happens in other contexts. When I hop in the car in the morning, Waze asks me if I am headed to work. An app called Random analyzes what you read and suggests something you might discover is of interest (Lomas 2014). And if it feels like this direct approach is too pushy and you start to get anxious, an app will tell you to take a deep breath (Mosendz 2014). These kinds of personal analytics draw from a heavily monitored stream of media and data that people produce, and apply the same kinds of analytics that businesses use at a human scale (Regalado 2013). Just as the search engine produces a kind of darkened mirror of society, attributing relevance to some topics and not to others, seeing yourself through your "data double" means a shift in perceptual bias (Ruckenstein 2014). Jill Walker Rettberg (2014) likens it to Parmigianino's sixteenth-century self-portrait using a convex mirror. We see ourselves through the technologies we choose and which are chosen for us.

This kind of interaction requires new ways to interface with the user, and new ways to "crawl" and index the physical world and the flows within it. In the first instance, we are finding new ways to interact with the network while on the move. Messages need not be spoken; they can be presented on the screens that may be around us at any time, sent to the computer in our pockets, to our wristwatches, pulsed secretly from our activity tracker, projected into our eyesight with augmented reality devices, or, eventually, directly to our brains. Under these conditions, the nature of "searching" changes fundamentally.

Likewise, we are really only at the outset of the Internet of Things, and the sensors that come along with it. At present, the greatest stumbling block is one of protocols: standardized ways of allowing these connected things to truly begin behaving like networks. That means not just being able to get online, but becoming easily discoverable and passing along data in a way that is easily understood by other systems. There is already a rapid adoption of wearable trackers, and this is being gradually joined by a new generation of home automation. For many of us, these connected devices are making their way into our lives without much active consideration: the television is suddenly a computer, the electronic lock on the door can talk to the alarm system, the music player connects to our virtual collection, all of them capable of sensing and reacting with a home network we did not plan to have. Likewise, our automobiles are becoming networked devices, even when we do not realize it. Certainly, we might take active measures, like installing a dongle that lets our insurance company monitor our driving habits, but in many cases we are not aware of the number of sensors in our own cars. At the extreme end, all Tesla automobiles are being shipped with the equipment needed to become self-driving – all that is needed is a software update at some point in the future.

This crawlable Internet of Things means never having to figure out where you left your sunglasses or remember where your friends live; you will be able to search the real world electronically. But it means so much more than this when those data streams can be used to find patterns and make sense of our personal and our social worlds. And, of course, this means that the search engines and social platforms will know at least as much about us as we know about ourselves.

The ascendance of the algorithm

When Ask.com was trying to vie for search users in the mid-2000s, they included the word "algorithm" in a number of campaigns because, as the CEO noted at the time, it was "a funny word that people don't hear every day" (Vascellaro &

Lacapra 2007). While the word may not find its way into conversation around the dinner table in many households, it does seem to show up with surprising frequency in other venues. At the moment, deep learning algorithms and approaches to predictive analytics seem poised to change not just search and discovery, but a range of social processes. If you were to take a sample of current popular coverage of deep learning, you would easily be convinced that we are on the precipice of fully functioning artificial intelligence and steps away from the singularity. Particularly when the networks used to classify images produce psychedelic dream images or when researchers detect indications of internal language structures in translation software (Johnson et al. 2016), it is easy to feel as if we are reaching an explosive period of development on this front – and it is likely we are. But figuring out which problems these approaches and their "unreasonable effectiveness" (as Yann LeCunn, director of Facebook's AI efforts, has called it – 2014) can help with and where the limits might be is difficult. The best that can be done is to sketch out where we are today and some of the directions this is leading.

As noted in an earlier chapter, "deep learning" refers to a subset of machine learning algorithms that are able to classify complex information based on patterns they have learned from past examples. It requires a significant amount of computing power, and huge numbers of examples to work well, but when it does, the outcome can be eerie in its accuracy. This has allowed for significant improvements in recognition tasks, particularly of images, and in some cases the ability to reconstitute patterns: accurately colorizing black-and-white movies, translating text from one language to another, or playing a solid game of go, for example. These have traditionally been considered very challenging problems in artificial intelligence. In fact, only a decade ago, Amazon created the Mechanical Turk precisely to harness what has been called "human computation" (Quinn & Bederson 2011). Although many of these Human Intelligence Tasks (HITs) require deep social knowledge that only humans possess, many of the initial uses of the system were to perform the kinds of visual recognition and translation services to which deep learning algorithms appear to be particularly well suited.

Open source frameworks now make the process of constructing deep learning systems much easier, and we have seen an acceleration of research into their application. They are rapidly becoming the motor that is revolutionizing a range of complex recognition and reproduction systems, search and discovery chief among them. Things like weather prediction, detecting anomalies in medical imaging, or making financial bets have been seen as the kinds of complex tasks for which human "wetware" was considered essential. It is likely that deep learning and related approaches will continue to be an area of substantial research investment, even as supporting hardware and software make such systems increasingly ubiquitous. What that means is that search engines are likely to get much better at finding relevant search results, but, more importantly, they will be able to make connections and see relationships that so far have eluded human observers. Machines will "see" the vast collections of data on the web and the new Internet of Things, in ways that humans never have or could. There are limits to how much such approaches will be able to accomplish, both on their own and in concert with other algorithms, but it will be some time before we reach the edges of those capabilities, and they are likely to lead to extraordinary changes in the tasks computers and robots are suited for.

They also will make search far less about an archive of the past and more involved in predicting (and shaping) the future. Knowing what you want to find before you know has long been the stated goal of Google, and early examples of predictive search like Google Now demonstrate that this aim remains (Miller 2013). As Hillis, Petit, and Jarrett (2012) argue, the idea that a networked computing system could ever answer the question "What shall I do tomorrow?" says far more about us and the kinds of faith we put in these algorithms than it does about the technology itself. Given the uncanny ability of these new algorithms to detect patterns and project those patterns forward, I suspect many will think of Google as even more of an oracle than we do today. It will no longer be enough to "know thyself," we will also need to be conscious of how we use these new thinking tools as tools, rather than allowing them to use us.

The history of right now

In the film *Strange Days* (1995), people entertain themselves by reliving the recorded experiences of others. By attaching electrodes to their head, everything they see and feel is recorded for later playback. Even without the brain interface this would necessitate, we are moving closer to the point where all of our experiences are recorded and accumulated as a personal history. Already, our personal histories, as recorded on our home computers, are searchable by Google, and can be made available to the global collection of data. Those collections are growing much richer, drawing on new ways of recording our lives, and organizing that complexity is staggeringly difficult (Gemmell, Bell, & Lueder 2006).

Those recordings recall the Borges story in which a king orders a map at 1:1 scale to cover his entire country.[2] A recording of our life is of very little value if we can only play it back at its original speed. The idea of a perfect memory is probably more attractive than the reality might be. Russian psychologist Aleksandr Luria (2006) describes the life of a man cursed by a perfect memory, and its crippling effects. Without being able to easily edit memories of his life experiences, he loses the ability to distinguish events and interact with the world. The solution requires that we capture the moments that we wish to remember, and delete those moments that are best forgotten without too much intervention on our part. Unfortunately, sometimes it takes us a while to know which are which. Search engine technology will be called upon to help us find valuable information in this large data stream, filtering out the normal experience of our lives to extract the most salient features.

It is hard to say whether we want to have a recording of the first glance at our future spouse, or the last conversation we have with a friend before her death. Some things may be best left to our own memories, or just beyond them. But if we are to record our lives, we will want to have search engines that manage our memories in the ways that we want, and share them only when we want them to. We are still far from having the majority of our lives recorded, but automatic metadata and analysis of video and audio recordings remain particularly important applications of deep learning approaches.

And, of course, this moves beyond personal history to the histories of organizations (which have become of particular interest to attorneys who seek to understand what a company may have done wrong) and to history of society more broadly. Historians and archeologists have always had to do the work of knitting together sparse information in order to better understand the whole. The conditions have become much different now, when they have to make sense not of the needles but of the haystack. The super-abundance of recorded information will change the task of the historian in some ways, as she is faced with finding what of the evidence is meaningful. In the cases where such histories are successful, it will fundamentally change what history does and its place in society. It will be difficult to discern who is a search engineer and who is a historian.

And the question becomes the degree to which she will be able to interrogate these archives with an index that is commercial and that is closed to investigation. The best she may be able to hope for is viewing history through the lens of Facebook or Google, assuming these indexes survive. The idea that they might is both frightening and appealing. Sergey Brin, in making the case for Google Books, claimed that it was necessary to immortalize libraries so that they did not meet the fate of the Alexandrian library (Hillis, Petit, & Jarrett 2012). The presumption that a digital, commercial archive is more resilient than a physical library is difficult to accept at face value – that Brin would consider it so, even more unsettling. In case this is too abstract an idea, we need only recall what happened to the search engine for Usenet, called DejaNews, after Google acquired it (Braga 2015). It was, at first, integrated into Google Groups, and searches would turn up posts from Usenet going back into the 1990s and further. Now such searches turn up nothing. Potentially the archive remains there, if unsearchable. It was as if Google slurped it up and then stored it away from private eyes in its own Goobliette. The idea that our lives may be memorialized by a company or companies that at any moment could sell their indexes or decide to make them inaccessible is troubling. As Tama Leaver (2013) makes clear, your collected data – the memories that make up a large part of who you are – revert to Google and Facebook when you die. Does your trust of these companies extend to their safeguarding your electronic spirit?

Platform wars II

Perhaps more important than these technological advances are the corporate structures that are fostering them. Deep learning is in large part a natural monopoly: it requires extraordinarily large computing resources and collections of data. In any rapidly developing field of technology, there will be room for innovation and start-ups that find solutions missed by the platform behemoths. But it is likely that most of these will be rapidly acquired by Google or Facebook to be applied in their battle for the information ecology. The largest platforms have the resources not only to acquire innovations, but to develop them into working applications at scale.

The search engine wars are over. Google is not the only search engine, but it is overwhelmingly large, and continues to acquire users. That does not mean that Baidu is going anywhere soon, nor does it mean that other search engines may not gain ground, particularly within certain verticals. But we will not see the kinds of vast efforts to attract users that we witnessed around the turn of the millennium. But another battle is shaping up, with new players. Those researching deep learning and new forms of organizing include not just Google and Facebook, both of which have global user bases. Amazon, which has access to both computing and storage capacity, is making a play to become an important part of this revolution. And there are others – though Tesla certainly does not have the resources of any of these three, they represent the kind of existing medium-sized company that is unlikely to be acquired by the giants but may produce innovations that put it into the fray.

All of these large companies share a product: you. In Amazon's case, that means not selling you to marketers, but directly to retailers and manufacturers who want to deliver products. While some of their hardware and mobile efforts have fallen relatively flat, it is interesting to see Google going head-to-head with Amazon's Alexa in an effort to become the voice point-of-contact within the home. It would be surprising not to see Apple move into this space, and perhaps even Facebook. The new platform war will be fought on both of these fronts. Companies will seek to find new ways of analyzing sensor data, as well as new kinds of sensors – from the personal to the infrastructural – that they can build into their analytics engines. It remains to be seen whether these are interoperable systems or if users will be forced to choose between providers.

Given resistance to closed "families" of products, I suspect the successful strategy is to be as open and interoperable as possible, and this has certainly been their *modus operandi* thus far (see Bechmann 2013). The ability to work with retailers and to provide computing services easily to all comers has led to success for Amazon. Likewise, Google's release of their deep learning code seems to suggest that they understand the value of relationships over closed development structures. Nonetheless, it will be interesting to see the degree to which open architectures and partnerships are embraced as these platforms seek our limited attention.

The other side of this war is, unfortunately, war. There is a resurgence of nationalism across the globe, and the threat of cyberwarfare and surveillance hangs over many of these technologies. The ascendancy of Baidu owes as much to Chinese control over their national web space as it does the capabilities of the engine itself. There are reasons to be hopeful about successes in analytics and sensors that could change our lives for the better, but a reluctance by national governments to allow for strong encryption, and of both companies and individuals to adopt secure systems that respect the privacy of the user, threatens the viability of large centralized systems.

There may be space for more distributed and federated approaches like the one embraced by the Diaspora project, which was created as an alternative to Facebook. Certainly, there is room for human-driven, distributed search to be developed, particularly if the centralized solutions are seen as vulnerable to attack. Several have argued, at least conceptually, that search systems that are more cooperative represent a fairer solution, and a number of proposals for, and prototypes of, peer-to-peer search engines have been produced (e.g., Michel, Trianafillou, & Weikum 2005; Felber et al. 2013). Given increased interest in "platform cooperativism" (Scholz & Schneider 2016), it seems as if there may be some impetus in this direction. Astrid Mager (2014) provides an overview of one such promising project: YaCy.

As Vaidhyanathan (2012) notes, creating a large-scale public index would have been much easier before Google became the go-to. He suggests it is not too late for a "Human Knowledge Project," an effort to align political will, technology, and funding toward an open and accessible alternative to Google. Perhaps, as Europe struggles with an external company indexing the web for it, they may manage to put together "several hundred million euros" toward a pan-European, state-sponsored alternative (Lewandowski 2014). Creating an alternative system would require more than money – a critical mass of users is needed. And that is unlikely to occur unless Google and other search engines do something to trigger mass abandonment. Nonetheless, right now all our eggs are in one basket, and we do not own the basket. Christian Fuchs (2014, p. 148) indicates that many of the issues that concern critics of Google could be eliminated if Google were made a public, non-profit, non-commercial entity, and that this would be preferable to an attempt to unseat this "sorcerer of capitalism." Barring that, efforts at the margin at least would provide users of the internet with an alternative view of the information spaces around them, for the sake of comparison.

Who will know?

Lyotard predicted, over 30 years ago, that global computerization would give rise to new legal challenges, and, with them, the central question: "Who will know?" (1984, p. 6). More recently, it has been suggested that modern military conflict will become knowledge-centric: "about who knows (or can be kept from knowing) what, when, where, and why" (Ronfeldt et al. 1998, p. 7). Search and discovery platforms operate at the nexus of such questions, and those interested in shaping the future are interested in shaping such systems. If for no other reason, search engines and social platforms are interesting to the person who wants to understand the exercise of power in the information society. In an era in which knowledge is the only real bankable commodity, search engines own the exchange floor. The term "search engine" is far too prosaic for the role that search plays.

In 1912, Rudyard Kipling wrote a short story called "As easy as A.B.C." (a sequel to an earlier story entitled "With the night mail"), in which he gives an account of the world in the year

2000. The airplane has been overtaken by the dirigible and an "Aerial Board of Control" is established to provide global control of air traffic and "all that implies." The reliance on global transportation – especially for communication, which is handled through the mails – has led to the decline and eventual disappearance of local control, and the A.B.C. has become a global regime:

> Transportation is Civilisation, our motto runs. Theoretically we do what we please, so long as we do not interfere with the traffic and all it implies. Practically, the A.B.C. confirms or annuls all international arrangements, and, to judge from its last report, finds our tolerant, humorous, lazy little Planet only too ready to shift the whole burden of public administration on its shoulders. (Kipling 1925)

Recent incidents provide an indication that national governments are not yet ready to cede power to the search and discovery giants – quite the opposite. Nonetheless, if we wish to understand the contours of social power in the information age, we need do little more than Google it.

Notes

1 THE ENGINES

1 For a more thorough overview of the technical elements of search engine construction, see Büttcher, Clarke, & Cormack (2010).
2 This section discusses search on networked computers, including what would come to be known as "the internet," in the decades preceding the emergence of the web. The web is so ubiquitous at this point that nearly four out of five American users equate the two (Smith 2014).

2 SEARCHING

1 www.unblinking.com/heh/googlewhack.htm.
2 In the first edition of this book, the example given was a failed search for the band "The The." In the interceding years, a Google query for "the the" easily provides links to the band. Searchers probably did not get smarter in the intervening years, but Google certainly did.

4 ATTENTION

1 See Adamic (n.d.) for a discussion of the relationship between Pareto distributions and Zipf's Law.
2 The posting may be found at alex.halavais.net/how-to-cheat-good/.
3 Note also that, since these searches were from the United States, they are probably different from the results for the same Google search in other countries. Also, the same repeated search at five-minute intervals results in different sites at the lower ranks, though the front page remains the same.
4 See, for example, Google Webmaster Guidelines, www.google.com/support/webmasters/bin/answer.py?answer=35769.

5 KNOWLEDGE AND DEMOCRACY

1 While dissemination of racist materials is a crime in Denmark, a search for the white supremacist organization that produced the

racist biography of King leads to that organization's site. So, once again, the reasons for the ranking remain opaque.

2 Ironically, in order to re-find this quote, I turned not to the original French version of the essay, nor to my own English copy in book form, but to Google Book Search.

3 In fact, the term "ideology" is perhaps not so clearly defined. Eagleton (1991) offers no fewer than 21 different potential definitions, but here I intend mostly the last of these: "the process whereby social life is converted to a natural reality" (p. 2).

4 "Blue feed, red feed: see liberal Facebook and conservative Facebook, side by side": graphics.wsj.com/blue-feed-red-feed/.

5 This particular claim, as presented in the quoted *Washington Post* article (C. Dewey 2016), did not appear in a search for "Taipei" by the author in late 2016. Despite trust in the knowledge presented by Google, it remains in flux, without a clear indication of why or when that presented knowledge is changed, as you might find on Wikipedia, for example.

6 CONTROL

1 Most famously the Vatican's Index Librorum Prohibitorum and Index Expurgatorius, though the term "index" was in use in other contexts as an indication of censored documents.

2 See the OpenNet Initiative (opennet.net/) for information on filters in various countries.

3 The same searches made today are likely to turn up a different set of results, perhaps thanks to tens of thousands of searches of the two phrases together. As is often the case, the Google search is an unstable beast, and the search only survives because it was archived in a video.

4 lumendatabase.org.

7 PRIVACY

1 An earlier paper published in the *Annals of Improbable Research* (Schulman 1999) used Alta Vista to quantify fame and determine how many hits were needed to reach the "A-list."

2 See www.aolstalker.com/.

3 When first asked to provide private data to the US government in 1945, ITT Communications flatly refused. After obtaining permission to tap Western Union's lines, a representative of US intelligence went back to ITT and suggested that "his company would not desire to be the only non-cooperative company on the project" (Bamford 1983, p. 304). Lyon (2015) suggests that this sort of pressure was exerted on the present carriers.

4 Andrejevic (2005) provides examples of deceptive searches and

secret investigations of people by other people and argues that "lateral surveillance" is merely an internalization of existing structures of control. It is important to note that the kind of transparency advocated here is open and obvious: not hidden cameras, but clearly visible cameras. When that condition is placed on lateral observation (I don't know that "surveillance" fits any longer), his argument loses some of its strength. But there can be little question that a watched society is a disciplined society, and no less so when the watchers are our neighbors, friends, and colleagues.

5 A more modest solution is proposed by Conti (2006): a browser plug-in that would catalog all the information a user was passing to Google. He argues that, along with notification laws, this would provide more awareness of what we are giving Google and other search engines. Mozilla provides some visualization of the kinds of connections websites make with their Lightbeam plug-in: www.mozilla.org/en-US/lightbeam/. An expansion of these capabilities would be helpful. In 2017, a US court found that the verb form ("to google") does not enjoy trademark protection, but the noun, as a name for a specific search engine, does.

8 FUTURE FINDING

1 Google must defend its trademark or it will lose it, through a process called "trademark dilution." When, like aspirin or (in many parts of the world) hoover, a brand name becomes a part of the language, it is no longer the sole property of the company that created it. Thus, when the Language Council of Sweden included "ungoogleable" among the top 10 new words of the year, it was forced by Google to remove the word (Fanning 2013).

2 See Borges (1975). Of course, it is even more reminiscent of his short story "Funes, the memorious" (Borges 1962), which no doubt was inspired by Luria's narrative (see below), and also ends badly for the protagonist.

Glossary

A/B testing A widely used method of iteratively testing innovations in an interface by automatically exposing a large portion of the user base to the new version and comparing their behavior with those who are served the original (or alternate) design.

Algorithm An algorithm is any methodical way of doing things, and, in the case of search engines, usually refers to the way in which a given engine processes the data from its crawlers and determines the relevance of pages to a particular query.

Anchor text The text that is highlighted as part of a hyperlink on a page.

Archie A search engine for FTP sites.

Backlink A term used to describe a hyperlink leading to a page, rather than leading away from it.

Behavioral targeting This term refers to the ability to target particular advertising messages according to "behaviors" of a user, including visiting or viewing some combination of pages, searching for particular keywords, and the like.

Berrypicking The process of assembling the answer to a query from a diverse set of documents. Coined by Marcia Bates in 1989.

Boolean operators Words that indicate how keywords should be used by a search engine – including AND, OR, and NOT – allowing for more control over what is returned.

Clickbait An often misleading headline that is intended to spur curiosity or an emotional reaction in order to encourage the user to click through to the site.

Cloaking Providing different versions of pages to visitors who are identified as crawlers rather than as humans. This can be used by spamdexers to hide the true content of a page, but may have legitimate uses for those who wish to provide an alternative version of the page for search engines that have trouble with various formats (Flash, video, and the like).

Content farm A large collection of sites that produce textual content based on automatic language generation or inexpensive freelancing in order to guide Google toward a particular site.

Crawler A program that automatically follows links from page to page on the World Wide Web, recording the content of each page.

Crowdsourcing A neologism rooted in the idea of "outsourcing" large-scale production to a widely distributed group of (usually) volunteers willing to contribute a small amount of effort toward the project.

Deep learning A group of machine learning algorithms that are particularly able to classify patterns without specific feature extraction. For example, when classifying an image, pixels alone are networked rather than first detecting features like lines or shapes.

Deep web Sometimes used as an alternative to "Invisible web," in order to clearly indicate that the pages may be visible, but that they are not indexed by the major search engines.

File Transfer Protocol (FTP) A protocol that allows for files to be uploaded and downloaded on the internet.

Golden triangle A triangular area in the upper left-hand side of (for example) a search engine results page that attracts the glance of a person's eye most readily.

Google bomb An attempt to associate a key phrase with a given website by collectively using that phrase in links to a site. The original example is linking the keyword "miserable failure" to the White House biography of George W. Bush.

Google bowling Making a competitor look like a search spammer by employing obvious spam techniques on their behalf.

Google dance The reordering of PageRank that occurred when Google completed a new crawl. Search engines now crawl continuously, so such changes are more gradual.

Google juice An imaginary representation of the reputational currency provided by linking from one site to another. Such links lead to higher PageRank on Google.

Gopher A distributed menu-driven protocol for publishing content to the internet, predating the World Wide Web.

Hits The number of results returned for a particular query. (Not to be confused with Hypertext Induced Topic Selection, or HITS, which is an algorithm developed by Jon Kleinberg designed to rank the authority of documents in a network. Nor with a Human Intelligence Task performed on the Mechanical Turk.)

Horizontal search Search of the broader web, undertaken by general-purpose search engines, which are considered "horizontal" in order to differentiate them from search engines focused on "vertical search."

Information foraging A theory developed by Pirolli and Card that suggests that humans search for information the way that animals search for food, making repeated, rapid decisions about the cost and potential benefit of following particular links.

Inline link The HTML code indicating the positioning of an image on a webpage includes the address where the image may be found. This is normally on the same server as the page itself, but such links can pull the image from anywhere on the web. This sort of lifting of images into a new context is sometimes called "hotlinking."

Internet of Things (IoT) Refers to the growing number of internet-connected sensors and appliances.

IP (Internet Protocol) address A unique four-digit hexadecimal code indicating a single numerical address for every device connected to the internet.

Keyword Word or series of words that makes up a search engine query.

Keyword stuffing Various techniques for hiding many unrelated keywords, and often a large number of the same keyword, on a page so that it is more likely to come up as a false result when people search for those keywords.

Link farms Large numbers of webpages created with the single intent of linking to a particular page and making it appear popular to search engines that rely on inbound links to determine page relevance.

Link spam Generally, links used to deceive search engines as to the reputation or authority of a target website. These may also include hidden links that are visible to search engines, but not to human users.

Metasearch engine A search engine that accepts a query, requests results from several different search engines, and then provides the combined results.

Metatag HTML allows for tags that convey information about the page, but are not displayed on the page. These can provide a summary, relevant keywords, information about authorship, and a number of other things.

Natural Language Processing (NLP) Any attempt to extract grammatical or semantic data from "natural" human language (as opposed to computer languages).

Network gatekeepers A term used by Nahon and Hemsley (2013) to describe those who act as bridges between clusters of networks of people.

Ontology An "ontology," within the field of computer science, refers to an explicit definition of concepts and their relationships within a particular domain. They are essential to the development of a "semantic web."

PageRank The Google algorithm for determining which results are most authoritative, based on the hyperlinked structure of pages linking to them.

Permalink The URL of a blog posting that remains stable so that references to it will continue to be valid.

Power law distribution A distribution for which there exists a scale-free inverse relationship between an observed magnitude of an event and its frequency.

Preferential attachment The idea that new links in a network are likely to lead to the nodes that already enjoy a large number of backlinks.

Relevance The degree to which a search engine's results correspond to a searcher's goal.

Robot exclusion protocol A way for content authors to instruct crawlers which pages should and should not be indexed.

RSS A file format that packages new additions to a website over time in a format easily parsed by other applications. Abbreviation of "Really Simple Syndication," "RDF Site Summary," or "Rich Site Summary."

Search engine optimization (SEO) The process (and industry) of creating pages that will receive more visibility on large search engines.

Semantic web The semantic web is a proposed way of extending the web to make it possible for computers to associate data with other data on the web, to act on that data, and to draw inferences from that data.

Spamdexing A term used to describe search spamming, or attempts to rise to the top of the search rankings for a set of keywords.

Spider See "Crawler."

Splog Spam blog, a blog set up in order to create links to a target page, in an effort to make it appear more authoritative and receive better placement on search engine results pages.

Stop words Words that are too common to be useful in a search, and are generally ignored by search engines.

Transaction Log Analysis (TLA) Records of many interactions on the internet, including search records, are kept in log files that can later be analyzed to provide information about search behaviors.

Usenet An internet-based news forum system that reached its peak just before the World Wide Web became popular. It was initially archived on the web by Dejanews, which, when purchased by Google, eventually became Google Groups.

User-generated media A broad term taking in amateur production of media: especially things like blogs, podcasts, and shared photos and video.

Veronica A search engine that was used with Gopher.

Vertical search Search engines that limit themselves in terms of topic, medium, region, language, or some other set of constraints, and cover that area in great depth, are often called "vertical" in order to differentiate them from general-purpose search engines.

Web analytics Tools to measure and understand the behavior of users on a given website.

Web robot (or "Bot") See "Crawler."

Zipf's Law Distribution of events such that there is an inverse relationship (with some fixed exponent) between the frequency of an event and its rank. Named for George Kingsley Zipf.

Bibliography

2600. 2010, "Google blacklist: words that Google Instant doesn't like," September 30, www.2600.com/googleblacklist/.

Abeles, T. P. 2002, "The Internet, knowledge and the academy," *foresight*, 4, 3, pp. 32–7.

Abrams, D., Baecker, R. & Chignell, M. 1998, "Information archiving with bookmarks: personal web space construction and organization," in *CHI '98 Proceedings of the SIGCHI Conference on Human Factors in Computing Systems, Los Angeles, California, April 18–23*, New York: ACM Press, pp. 41–8.

Acquisti, A. & Fong, C. 2015, "An experiment in hiring discrimination via online social networks," July 17, ssrn.com/abstract=2031979.

Adamic, L. A. n.d., "Zipf, power-laws, and Pareto: a ranking tutorial," www.hpl.hp.com/research/idl/papers/ranking/ranking.html.

Adamic, L. A. & Adar, E. 2005, "How to search a social network," *Social Networks*, 27, 3, pp. 187–203.

Adamic, L. A. & Glance, N. 2005, "The political blogosphere and the 2004 US election: divided they blog," in *Proceedings of the 3rd International Workshop on Link Discovery*, Chicago: ACM Press, pp. 36–43.

Adams, S. 2013, "6 steps to managing your online reputation," *Forbes*, March 14, www.forbes.com/sites/susanadams/2013/03/14/6-steps-to-managing-your-online-reputation/.

Adar, E., Weld, D. S., Bershad, B. N. & Gribble, S. D. 2007, "Why we search: visualizing and predicting user behavior," in *WWW '07 Proceedings of the 16th International Conference on World Wide Web, Banff, May 8–12*, New York: ACM Press, pp. 161–70.

Adler, S. 1999, "The Slashdot Effect, an analysis of three internet publications," *Linux Gazette*, 38.

Adomavicius, G. & Tuzhilin, A. 2005, "Towards the next generation of recommender systems: a survey of the state-of-the-art and possible extensions," *IEEE Transactions on Knowledge and Data Engineering*, 17, 6, pp. 734–49.

Agrawal, R., Gollapudi, S., Halverson, A. & Ieong, S. 2009, "Diversifying search results," in *WSDM '09 Proceedings of the Second ACM International Conference on Web Search and Data Mining, Barcelona, February 9–12*, New York: ACM Press, pp. 5–14.

Agre, P. 1998, "The internet and public discourse," *FirstMonday*, 3, 3, www.firstmonday.org/ojs/index.php/fm/article/view/581.

Alexander, B., Adams Becker, S. & Cummins, M. 2016, *Digital literacy: an NMC horizon project strategic brief*, Austin, Tex.: The New Media Consortium.

Allgrove, B. 2007, "The search engine's dilemma: implied license to crawl and cache?" *Journal of Intellectual Property Law Practice*, 2, 7, pp. 437–8.

Alli, K. 2016, "YOOOOOO LOOK AT THIS," Twitter, June 6, twitter.com/ibeKabir/status/740005897930452992.

Anakata. 2004, "Re: unauthorized use of DreamWorks SKG properties," www.automotiveforums.com/t361188–re_unauthorized_use_of_dreamworks_skg_properties.html.

Ananny, M. 2011, "The curious connection between apps for gay men and sex offenders," *The Atlantic*, April 14, www.theatlantic.com/technology/archive/2011/04/the-curious-connection-between-apps-for-gay-men-and-sex-offenders/237340/.

Anderson, C. 2004, "The long tail," *Wired*, 12, 10, www.wired.com/wired/archive/12.10/tail.html.

Anderson, N. 2007, "US intelligence wants ability to censor satellite images," *Ars Technica*, May 9, arstechnica.com/security/2007/05/us-intelligence-wants-ability-to-censor-satellite-images/.

Andrejevic, M. 2005, "The work of watching one another: lateral surveillance, risk, and governance," *Surveillance & Society*, 2, 4, pp. 479–97.

Ang, P. H. & Nadarajan, B. 1996, "Censorship and the internet: a Singapore perspective," *Communications of the ACM*, 39, 6, pp. 72–8.

Answers Corporation. 2007, "Answers.com seeing lower traffic," *PR Newswire*, August 2, www.prnewswire.com/news-releases/answersc om-seeing-lower-traffic-57802832.html.

Aonghusa, P. M. & Leith, D. J. 2016, "It wasn't me! Plausible deniability in web search," arXiv.org, September 26, arxiv.org/abs/1609.07922.

Arel, I., Rose, D. C. & Kamowski, T. P. 2010, "Deep machine learning: a new frontier in artificial intelligence research," *IEEE Computational Intelligence Magazine*, 5, 4, pp. 13–18.

Argenti, P., MacLeod, S. & Capozzi, L. 2007, "The experts offer advice on Google," *Journal of Business Strategy*, 28, 3, pp. 23–5.

Arlin, P. K. 1990, "Wisdom: the art of problem finding," in R. J. Sternberg (ed.), *Wisdom: its nature, origins, and development*, Cambridge University Press, pp. 23–43.

Arrington, M. 2006, "AOL proudly releases massive amounts of private data," *TechCrunch*, August 6, techcrunch.com/2006/08/06/aol-proudly-releases-massive-amounts-of-user-search-data/.

Arroyo, E., Selker, T. & Wei, W. 2006, "Usability tool for analysis of web designs using mouse tracks," in *Proceedings of Conference on Human Factors in Computing Systems*, Montreal: ACM Press, pp. 484–9.

Arthur, C. 2014, "Explaining the 'right to be forgotten': the newest cultural shibboleth," *The Guardian*, May 14, www.theguardian.com/technology/2014/may/14/explainer-right-to-be-forgotten-the-newest-cultural-shibboleth.

Aul, W. R. 1972, "Herman Hollerith," *Think*, IBM Archives, pp. 22–4, November, www-03.ibm.com/ibm/history/exhibits/builders/builders_hollerith.html.

Aula, A., Jhaveri, N. & Käki, M. 2005, "Information search and reaccess strategies of experienced web users," in *Proceedings of the 14th International Conference on the World Wide Web*, Chiba: ACM Press, pp. 583–92.

Aula, A., Päivi, M. & Räihä, K.-J. 2005, "Eye-tracking reveals the personal styles for search result evaluation," in *Proceedings of Human–Computer Interactions – INTERACT 2005*, Berlin: Springer, pp. 954–7.

Bagdikian, B. H. 1983, *The media monopoly*, Boston: Beacon Press.

Bagrow, J. P. & ben-Avraham, D. 2005, "On the Google-fame of scientists and other populations," in J. Marro, P. L. Garrido, & M. A. Muñoz (eds.), *AIP Conference Proceedings*, 779, 1, pp. 81–9.

Baker, P. & Potts, A. 2013, "'Why do white people have thin lips?' Google and the perpetuation of stereotypes via auto-complete search forms," *Critical Discourse Studies*, 10, 2, pp. 187–204.

Bakshy, E., Messing, S. & Adamic, L. A. 2015, "Exposure to ideologically diverse news and opinion on Facebook," *Science*, 348, 6239, pp. 1130–2.

Balkin, J. M. 2004, "Digital speech and democratic culture: a theory of freedom of expression for the information society," *New York University Law Review*, 79, 1, pp. 1–55.

Ballatore, A. 2015, "Google chemtrails: a methodology to analyse topic representation in search engine results," *First Monday*, 20, 7, firstmonday.org/ojs/index.php/fm/article/view/5597.

Bamford, J. 1983, *The puzzle palace: a report on America's most secret agency*, Harmondsworth, Middx.: Penguin Books.

Bar-Zeev, A. 2007, "The value of censoring Google Earth," RealityPrime, July 9, www.realityprime.com/articles/the-value-of-censoring-google-earth.

Barbaro, M. & Zellner, T. 2006, "A face is exposed for AOL searcher 4417749," *New York Times*, August 9, www.nytimes.com/2006/08/09/technology/09aol.html.

Barber, B. R. 1996, *Jihad vs. McWorld*, New York: Ballantine Books.

Barlow, J. P. 1996, *A declaration of the independence of cyberspace*, Electronic Frontier Foundation, www.eff.org/cyberspace-independence.

Bates, M. J. 1989, "The design of browsing and berrypicking techniques for the online search interface," *Online Review*, 13, 5, pp. 407–24.

Battelle, J. 2005, *The search: how Google and its rivals rewrote the rules of business and transformed our culture*, New York: Portfolio.

Bauman, Z. 2000, *Liquid modernity*, Cambridge: Polity.

Becerra-Fernandez, I. 2006, "Searching for experts on the web: a review of contemporary expertise locator systems," *ACM Transactions on Internet Technology*, 6, 4, pp. 333–55.

Bechmann, A. 2013, "Internet profiling: the economy of data interoperability on Facebook and Google," *MedieKultur*, 55, pp. 72–91.

Becker, D. 2004, "Google caught in anti-Semitism flap," *CNet*, April 7, www.cnet.com/news/google-caught-in-anti-semitism-flap/.

Beitzel, S. M., Jensen, E. C., Chowdhury, A., Grossman, D. & Ophir, F. 2004, "Hourly analysis of a very large topically categorized web query log," in *SIGIR '04 Proceedings of the 27th Annual International ACM SIGIR Conference on Research and Development in Information Retrieval, Sheffield, July 25–29*, New York: ACM Press, pp. 321–8.

Belkin, N. J., Oddy, R. N. & Brooks, H. M. 1982, "ASK for information retrieval: Part I: background and theory," *Journal of Documentation*, 38, 2, pp. 61–71.

Bender, W. 2002, "Twenty years of personalization: all about the 'Daily Me,'" *Educause Review*, 37, 5, pp. 21–9.

Benkler, Y. 2006, *The wealth of networks: how social production transforms markets and freedom*, New Haven: Yale University Press.

Bennett, R. J. 2012, "Supporting trust: credit assessment and debt recovery through Trade Protection Societies in Britain and Ireland, 1776–1992," *Journal of Historical Geography*, 38, pp. 123–42.

Bennett, W. L. & Manheim, J. B. 2006, "The one-step flow of communication," *The Annals of the American Academy of Political and Social Science*, 608, 1, pp. 213–32.

Benyon, D. 1998, "Cognitive engineering as the development of information spaces," *Ergonomics*, 41, 2, pp. 153–55.

Berners-Lee, T., Hendler, J. & Lassila, O. 2001, "The semantic web," *Scientific American*, 284, 5, pp. 34–43.

Bershidsky, L. 2015, "Europe could learn from Russia's Google ruling," BloombergView, October 6, www.bloomberg.com/view/articles/2015-10-06/europe-could-learn-from-russia-s-google-ruling.

Bharat, K. & Broder, A. 1998, "A technique for measuring the relative size and overlap of public Web search engines," *Computer Networks and ISDN Systems*, 30, 1–7, pp. 379–88.

Bilić, P. 2016, "Search algorithms, hidden labour and information control," *Big Data & Society*, 3, 1, dx.doi.org/10.1177/2053951716652159.

Bishop, T. 2007, "Google takes its ad system into the video-game market," *Seattle P-I*, July 18, www.seattlepi.com/business/article/Google-takes-its-ad-system-into-the-video-game-1244047.php.

Biundo, J. & Enge, E. 2006, "Creating advanced custom search engines," blogoscoped.com/archive/2006–11–15–n50.html.

Blacharski, D. 2016, "Is Google trying to kill SEO?" *Entrepreneur*, June 21, www.entrepreneur.com/article/277007.

Blake, W. 1982, *The complete poetry and prose of William Blake*, Berkeley: University of California Press.

Blanke, T. 2005, "Ethical subjectification and search engines: ethics reconsidered," *International Review of Information Ethics*, 3, pp. 33–8.

Blanzieri, E. & Giorgini, P. 2000, "From collaborative filtering to implicit culture: a general agent-based framework," presented at the Workshop on Agents and Recommender Systems, Barcelona, June 4, citeseerx.ist.psu.edu/viewdoc/download?doi=10.1.1.2.894&rep=rep1&type=pdf.

Bloom, Beth S. & Deyrup, M. 2012, "The truth is out: how students REALLY search," Charleston Library Conference, Purdue e-Pubs, docs.lib.purdue.edu/cgi/viewcontent.cgi?article=1360&context=Charleston.

Bogatin, D. & Sullivan, D. 2007, "Resolved: Google is overrated," *Fast Company*, 113, March, p. 116.

Bogost, I. 2015, "The cathedral of computation," *The Atlantic*, January 15 www.theatlantic.com/technology/archive/2015/01/the-cathedral-of-computation/384300/.

Boguslaw, R. 1971, "Systems of power and the power of systems," in A. Westin (ed.), *Information technology in a democracy*, Cambridge, Mass.: Harvard University Press, pp. 419–31.

Borges, J. L. 1962, "Funes, the memorious," in *Ficciones*, New York: Grove Press, pp. 107–16.

1975, "Of exactitude in science," in *A Universal History of Infamy*, Harmondsworth, Middx.: Penguin, p. 131.

Bourdieu, P. 1986, "The forms of capital," in J. Richardson (ed.), *Handbook of theory and research for the sociology of education*, New York: Greenwood Press, pp. 241–58.

2000, *Pascalian meditations*, Stanford University Press.

2003, "The Berber house," in S. M. Low & D. Lawrence-Zúñiga (eds.), *The anthropology of space and place: locating culture*, Malden, Mass.: Blackwell, pp. 131–41.

Bowman, C. M., Danzig, P. B., Manber, U. & Schwartz, M. F. 1994, "Scalable internet resource discovery: research problems and approaches," *Communications of the ACM*, 37, 8, pp. 98–107, 114.

Boydell, O. & Smyth, B. 2007, "From social bookmarking to social summarization: an experiment in community-based summary generation," in *IUI '07 Proceedings of the 12th International Conference on Intelligent User Interfaces, Honolulu, January 28–31*, New York: ACM Press, pp. 42–51.

Bozdag, E. 2013, "Bias in algorithmic filtering and personalization," *Ethics and Information Technology*, 15, 3, pp. 209–27.

Brabham, D. C. 2008, "Crowdsourcing as a model for problem solving: an introduction and cases," *Convergence: The International Journal of Research into New Media Technologies*, 14, 1, pp. 75–90.

Braga, M. 2015, "Google, a search company, has made its internet archive impossible to search," Motherboard, February 13, motherboard.vice.com/read/google-a-search-company-has-made-its-internet-archive-impossible-to-search.

Brand, S. 1987, *The Media Lab: inventing the future at MIT*, New York: Viking.

Brenner, D. L. 1996, *Law and regulation of common carriers in the communications industry*, Boulder: Westview Press.

Brewer, E. 2001, "When everything is searchable," *Communications of the ACM*, 44, 3, pp. 53–5.

Brin, D. 1998, *The transparent society: will technology force us to choose between privacy and freedom?* Reading, Mass.: Perseus Books.

Brin, S. & Page, L. 1998, "The anatomy of a large-scale hypertextual web search engine," *Computer Networks*, 30, 1–7, pp. 107–17.

Broder, A. 2002, "A taxonomy of web search," *ACM SIGIR Forum*, 36, 2, pp. 3–10.

Broder, A., Kumar, R., Maghoul, F., et al. 2000, "Graph structure in the web," *Computer Networks*, 33, 1–6, pp. 309–20.

Brooks, F. P. 1995, *The mythical man-month: essays on software engineering*, anniversary edn., Reading, Mass.: Addison-Wesley Pub. Co.

Brophy, J. & Bawden, D. 2005, "Is Google enough? Comparison of an internet search engine with academic library resources," *Aslib Proceedings: New Information Perspectives*, 57, 6, pp. 498–512.

Brown, D. J. 2004, "Web search considered harmful," *Queue*, 2, 2, pp. 84–3.

Brunelli, R. & Poggio, T. 1993, "Face recognition: features versus templates," *IEEE Transactions on Pattern Analysis and Machine Intelligence*, 15, 10, pp. 1042–52.

Brynjolfsson, E., Hu, Y. J. & Smith, M. D. 2003, "Consumer surplus in the digital economy: estimating the value of increased product variety at online booksellers," MIT Sloan Working Paper, vol. 4305–03, papers.ssrn.com/sol3/papers.cfm?abstract_id=400940.

Bucher, T. 2012, "Want to be on the top? Algorithmic power and the threat of invisibility on Facebook," *New Media & Society*, 14, 7, pp. 1164–80.

Buckley, C. & Rashbaum, W. K. 2007, "4 men accused of plot to blow up Kennedy airport terminals and fuel lines," *The New York Times*, June 3, www.nytimes.com/2007/06/03/nyregion/03plot.html.

Burri, M. 2016, "Cultural diversity in the internet age: in search of new tools that work," *Digiworld Economic Journal*, 101, 1, ssrn.com/abstract=2748051.

Burton, J. 1972, *World society*, Cambridge University Press.

Bush, V. 1945, "As we may think," *Atlantic Monthly*, 176, July, pp. 101–8.

Büttcher, S., Clarke, C. L. A. & Cormack, G. V. 2010, *Information retrieval: implementing and evaluating search engines*, Cambridge, Mass.: MIT Press.

Calishain, T. 2007, *Information trapping: real-time research on the web*, Berkeley, Calif.: New Riders.

Calori, R. 2002, "Organizational development and the ontology of creative dialectical evolution," *Organization*, 9, 1, pp. 127–50.

Campbell-Kelly, M. & Aspray, W. 1996, *Computer: a history of the information machine*, New York: Basic Books.

Capra, R. G. & Pérez-Quiñones, M. A. 2005, "Using web search engines to find and refind information," *IEEE Computer*, 38, 10, pp. 36–42.

Carey, J. 1969, "The communications revolution and the professional communicator," *Sociological Review Monograph*, 13, pp. 23–8.

Carey, K. 2012, "Show me your badge," *The New York Times*, November 2, www.nytimes.com/2012/11/04/education/edlife/show-me-your-badge.html.

Carlton, A. 2016, "Web search engines for IoT: the new frontier," *NetworkWorld*, August 25, www.networkworld.com/article/3111984/internet-of-things/web-search-engines-for-iot-the-new-frontier.html.

Carmel, D., Zwerdling, N., Guy, I., et al. 2009, "Personalized social search based on the user's social network," in *CIKM '09 Proceedings of the 18th ACM Conference on Information and Knowledge Management*, Hong Kong, November 2–6, New York: ACM Press, pp. 1227–36.

Carmel, Y. & Ben-Haim, Y. 2005, "Info-gap robust-satisficing model of foraging behavior: do foragers optimize or satisfice?" *American Naturalist*, 166, 5, pp. 634–41.

Carr, N. 2008, "Is Google making us stupid? What the internet is doing to our brains," *The Atlantic*, July/August, www.theatlantic.com/magazine/archive/2008/07/is-google-making-us-stupid/306868/.

2010, *The shallows: what the internet is doing to our brains*, New York: W. W. Norton.

Catone, J. 2009, "Local tweets: 9 ways to find Twitter users in your town," Mashable, June 8, http://mashable.com/2009/06/08/twitter-local-2/.

Caufield, J. 2005, "Where did Google get its value?" *Libraries and the Academy*, 5, 4, pp. 555–72.

Charette, R. N. 2012, "Do you need to worry about DHS looking at your social media conversations?" *IEEE Spectrum* Risk Factor, May 29, spectrum.ieee.org/riskfactor/telecom/internet/do-you-need-to-be-careful-about-the-words-you-use-in-social-media-conversations.

Chellapilla, K. & Chickering, D. M. 2006, "Improving cloaking detection using search query popularity and monetizability," presented at 2nd International Workshop on Adversarial Information Retrieval on the Web, Seattle, August 10.

Chi, E. H. & Pirolli, P. 2006, "Social information foraging and collaborative search," presented at Human Computer Interaction Consortium (HCIC) Workshop, Fraser, Colorado, USA.

Cho, C.-H. & Cheon, H. J. 2004, "Why do people avoid advertising on the internet?" *Journal of Advertising*, 33, 4, pp. 89–97.

Cho, J. & Roy, S. 2004, "Impact of search engines on page popularity," in *WWW '04 Proceedings of the 13th International Conference on World Wide Web, New York, May 17–20*, New York: ACM Press, pp. 20–9.

Church, K., Smyth, B., Cotter, P. & Bradley, K. 2007, "Mobile information access: a study of emerging search behavior on the mobile internet," *ACM Transactions on the Web*, 1, 1, pp. 1–38.

Clark, J. 2015, "Google turning its lucrative web search over to AI machines," Bloomberg Technology, October 26, www.bloomberg.com/news/articles/2015-10-26/google-turning-its-lucrative-web-search-over-to-ai-machines.

Clarke, R. 1988, "Information technology and dataveillance," *Communications of the ACM*, 31, 5, pp. 498–512.

Cohen, B. 1963, *The press and foreign policy*, Princeton University Press.

Colin, C. 2007, "Pig balls and stuck skunks: a 311 customer service rep has a window onto San Francisco's secret heart," SFGate, www.sfgate.com/news/article/Pig-balls-and-stuck-skunks-A-311-customer-2523555.php.

comScore 2016, "Latest rankings: top 50 multi-platform properties (desktop & mobile)," August, www.comscore.com/Insights/Rankings.

Connolly, K. 2016, "Angela Merkel: internet search engines are 'distorting perception,'" *The Guardian*, October 27, www.theguardian.com/world/2016/oct/27/angela-merkel-internet-search-engines-are-distorting-our-perception.

Constine, J. 2016, "Facebook sees 2 billion searches per day, but it's attacking Twitter not Google," TechCrunch, July 27, techcrunch.com/2016/07/27/facebook-will-make-you-talk/.

Conti, G. 2006, "Googling considered harmful," in *NSPW '06 Proceedings of the 2006 Workshop on New Security Paradigms, Germany, September 19–22*, New York: ACM Press, pp. 67–76.

Cooper, J. F. 2004, *The American democrat*, New York: Barnes & Noble Books.

Crawford, K. & Schultz, J. 2014, "Big data and due process: toward a framework to redress predictive privacy harms," *Boston College Law Review*, 55, 1, a. 4, lawdigitalcommons.bc.edu/cgi/viewcontent.cgi?article=3351&context=bclr.

Crist, R. 2016, "'Alexa, where are my keys?' TrackR syncs with Amazon

Echo to help you find your stuff," *CNET*, January 6, www.cnet.com/
news/alexa-where-are-my-keys-trackr-syncs-with-amazon-echo-to-
help-you-find-your-stuff/.

Czitrom, D. J. 1982, *Media and the American mind: from Morse to McLuhan*, Chapel Hill: University of North Carolina Press.

Daniel, C. & Palmer, M. 2007, "Google's goal: to organize your daily life," *Financial Times*, www.ft.com/content/c3e49548–088e-11dc-b11e-000b5df10621.

Datta, A., Tschantz, M. C. & Datta, A. 2015, "Automated experiments on ad privacy settings: a tale of opacity, choice, and discrimination," in *Proceedings on Privacy Enhancing Technologies, 1, Philadelphia, June 30 – July 2*, Warsaw: De Gruyter, pp. 92–112.

Davies, P., Chapman, S. & Leask, J. 2002, "Anti-vaccination activists on the world wide web," *Archives of Disease in Childhood*, 87, 1, pp. 22–5.

Delgado López-Cózar, E. & Cabezas-Clavijo, Á. 2012, "Google Scholar metrics: an unreliable tool for assessing scientific journals," *Professional Information*, 21, 4, pp. 319–427.

Department of Homeland Security. 2010, *Terrorist use of social networking sites: Facebook case study*, December 5, publicintelligence.net/ufouoles-dhs-terrorist-use-of-social-networking-facebook-case-study/.

Deutsch, K. 1966, *The nerves of government: models of political communication and control*, New York: The Free Press.

Deutsch, P. 2000, "Archie: a Darwinian development process," *Internet Computing*, 4, 1, pp. 89–97.

Dewey, C. 2015a, "Facebook is embroiled in yet another breastfeeding photo controversy," *The Washington Post*, February 26, www.washingtonpost.com/news/the-intersect/wp/2015/02/26/facebook-is-embroiled-in-yet-another-breastfeeding-photo-controversy/.
2015b, "Censorship, fat-shaming and the 'Reddit revolt': how Reddit became the Alamo of the internet's ongoing culture war," *The Washington Post*, June 12, www.washingtonpost.com/news/the-intersect/wp/2015/06/12/censorship-fat-shaming-and-the-reddit-revolt-how-reddit-became-the-alamo-of-the-internets-ongoing-culture-war/.
2016, "You probably haven't even noticed Google's sketchy quest to control the world's knowledge," *The Washington Post*, May 11, www.washingtonpost.com/news/the-intersect/wp/2016/05/11/you-probably-havent-even-noticed-googles-sketchy-quest-to-control-the-worlds-knowledge/.

Dewey, J. 1927, *The public and its problems*, New York: H. Holt & Co.

Diaz, A. 2008, "Through the Google goggles: socio-political bias in search engine design," in A. Spink & M. Zimmer (eds.), *Web search: multidisciplinary perspectives*, Berlin: Springer-Verlag, pp. 11–34.

Dickinson, A., Smith, M., Arnott, N. & Robin, H. 2007, "Approaches to web search and navigation for older computer novices," in *CHI*

'07 *Proceedings of the SIGCHI Conference on Human Factors in Computing Systems*, San Jose, Calif.: ACM Press, pp. 281–90.

DiMaggio, P., Hargittai, E., Celeset, C. & Shafer, S. 2004, "Digital inequality: from unequal access to differentiated use," in K. Neckerman (ed.), *Social inequality*, New York: Russell Sage Foundation, pp. 355–400.

DiMaggio, P., Hargittai, E., Neuman, W. R. & Robinson, J. P. 2001, "Social implications of the internet," *Annual Review of Sociology*, 27, pp. 307–36.

Dittenbach, M., Berger, H. & Merkl, D. 2006, "Automated concept discovery from web resources," in *Proceedings of the 2006 IEEE/WIC/ACM International Conference on Web Intelligence*, Washington, DC: IEEE Computer Society, pp. 309–12.

Doctorow, C. 2003, *Down and out in the Magic Kingdom*, New York: Tor.

2007, "Scroogled," *Radar*, September 12, www.crimeflare.com/doc torow.html.

Donath, J. 2004, "Sociable media," in W. S. Bainbridge (ed.), *The encyclopedia of human–computer interaction*, Great Barrington, Mass.: Berkshire Publishing Group.

Döpfner, M. 2014, "Why we fear Google: an open letter to Eric Schmidt," *Frankfurter Allgemeine*, November 26, www.faz.net/aktuell/feuilleton/debatten/mathias-doepfner-s-open-letter-to-eric-schmidt-12900860.html.

Douglas, D. D. 2016, "Doxing: a conceptual analysis," *Ethics and Information Technology*, 18, 3, pp. 199–210.

Duhigg, C. 2012, "How companies learn your secrets," *New York Times Magazine*, February 12, www.nytimes.com/2012/02/19/magazine/shopping-habits.html.

Duke, Lynda M. & Asher, Andrew D. 2011, *College libraries and student culture: what we now know*, Chicago: ALA Editions.

Dvir-Gvirsman, S., Tsfati, Y. & Menchen-Trevino, E. 2014, "The extent and nature of ideological selective exposure online: combining survey responses with actual web log data from the 2013 Israeli elections," *New Media & Society*, 18, 5, pp. 857–77.

Eagleton, T. 1991, *Ideology: an introduction*, London: Verso.

Eco, U. 1989, *Foucault's pendulum*, New York: Harcourt.

1995, *The search for the perfect language*, Oxford: Blackwell.

Economist. 2014, "Now or Naver," March 1, www.economist.com/news/business/21597937-home-south-koreas-biggest-web-portal-has-thrashed-yahoo-and-kept-google-bay-now-its.

Edelman. 2016, "2016 Edelman trust barometer: leadership in a divided world," www.edelman.com/assets/uploads/2016/01/2016–Edelman-Trust-Barometer-Global-_-Leadership-in-a-Divided-World.pdf.

Edelman, B. & Gilchrist, 2012, "Advertising disclosures: measuring labelling alternatives in internet search engines," *Information Economics and Policy*, 24, 1, pp. 75–89.

Edwards, J. 2007, "Google, DoubleClick throw punches in privacy war," *Adweek.com*, July 16.

Ehet-Alkalai, Y. & Chajut, E. 2009, "Changes over time in digital literacy," *CyberPsychology & Behavior*, 12, 6, pp. 713–15.

Eichmann, D. 1994, "The RBSE spider: balancing effective search against web load," *Computer Networks and ISDN Systems*, 4, 2, pp. 281–8.

Eisenstein, E. L. 1979, *The printing press as an agent of change: communications and cultural transformations in early modern Europe*, Cambridge University Press.

El Akaad, O. 2015, "Startup Echosec collects social media from world's most volatile hot spots," *The Globe and Mail*, October 16, www.theglobeandmail.com/news/world/startup-echosec-collects-social-media-from-worlds-most-volatile-hot-spots/article26859284/.

Ellison, N. B., Steinfield, C. & Lampe, C. 2007, "The benefits of Facebook 'friends': social capital and college students' use of online social network sites," *Journal of Computer-Mediated Communication*, 12, 4, pp. 1143–68.

Elmer, G. 2006, "The vertical (layered) net," in D. Silver & A. Massanari (eds.), *Critical cyberculture studies*, New York University Press.

Engelbart, D. & Lehtman, H. 1988, "Working together," *BYTE*, 13, 13, pp. 245–52.

Epstein, R. & Robertson, R. E. 2015, "The search engine manipulation effect (SEME) and its possible impact on the outcomes of elections," *Proceedings of the National Academy of Sciences of the United States of America*, 112, 33, pp. E4512–E4521.

Erickson, T. 1996, "The World-Wide Web as social hypertext," *Communications of the ACM*, 39, 1, pp. 15–17.

Erickson, T. & Kellogg, W. 2000, "Social translucence: an approach to designing systems that support social processes," *ACM Transactions on Computer–Human Interaction*, 7, 1, pp. 59–83.

Escarrabill, J., Marti, T. & Torrente, E. 2011, "Good morning, Doctor Google (Bom dia, Doutor Google)," *Revista Portuguesa de Pneumologia*, 17, 4, pp. 177–81.

Eshet-Alkalai, Y. & Chajut, E. 2009, "Changes over time in digital literacy," *CyberPsychology & Behavior*, 12, 6, pp. 713–15.

Etzioni, A. 1999, *The limits of privacy*, New York: Basic Books.

Evans, B. M. & Chi, E. H. 2009, "Towards a model of understanding social search," in *CSCW '08 Proceedings of the 2008 ACM Conference on Computer Supported Cooperative Work, San Diego, November 8–12*, New York: ACM Press, pp. 485–94.

Ewen, S. 1976, *Captains of consciousness*, New York: McGraw-Hill.

Facebook. 2016, "Search FYI: an update to Trending," Facebook

Newsroom, August 26, newsroom.fb.com/news/2016/08/search-fyi-an-update-to-trending/.

Fallows, D. 2005, "Search engine users," Pew Internet and American Life, Washington, DC, www.pewinternet.org/files/old-media/Files/Reports/2005/PIP_Searchengine_users.pdf.pdf.

Fanning, S. 2013, "Google gets ungoogleable off Sweden's new word list," *BBC News*, March 26, www.bbc.com/news/world-europe-21944834.

Farrell, W. 1998, *How hits happen*, New York: HarperBusiness.

Fehr, E. 2004, "Don't lose your reputation," *Nature*, 432, pp. 449–50.

Felber, P., Kropf, P., Leonini, L., et al. 2013, "CoFeed: privacy-preserving Web search recommendation based on collaborative aggregation of interest feedback," *Software: Practice and Experience*, 43, 10, pp. 1165–84.

Ferguson, R., Faulkner, D., Whitelock, D. & Sheehy, K. 2015, "Pre-teens' informal learning with ICT and Web 2.0," *Technology, Pedagogy and Education*, 24, 2, pp. 247–65.

Finkelstein, S. 2003, "Chester's guide to molesting Google," sethf.com/anticensorware/general/chester.php.

Fiormonte, D. 2016, "Search engine with(out) a difference," April 6, infolet.it/2016/04/06/search-engine-without-a-difference/.

Foley, M. W. & Edwards, B. 1999, "Is it time to disinvest in social capital?" *Journal of Public Policy*, 19, pp. 141–73.

Freyne, J., Farzan, R., Brusilovsky, P., Smyth, B. & Coyle, M. 2007, "Collecting community wisdom: integrating social search and social navigation," in *IUI '07 Proceedings of the 12th International Conference on Intelligent User Interfaces, Honolulu, January 28–31*, New York: ACM Press, pp. 52–61.

Froomkin, D. 2015, "The computers are listening: how the NSA converts spoken words into searchable text," *The Intercept*, May 5, theintercept.com/2015/05/05/nsa-speech-recognition-snowden-searchable-text/.

Fry, J. 2006, "Google's privacy responsibilities at home and abroad," *Journal of Librarianship and Information Science*, 38, 3, pp. 135–9.

Fu, L. Y., Zook, K., Spoehr-Labutta, Z., Hu, P. & Joseph, J. G. 2016, "Search engine ranking, quality, and content of web pages that are critical versus noncritical of human papillomavirus vaccine," *Journal of Adolescent Health*, 58, 1, pp. 33–9.

Fuchs, C. 2011, "A contribution to the critique of the political economy of Google," *Fast Capitalism*, 8, 1, www.uta.edu/huma/agger/fastcapitalism/8_1/fuchs8_1.html.

2014, *Social media: a critical introduction*, Los Angeles: Sage.

Fulgoni, G. 2007, "Younger consumers receptive to advertising on user-generated content sites," www.comscore.com/ita/Insights/Blog/Younger-Consumers-Receptive-to-Advertising-on-User-Generated-Content-Sites.

Fulton, S. 2014, "Beware the dangers of Congress' latest cybersecurity bill," American Civil Liberties Union, June 27, www.aclu.org/blog/beware-dangers-congress-latest-cybersecurity-bill.

Gadkari, P. 2013, "How does Twitter make money?" BBC News, November 7, www.bbc.com/news/business-24397472.

Galin, J. R. & Latchaw, J. 1998, "Heterotopic spaces online: a new paradigm for academic scholarship and publication," *Kairos*, 3, 1, kairos.technorhetoric.net/3.1/.

Gandy, O. 1993, "Toward a political economy of personal information," *Critical Studies in Mass Communication*, 10, 1, pp. 70–97.

Gardner, H. 1983, *Frames of mind: the theory of multiple intelligences*, New York: Basic Books.

Gartner, 2011, "Gartner says by 2015, digital strategies, such as social and mobile marketing, will influence at least 80 percent of consumers' discretionary spending," Gartner Newsroom, March 29, www.gartner.com/newsroom/id/1607814.

Gay, G. 2007, "Evaluating the accuracy of implicit feedback from clicks and query reformulations in web search," *ACM Transactions on Information Systems*, 25, 2, pp. 7, 1–27.

Geertz, C. 1983, *Local knowledge*, New York: Basic Books.

Gemmell, J., Bell, G. & Lueder, R. 2006, "MyLifeBits: a personal database for everything," *Communications of the ACM*, 49, 1, pp. 88–95.

Georgas, H. 2014, "Google v. the library (part II): student search patterns and behaviors when using Google and a federated search tool," *portal: Libraries and the Academy*, 14, 4, pp. 503–32.

Gerhards, J. & Schäfer, M. S. 2010, "Is the internet a better public sphere? Comparing old and new media in the USA and Germany," *New Media & Society*, 12, 1, pp. 143–60.

Gevelber, L. 2016, "How mobile has changed how people get things done: new consumer behavior data," Think with Google, September, www.thinkwithgoogle.com/articles/mobile-search-consumer-behavior-data.html.

Gibson, O. 2006, "Google to appeal, as court rules news site is illegal," *Guardian International*, September 19, www.guardian.co.uk/international/story/0,,1875616,00.html.

Giddens, A. 1984, *The constitution of society*, Berkeley: University of California Press.

Gillespie, T. 2011, "Can an algorithm be wrong? Twitter Trends, the specter of censorship, and our faith in the algorithms around us," Culture Digitally, October 19, culturedigitally.org/2011/10/can-an-algorithm-be-wrong/.

2012, "The dirty job of keeping Facebook clean," Culture Digitally, February 22, culturedigitally.org/2012/02/the-dirty-job-of-keeping-facebook-clean/.

2014, "The relevance of algorithms," in T. Gillespie, P. J. Boczkowski, & K. A. Foot (eds.), *Media technologies: essays on com-*

munication, materiality, and society, Cambridge, Mass.: MIT Press, pp. 167–94.

Ginsparg, P. 1997, "Winners and losers in the global research village," *The Serials Librarian*, 30, 3/4, pp. 83–95.

Gjorgievska, A. 2016, "Google and Facebook lead digital ad industry to revenue record," Bloomberg, April 21, www.bloomberg.com/news/articles/2016-04-22/google-and-facebook-lead-digital-ad-industry-to-revenue-record.

Glanz, J. 2011, "Google details, and defends, its use of electricity," *The New York Times*, September 8, www.nytimes.com/2011/09/09/technology/google-details-and-defends-its-use-of-electricity.html.

Glaser, M. 2005, "Companies subvert search results to squelch criticism," *Online Journalism Review*, June 1, www.ojr.org/ojr/stories/050601glaser/.

Goffman, E. 1997, "Self-presentation," in E. Goffman, C. C. Lemert, & A. Branaman (eds.), *The Goffman Reader*, Oxford: Blackwell, pp. 21–6.

Goggin, G. 2017, "Locating mobile media audiences: in plain view with Pokémon GO," in C. Hight & R. Harindranath (eds.), *Studying digital media audiences: perspectives from Australasia*, New York: Routledge, pp. 39–59.

Goh, D. H.-L., Lee, C. S. & Razikin, K. 2015, "Interfaces for accessing location-based information on mobile devices: an empirical evaluation," *Journal of the Association for Information Science and Technology*, June 23 (Early View), DOI: 10.1002/asi.23566.

Goldhaber, M. H. 1997, "The attention economy and the net," *FirstMonday*, 2, 4, a. 1, www.firstmonday.org/ojs/index.php/fm/article/view/519.

Goldman, E. 2005, "Search engine bias and the demise of search engine utopianism," *Yale Journal of Law & Technology*, 8, pp. 188–200.

Golumbia, D. 2009, *The cultural logic of computation*, Cambridge, Mass.: Harvard University Press.

Google. 2007, "Corporate information," July 1, www.google.com/about/company/history/.

2014, "Understanding web pages better," Webmaster Central Blog, May 23, webmasters.googleblog.com/2014/05/understanding-web-pages-better.html.

"Google y Yahoo, denunciados ante Consumo por publicidad engañosa," 2007, *El Pais.com*, August 13, tecnologia.elpais.com/tecnologia/2007/08/13/actualidad/1186993683_850215.html.

Gordon, M., Lindsay, R. K. & Fan, W. 2002, "Literature-based discovery on the World Wide Web," *ACM Transactions on Internet Technology*, 2, 4, pp. 261–75.

Gori, M. & Numerico, T. 2003, "Social networks and web minorities," *Cognitive Systems Research*, 4, 4, pp. 355–64.

Gorman, G. E. 2006, "Giving way to Google," *Online Information Review*, 30, 2, pp. 97–9.

Gottfried, J. & Shearer, E. 2016, "News use across social media platforms 2016," Pew Research Center, May 26, www.journalism.org/2016/05/26/news-use-across-social-media-platforms-2016/.

Graff, D. 2016, "An update to our AdWords policy on lending products," Google: The Keyword, May 11, blog.google/topics/public-policy/an-update-to-our-adwords-policy-on/.

Graham, L. & Metaxas, P. T. 2003, "'Of course it's true; I saw it on the Internet!': critical thinking in the internet era," *Communications of the ACM*, 46, 5, pp. 70–5.

Gramsci, A. 1957, *The modern prince and other writings*, New York: International Publishers.

Granka, L. A., Joachims, T. & Gay, G. 2004, "Eye-tracking analysis of user behavior in WWW search," in *SIGIR '04 Proceedings of the 27th Annual International ACM SIGIR Conference on Research and Development in Information Retrieval, Sheffield, July 25–29*, New York: ACM Press, pp. 478–9.

Greenberg, A. 2007a, "Condemned to Google hell," Forbes.com, April 30, www.forbes.com/2007/04/29/sanar-google-skyfacet-tech-cx_ag_0430googhell.html.

2007b, "The Google blogger vs. Sicko," Forbes.com, July 2, www.forbes.com/2007/07/02/google-sicko-blogs-tech-techbiz-cx_ag_0702sicko.html.

Greenwald, G. 2013, "XKeyscore: NSA tool collects 'nearly everything a user does on the internet,'" *The Guardian*, July 31, www.theguardian.com/world/2013/jul/31/nsa-top-secret-program-online-data.

Greenwood, S., Perrin, A. & Duggan, M. 2016, "Social media update 2016," Pew Research Center, November 11, www.pewinternet.org/2016/11/11/social-media-update-2016/.

Grimmelmann, J. T. 2008, "The structure of search engine law," *Iowa Law Review*, 93, 1, ssrn.com/abstract=979568.

2010, "Some scepticism about search neutrality," in B. Szoka & A. Marcus, *The next digital decade*, Washington, DC: TechFreedom, pp. 435–60.

Gross, A. M. 2014, "Search engine behavior and satisfaction of Arab students from a user perspective," *International Journal of Computational Linguistics Research*, 5, 3, pp. 85–98.

Gruman, G. 2014, "Too big to trust? Google's growing credibility gap," *InfoWorld*, April 15, www.infoworld.com/article/2610866/technology-business/too-big-to-trust--google-s-growing-credibility-gap.html.

Guan, Z. & Cutrell, E. 2007, "An eye tracking study of the effect of target rank on web search," in *CHI '07 Proceedings of the SIGCHI Conference on Human Factors in Computing Systems, San Jose, Calif., April 28 – May 3*, New York: ACM Press, pp. 417–20.

Guinee, K., Eagleton, M. B. & Hall, T. E. 2003, "Adolescents' internet search strategies: drawing upon familiar cognitive paradigms when accessing electronic information sources," *Journal of Educational Computing Research*, 29, 3, pp. 363–74.

Hachten, W. A. 1992, *The world news prism*, 5th edn., Ames: Iowa State University Press.

Haigh, G. 2006, "Information idol: how Google is making us stupid," *The Monthly*, 9, pp. 25–33, www.themonthly.com.au/monthly-essays-gideon-haigh-information-idol-how-google-making-us-stupid-170.

Halavais, A. 2000, "National borders on the World Wide Web," *New Media and Society*, 2, 1, pp. 7–28.

2006, "The visible college: blogs as transparent research journals," in A. Bruns & J. Jacobs (eds.), *Uses of Blogs*, New York: Peter Lang, pp. 117–26.

2008, "The hyperlink as organizing principle," in J. Turow & L. Tsui (eds.), *The hyperlinked society: questioning connections in the digital age*, Ann Arbor: University of Michigan Press.

2009, "Do dugg diggers Digg diligently? Feedback as motivation in collaborative moderation systems," *Information, Communication & Society*, 12, 3, pp. 444–59.

2016, "The blogosphere and its problems: Web 2.0 undermining civic webspaces," *First Monday*, 21, 6, ojs-prod-lib.cc.uic.edu/ojs/index.php/fm/article/view/6788.

Hamilton, K., Karahalios, K., Sandvig, C. & Eslami, M. 2014, "A path to understanding the effects of algorithm awareness," in *CHI EA '14 Extended Abstracts on Human Factors in Computing Systems, Toronto, April 26 – May 1*, New York: ACM Press, pp. 631–42.

Hargittai, E. 2002a, "Second-level digital divide: differences in people's online skills," *FirstMonday*, 7, 4, firstmonday.org/ojs/index.php/fm/article/view/942.

2002b, "Beyond logs and surveys: in-depth measures of people's online skills," *Journal of the American Society of Information Science and Technology*, 53, 14, pp. 1239–44.

2004, "Do you 'Google?' Understanding search engine use beyond the hype," *FirstMonday*, 9, 3, firstmonday.org/ojs/index.php/fm/article/view/1127.

2006, "Hurdles to information seeking: spelling and typographical mistakes during users' online behavior," *Journal of the Association of Information Systems*, 7, 1, pp. 52–67.

2008, "The role of experience in navigating links of influence," in J. Turow & L. Tsui (eds.), *The hyperlinked society: questioning connections in the digital age*, Ann Arbor: University of Michigan Press, pp. 85–103.

Hargittai, E., Fullerton, E., Menchen-Trevino, E. & Thomas, K. Y. 2010, "Trust online: young adults' evaluation of web content," *International Journal of Communication*, 4, pp. 468–94.

Hargittai, E. & Marwick, A. E. 2016, "'What can I really do?' Explaining the privacy paradox with online apathy," *International Journal of Communication*, 10, pp. 3737–57.

Harper, J. 2007, "Google 'get a life': ignore the roar of the JFK plotters," *National Review Online*, www.nationalreview.com/article/221221/google-get-life-jim-harper.

Harris, S. 2006, "TIA lives on," *National Journal*, 38, 8, pp. 66–7.

2014, *@ War: the rise of the military-internet complex*, Boston: Mariner Books.

Head, A. J. & Eisenberg, M. B. 2011, "How college students use the web to conduct everyday life research," *First Monday*, 16, 4, firstmonday.org/article/view/3484/2857.

"Hearing of the Africa, Global Human Rights and International Operations Subcommittee of the House International Relations Committee: The Internet in China, a tool for freedom or suppression," February 15, 2006, commdocs.house.gov/committees/intlrel/hfa26075.000/hfa26075_of.htm.

Hecht, B., Teevan, J., Morris, M. R. & Liebling, D. 2012, "SearchBuddies: bringing search engines into the conversation," in *ICWSM '12 Proceedings of the AAAI Conference on Web and Social Media, Dublin, June*, New York: ACM Press, pp. 138–45.

Heine, C. 2007, "Five things today's digital generation cannot do," 21st Century Information Fluency Project / Illinois Mathematics and Science Academy, 21cif.com/rkitp/features/v1n2/leadarticle_v1_n2.html.

Hendrikx, F., Bubendorfer, K. & Chard, R. 2015, "Reputation systems: a survey and taxonomy," *Journal of Parallel and Distributed Computing*, 75, pp. 184–97.

Heyamoto, L. 2007, "How to best your Google twin," *Chicago Sun-Times*, March 14, www.highbeam.com/doc/1P2-3742044.html.

Higginbotham, S. 2016, "Inside Facebook's biggest artificial intelligence project ever," *Fortune*, April 13, fortune.com/facebook-machine-learning/.

Hilbert, M., Vásquez, J., Halpern, D., Valenzuela, S. & Arriagada, E. 2016, "One step, two step, network step? Complementary perspectives on communication flows in Twittered citizen protests," *Social Science Computer Review*, online first, ssc.sagepub.com/content/early/2016/04/11/0894439316639561.abstract.

Hill, K. 2011, "Fitbit moves quickly after users' sex stats exposed," *Forbes*, July 5, www.forbes.com/sites/kashmirhill/2011/07/05/fitbit-moves-quickly-after-users-sex-stats-exposed/.

Hillis, K., Petit, M. & Jarrett, K. 2012, *Google and the culture of search*, New York: Routledge.

Hindman, M. 2008, *The myth of digital democracy*, Princeton University Press.

Hines, J. 2007, "Remarks in panel session: Beyond Simple Search," at Director of National Intelligence Conference on Open Source Intelligence, Washington, DC, July 16–17.

Hinman, L. M. 2005, "Esse est indicato in Google: ethical and political issues in search engines," *International Review of Information Ethics*, 3, pp. 19–25.

Hodson, H. 2015, "Inside China's plan to give every citizen a character score," *New Scientist*, October 9, www.newscientist.com/article/dn28314–inside-chinas-plan-to-give-every-citizen-a-character-score/.

Hogan, C. 1998, "Search engine survey: prospect researchers report their favorites, PRSPCT-L," www2.ups.edu/our/adi/research/survey.htm.

Holderness, M. 1998, "Who are the world's information-poor?" in B. D. Loader (ed.), *Cyberspace divide*, London: Routledge, pp. 35–56.

Hölscher, C. & Strube, G. 2000, "Web search behavior of Internet experts and newbies," *Computer Networks*, 33, 1, pp. 337–46.

Hong, J. 2013, "Considering privacy issues in the context of Google Glass," *Communications of the ACM*, 56, 11, pp. 10–11.

Horowitz, D. & Kamvar, S. 2010, "The anatomy of a large-scale *social* search engine," in *WWW '10 Proceedings of the 19th International Conference on the World Wide Web, April 26–30, Raleigh, North Carolina*, New York: ACM Press, pp. 431–40.

Howard, P. & Massanari, A. 2007, "Learning to search and searching to learn: income, education, and experience online," *Journal of Computer-Mediated Communication*, 12, 3, pp. 846–65.

Howe, A. E. & Dreilinger, D. 1997, "SavvySearch: a metasearch engine that learns which search engines to query," *AI Magazine*, 18, pp. 19–25.

Hoy, M. G. & Milne, G. 2010, "Gender differences in privacy-related measures for young adult Facebook users," *Journal of Interactive Advertising*, 10, 2, pp. 28–45.

Hoyt, C. 2007, "When bad news follows you," *New York Times*, August 26, www.nytimes.com/2007/08/26/opinion/26pubed.html.

Huberman, B. A. 2001, *The laws of the Web: patterns in the ecology of information*, Cambridge, Mass.: MIT Press.

Huberman, B. A., Pirolli, P. L. T., Pitkow, J. E. & Lukose, R. M. 1998, "Strong regularities in World Wide Web surfing," *Science*, 280, pp. 95–7.

Hugo, V. 1999, *Notre-Dame de Paris*, Oxford University Press.

Introna, L. D. & Nissenbaum, H. 2000, "Shaping the web: why the politics of search engines matters," *The Information Society*, 16, 3, pp. 169–85.

Jack, K. 2013, "What makes a search engine different from a recommender system?" Making Tools for Researchers, October 1, krisjack.wordpress.com/2013/10/01/what-makes-a-search-engine-different-from-a-recommender-system/.

James, B. 1995, "The Web: out of the lab and spun around the world," *The New York Times*, March 20, www.nytimes.com/1995/03/20/news/20iht-web.html.

Jansen, B. J. 2003, "Operators not needed? The impact of query structure on web searching results," in *Proceedings of the Information Resource Management Association International Conference*, Hainburg, Penn.: Idea Group, pp. 814–17.

Jansen, B. J. & Pooch, U. 2000, "Web user studies: a review and framework for future work," *Journal of the American Society of Information Science and Technology*, 52, 3, pp. 235–46.

Jansen, B. J., Spink, A. & Saracevic, T. 2000, "Real life, real users, and real needs: a study and analysis of user queries on the web," *Information Processing & Management*, 36, pp. 207–27.

Jasco, P. 2005, "As we may search: comparison of major features of the Web of Science, Scopus, and Google Scholar citation-based and citation-enhanced databases," *Current Science*, 89, 9, pp. 1537–47.

Jeanneney, J. N. 2007, *Google and the myth of universal knowledge*, trans. T. L. Fagan, University of Chicago Press.

Jefferson, T. 1903, *The writings of Thomas Jefferson*, Washington, DC: Thomas Jefferson Memorial Association.

Jeon, G. Y. & Rieh, S. Y. 2013, "The value of social search: seeking collective personal experience in social Q & A," *Proceedings of the Association for Information Science and Technology*, 50, 1, pp. 1–10.

Jiang, M. 2014, "Search concentration, bias, and parochialism: a comparative study of Google, Baidu, and Jike's search results from China," *Journal of Communication*, 64, 6, pp. 1088–110.

Joachims, T., Granka, L. A., Pan, B., Hembrooke, H., Radlinski, F. & Johnson, D. G. 1997, "Is the Global Information Infrastructure a democratic technology?" *Computers and Society*, 27, 3, pp. 20–6.

Johnson, M., Schuster, M., Le, Q. V., Krikum, M., Wu, Y., Chen, Z. & Thorat, N. 2016, "Google's multilingual neural machine translation system: enabling zero-shot translation," arXiv, arxiv.org/abs/1611.04558.

Jones, M. 2007, "Classical and alternative mobile search: a review and agenda," in J. Lumsden (ed.), *Developments in Technologies for Human-Centric Mobile Computing and Applications*, Hershey, Penn.: IGI Global, pp. 22–37.

Jupiter Communications. 1999, "Europeans opt for local eMerchants," NUA Internet Surveys, October 4, anciensdefcr.eu/histoire/ASE_web_janv2000/alertes/actualites/economie_internet/web_etude/global.html.

Kane, L. T. 1997, "Access vs. ownership: do we have to make a choice?" *College & Research Libraries*, 58, 1, pp. 59–67.

Karpf, D. A. 2011, "Social science research methods in internet time," SSRN, September 16, ssrn.com/abstract=1929095.

Kaser, D. 1962, "In principium erat verbum," *Peabody Journal of Education*, 39, 5, pp. 258–63.

Katz, E. & Lazarsfeld, P. F. 1955, *Personal influence, the part played by people in the flow of mass communications*, New York: The Free Press.

Kautz, H., Selman, B. & Shah, M. 1997, "Referral Web: combining social networks and collaborative filtering," *Communications of the ACM*, 40, 3, pp. 63–5.

Kavilanz, P. 2013, "Google's dreaded 'blacklist,'" CNN Money, November 5, money.cnn.com/2013/11/04/smallbusiness/google-blacklist/.

Kay, M., Matuszek, C. & Munson, S. A. 2015, "Unequal representation and gender stereotypes in image search results for occupations," in *CHI '15 Proceedings of the 33rd Annual ACM Conference on Human Factors in Computing Systems, Seoul, April 17–23*, New York: ACM Press, pp. 3819–28.

Kellner, D. 1997, "Intellectuals, the new public spheres, and techno-politics," in C. Toulouse & T. W. Luke (eds.), *The politics of cyberspace: a new political science reader*, London: Routledge, pp. 167–86.

Kenney, B. 2004, "Googlizers vs. resistors," *Library Journal*, December 15, lj.libraryjournal.com/2004/12/ljarchives/googlizers-vs-resistors/.

Kim, Y. A. & Park, G. W. 2013, "Topic-driven SocialRank: personalized search result ranking by identifying similar, credible users in a social network," *Knowledge-Based Systems*, 54, pp. 230–42.

Kipling, R. 1925, "As easy as A.B.C.," in *A diversity of creatures – letters of travel, 1892–1913*, Garden City, NY: Doubleday, pp. 3–40.

Klein, G. A. 1999, *Sources of power: how people make decisions*, Cambridge, Mass.: MIT Press.

Kleinberg, J. M. 1999, "Authoritative sources in a hyperlinked environment," *Journal of the ACM*, 46, 5, pp. 604–32.

Koene, A., Perez, E., Carter, C. J., et al. 2015, "Privacy concerns arising from internet service personalization filters," *ACM SIGCAS Computers and Society*, 45, 3, pp. 167–71.

Kornhauser, W. 1960, *The politics of mass society*, London: Routledge.

Kramer, A. D. I., Guillory, J. E. & Hancock, J. T. 2014, "Experimental evidence of massive-scale emotional contagion through social networks," *Proceedings of the National Academy of Sciences of the United States*, 111, 24, pp. 8788–90.

Krikorian, R. 2010, "Twitter by the numbers," Slideshare, September 11, www.slideshare.net/raffikrikorian/twitter-by-the-numbers/12-8_TBper_day_in_total_100.

Krug, S. 2006, *Don't make me think! A common sense approach to Web usability*, 2nd edn., Berkeley, Calif.: New Riders Pub.

Küçüktunç, O., Saule, E., Kaya, K. & Çatalyürek, Ü. V. 2015,

"Diversifying citation recommendations," *ACM Transactions on Intelligent Systems and Technology (TIST), Special Sections on Diversity and Discovery in Recommender Systems*, 5, 4, a. 55.

Kulp, P. 2016, "Google brags it's keeping you safe from weight-loss scams and malware," *Mashable*, January 22, mashable.com/2016/01/22/google-bad-ads/.

Kumar, R., Ragbaven, P., Rajagopalan, S. & Tomkins, A. 2002, "The Web and social networks," *Computer*, 35, 11, pp. 32–6.

Labbo, L. D., Reinking, D. & McKenna, M. C. 1998, "Literacy education in the 21st century," *Peabody Journal of Education*, 73, 3/4, pp. 273–89.

Lachance, N. 2016, "Facebook's facial recognition software is different from the FBI's. Here's why," All Tech Considered, May 18, www.npr.org/sections/alltechconsidered/2016/05/18/477819617/facebooks-facial-recognition-software-is-different-from-the-fbis-heres-why.

LaFrance, A. 2015, "Not even the people who write algorithms really know how they work," *The Atlantic*, September 18, www.theatlantic.com/technology/archive/2015/09/not-even-the-people-who-write-algorithms-really-know-how-they-work/406099/.

Lampe, C., Ellison, N. & Steinfield, C. 2006, "A face(book) in the crowd: social searching vs. social browsing," in *Proceedings of the 20th Anniversary Conference on Computer Supported Cooperative Work, Banff*, Alberta, Canada: ACM Press, pp. 167–70.

Lardinois, F. 2014, "Good riddance to social search," TechCrunch, December 28, techcrunch.com/2014/12/28/good-riddance-to-social-search/.

Latimer, K. 2011, "Collections to connections: changing spaces and new challenges in academic library buildings," *Library Trends*, 60, 1, pp. 112–33.

Latour, B. 2016, "Two bubbles of unrealism: learning from the tragedy of Trump," *Los Angeles Review of Books*, November 16, trans. C. Soudan & J. Park from the original published in *Le Monde*, lareviewofbooks.org/article/two-bubbles-unrealism-learning-tragedy-trump/.

Law, J. 1989, "Technology and heterogeneous engineering: the case of Portuguese expansion," in W. Bijker, T. Hughes & T. Pinch (eds.), *The social construction of technological systems: new directions in the sociology and history of technology*, Cambridge, Mass.: MIT Press, pp. 111–34.

Lazazrinis, F., Vilares, J., Tait, J. & Efthimiadis, E. 2009, "Current research issues and trends in non-English web searching," *Information Retrieval*, 12, pp. 230–50.

Leary, P. 2005, "Googling the Victorians," *Journal of Victorian Culture*, 10, 1, pp. 72–86.

Leaver, T. 2013, "The social media contradiction: data mining and digital death," *M/C Journal*, 16, 2, journal.media-culture.org.au/index. php/mcjournal/article/viewArticle/625.

LeCunn, Y. 2014, "The unreasonable effectiveness of deep learning," presented at Johns Hopkins University, Center for Language and Speech Processing, November 18, youtube/sc-KbuZqGkI.

Lenhart, A., Simon, M. & Graziano, M. 2001, "The internet and education," Pew Internet and American Life, September 1, www. pewinternet.org/2001/09/01/the-internet-and-education/.

Levin, D. & Arafeh, S. 2002, "The digital disconnect: the widening gap between internet-savvy students and their schools," Washington, DC: Pew Internet & American Life Project, August 14.

Levy, S. 2014, "How the NSA almost killed the internet," *Wired*, January 7, www.wired.com/2014/01/how-the-us-almost-killed-the-internet/.

Lewandowski, D. 2014, "Why we need an independent index of the web," in R. König & M. Rasch (eds.), *Society of the query reader: reflections on web search*, Amsterdam: Institute of Network Cultures, pp. 49–58.

Li, G., Ji, S., Li, C. & Feng, J. 2009, "Efficient type-ahead search on relational data: a TASTIER approach," in *SIGMOD '09 Proceedings of the 2009 ACM SIGMOD International Conference on Management of Data, Providence, R.I., June 29 – July 2*, New York: ACM Press, pp. 695–706.

Liebel, U., Kindler, B. & Pepperkok, R. 2005, "Bioinformatic 'Harvester': a search engine for genome-wide human, mouse, and rat protein resources," *Methods in Enzymology*, 404, pp. 19–26.

Liebelson, D. 2014, "Why Facebook, Google, and the NSA want computers that learn like humans," *Mother Jones*, September/October, www.motherjones.com/media/2014/09/deep-learning-artificial-intelligence-facebook-nsa.

Lithwick, D. 2003, "Google-Opoly: the game no one but Google can play," *Slate*, January 29, www.slate.com/articles/news_and_politics/jurisprudence/2003/01/googleopoly_the_game_no_one_but_google_can_play.html.

Liu, J., Liu, Y., Zhang, M. & Ma, S. 2013, "How do users grow up along with search engines? A study of long-term users' behavior," in *CIKM '13 Proceedings of the 22nd ACM International Conference on Information & Knowledge Management, San Francisco, October 27 – November 1*, New York: ACM Press, pp. 1795–800.

Ljunggren, D. 2007, "Global web privacy rules needed in 5 years: Google," Reuters, September 24, www.reuters.com/article/us-google-privacy-idUSN2429959320070924.

Lomas, N. 2014, "Futureful, the Janus Friis-backed AI predictive discovery engine, rebrands as Random," TechCrunch, April 4, techcrunch.com/2014/04/04/futureful-becomes-random/.

Long, J., Skoudis, E. & van Eikelenborg, A. 2004, *Google hacking for penetration testers*, Rockland, Md.: Syngress.

Longo, L., Barrett, S. & Dondio, P. 2009, "Information foraging theory as a form of collective intelligence for social search," in *Proceedings of International Conference on Computational Collective Intelligence, Semantic Web, Social Networks and Multiagent Systems, Wrocław, Poland, October 5–7*, Berlin: Springer, pp. 63–74.

Luria, A. R. 2006, *The mind of a mnemonist: a little book about a vast memory*, Cambridge, Mass.: Harvard University Press.

Lyon, D. 2015, *Surveillance after Snowden*, Cambridge: Polity.

Lyotard, J.-F. 1984, *The postmodern condition*, Minneapolis: University of Minnesota Press.

MacKinnon, R., Hickok, E., Bar, A. & Lim, H. 2014, *Fostering freedom online: the role of internet intermediaries*, UNESCO series on internet freedom, Paris: UNESCO, unesdoc.unesco.org/images/0023/002311/231162e.pdf.

Madden, M. 2005, "Do-it-yourself information online," Pew Internet & American Life, June, web.archive.org/web/20060626125713/http://www.pewinternet.org/pdfs/PIP_DIY_June2005.pdf.

2014, "Most would like to do more to protect their personal information online," Pew Research Center, November 12, www.pewinternet.org/2014/11/12/most-would-like-to-do-more-to-protect-their-pers onal-information-online/.

Mager, A. 2012, "Algorithmic ideology: how capitalism shapes our search engines," *Information, Communication and Society*, 15, 5, pp. 769–87.

2014, "Is small really beautiful? Big search and its alternatives," in R. König & M. Rasch (eds.), *Society of the query reader: reflections on web search*, Amsterdam: Institute of Network Cultures, pp. 60–72.

Mahle, M. B. 2006, *Denial and deception: an insider's view of the CIA*, New York: Nation Books.

Manjoo, F. 2008, *True enough: learning to live in a post-fact society*, Hoboken, NJ: John Wiley & Sons.

Mann, S., Nolan, J. & Wellman, B. 2003, "Sousveillance: inventing and using wearable computing devices for data collection in surveillance environments," *Surveillance & Society*, 1, 3, pp. 331–55.

Marchi, R. 2012, "With Facebook, blogs, and fake news, teens reject journalistic 'objectivity,'" *Journal of Communication Inquiry*, 36, 3, pp. 246–62.

Marcuse, H. 1964, *One-dimensional man*, Boston: Beacon Press.

Marvin, C. 1988, *When old technologies were new: thinking about electric communication in the late nineteenth century*, New York: Oxford University Press.

Marwick, A. E. 2014, "How your data are being deeply mined," *The New York Review of Books*, 61, 1, www.nybooks.com/articles/2014/01/09/how-your-data-are-being-deeply-mined/.

Masahiro, H., Goto, M. & Nakano, T. 2014, "Songrium: a music browsing assistance service with interactive visualization and exploration of a web of music," presented at World Wide Web 14 Companion, April 7–11, Seoul, Korea, wwwconference.org/proceedings/www2014/companion/p523.pdf.

Massanari, A. 2015, "#Gamergate and The Fappening: how Reddit's algorithm, governance, and culture support toxic technocultures," *New Media & Society*, published online before print, October 9, doi: 10.1177/1461444815608807.

Mattelart, A. 2000, *Networking the world: 1794–2000*, trans. L. Carey-Libbrecht & J. A. Cohen, Minneapolis: University of Minnesota Press.

Mayer-Schönberger, V. 2011, *Delete: the virtue of forgetting in the digital age*, Princeton University Press.

McChesney, R. R. 1996, "The Internet and U.S. communication policy-making in historical and critical perspective," *Journal of Communication*, 46, 1, pp. 98–124.

McCullagh, D. 2006, "AOL's disturbing glimpse into users' lives," CNET News.com, August 7, news.cnet.com/2100–1030_3-6103098.html.

McFedries, P. 2003, "Google this," *IEEE Spectrum*, 40, 2, p. 68.

McHugh, J. 2003, "Google vs. evil," *Wired*, 11, 1, www.wired.com/wired/archive/11.01/google_pr.html.

McKelvey, N., Diver, C. & Curran, C. 2015, "Drones and privacy," *International Journal of Handheld Computing Research*, 6, 1, pp. 44–57.

McLuhan, M. 1962, *The Gutenberg galaxy: the making of typographic man*, University of Toronto Press.

McPherson, M., Smith-Lovin, L. & Cook, J. M. 2001, "Birds of a feather: homophily in social networks," *Annual Review of Sociology*, 27, pp. 415–44.

Menchen-Trevino, E. & Karr, C. 2012, "Researching real-world web use with Roxy: collecting observational web data with informed consent," *Journal of Information Technology & Politics*, 9, 3, pp. 254–68.

Menn, J. 2016, "Exclusive: Yahoo secretly scanned customer emails for U. S. intelligence – sources," *Reuters*, October 4, www.reuters.com/article/us-yahoo-nsa-exclusive-idUSKCN1241YT.

Merton, R. K. & Barber, E. 2003, *The travels and adventures of serendipity: a study in sociological semantics and the sociology of science*, Princeton University Press.

Mesbah, A., van Deursen, A. & Lenselink, S. 2011, "Crawling AJAX-based web applications through dynamic analysis of user interface state changes," *ACM Transactions on the Web (TWEB)*, 6, 1, art. 3.

Meyer, J. 2006, "France searches for its own Google," *Business Week Online*, March 30, web.archive.org/web/20110416032702/http://www.businessweek.com/globalbiz/content/mar2006/gb20060330_385311.htm.

Michel, J., Julien, C. & Payton, J. 2014, "Gander: mobile, pervasive search of the here and now in the here and now," *IEEE Internet of Things Journal*, 1, 5, pp. 483–96.

Michel, S., Trianafillou, P. & Weikum, G. 2005, "MINERVA∞: a scalable efficient peer-to-peer search engine," in *Middleware '05 Proceedings of the ACM/IFIP/USENIX 6th International Conference on Middleware, Grenoble, November 28 – December 2*, Berlin: Springer-Verlag, pp. 60–81.

Mihailidis, P. & Cohen, J. 2013, "Exploring curation as a core competency in digital and media literacy education," *Journal of Interactive Media in Education*, 1, www-jime.open.ac.uk/articles/10.5334/2013-02/.

Miles, S. 2006, "Google delists BMW Germany for foul play," *Pocketlint*, February 5, www.pocket-lint.com/news/75471–bmw-germany-google-ranking-search.

Miller, C. C. 2013, "Apps that know what you want, before you do," *The New York Times*, July 29, www.nytimes.com/2013/07/30/technology/apps-that-know-what-you-want-before-you-do.html.

Miller, G. A. 1956, "The magical number seven, plus or minus two: some limits on our capacity for processing information," *Psychological Review*, 63, pp. 84–97.

Mills, C. W. 1959, *The sociological imagination*, New York: Oxford University Press.

Mislove, A., Gummadi, K. & Druschel, P. 2006, "Exploiting social networks for internet search," presented at the Fifth Workshop on Hot Topics in Networks, Irvine, California, November 29–30.

Mitchell, A., Jurkowitz, M. & Olmstead, K. 2014, "Audience routes: direct, search & Facebook," Pew Research Center, March 13, www.journalism.org/2014/03/13/audience-routes-direct-search-facebook/.

Moise, D., Shestakov, D., Gudmundsson, G. & Amsaleg, L. 2013, "Indexing and searching 100M images with Map-Reduce," in *ICMR '13 Proceedings of the 3rd ACM International Conference on Multimedia Retrieval, Dallas, April 16–20*, New York: ACM Press, pp. 17–24.

Mordvintsev, A., Olah, C. & Tyka, M. 2015, "DeepDream: a code example for visualizing neural networks," *Google Research Blog*, July 1, research.googleblog.com/2015/07/deepdream-code-example-for-visualizing.html.

Morris, M. R. 2013, "Collaborative search revisited," in *CSCW '13 Proceedings of the 2013 Conference on Computer Supported Cooperative Work, San Antonio, Texas, February 23–27*, New York: ACM Press, pp. 1181–92.

Morris, M. R., Teevan, J. & Panovich, K. 2010, "What do people ask their social networks, and why? A survey study of status message Q&A behavior," in *Proceedings of the SIGCHI Conference on Human Factors in Computing Systems*, New York: ACM Press, pp. 1739–48.

Mosendz, P. 2014, "Wearable gadget monitors your breathing, so it can tell you to calm down," *The Atlantic*, June 17, www.theatlantic.com/technology/archive/2014/06/spire-would-like-you-to-calm-down/372938/.

Mowshowitz, A. & Kawaguchi, A. 2002, "Bias on the web," *Communications of the ACM*, 45, 9, pp. 56–60.

Mullins, B., Winkler, R. & Kendall, B. 2015, "Inside the U.S. antitrust probe of Google," *The Wall Street Journal*, March 19, www.wsj.com/articles/inside-the-u-s-antitrust-probe-of-google-1426793274.

Mumford, L. 1964, "Authoritarian and democratic technics," *Technology and Culture*, 5, 1, pp. 1–8.

Munro, A., Höök, K. & Benyon, D. 1999, *Social navigation of information space*, London: Springer.

Murphy, M. 2016, "Facebook is using artificial intelligence to become a better search engine," *Quartz*, June 1, qz.com/696827/facebook-is-using-artificial-intelligence-to-become-a-better-search-engine/.

Nahon, K. 2016, "Where there is social media there is politics," in A. Bruns, G. Enli, E. Skogerbø, A. O. Larsson, & C. Christensen (eds.), *The Routledge companion to social media and politics*, New York: Routledge, pp. 39–55.

Nahon, K. & Hemsley, J. 2013, *Going viral*, Cambridge: Polity.

Napoli, P. 2014, "Automated media: an institutional theory perspective on algorithmic media production and consumption," *Communication Theory*, 24, 3, pp. 340–60.

Nathanson, I. S. 1998, "Internet infoglut and invisible ink: spamdexing search engines with meta tags," *Harvard Journal of Law & Technology*, 12, 1.

NetMarketShare. 2016, "Desktop search engine market share, September 2016," www.netmarketshare.com/search-engine-market-share.aspx?qprid=4&qpcustomd=0.

Neyland, D. 2016, "Bearing account-able witness to the ethical algorithmic system," *Science, Technology & Human Values*, 41, 1, pp. 50–76.

Nielsen, J. 2003, "Diversity is power for specialized sites," Alertbox, June 16, www.nngroup.com/articles/diversity-is-power-for-special ized-sites/.

Nixon, R. 2016, "Visitors to the U.S. may be asked for social media information," *The New York Times*, June 28, www.nytimes.com/2016/06/29/us/homeland-security-social-media-border-protection.html.

Noam, E. 1997, "An unfettered internet? Keep dreaming," *The New York Times*, July 11, www.nytimes.com/1997/07/11/opinion/an-unfettered-internet-keep-dreaming.html.

Noble, S. U. 2013, "Google search: hyper-visibility as a means of rendering black women and girls invisible," *InVisible Culture*, 19, hdl.handle.net/1802/28018.

Noruzi, A. 2004, "Application of Ranganathan's laws of the web," *Webology*, 2, 1, www.webology.org/2004/vin2/a8.html.

Ntoulas, A., Zerfos, P. & Cho, J. 2005, "Downloading textual hidden web content through keyword queries," in *Proceedings of the Joint Conference on Digital Libraries (JCDL)*, New York: ACM Press, pp. 100–9.

Nunez, M. 2016, "Former Facebook workers: we routinely suppressed conservative news," Gizmodo, May 9, gizmodo.com/former-face book-workers-we-routinely-suppressed-conser-1775461006.

O'Brien, J. 2006, "The race to create a 'smart' Google," *Fortune*, November 20, archive.fortune.com/magazines/fortune/fortune_ archive/2006/11/27/8394347/index.htm.

Oliver, J. 2014, "Right to be forgotten," Last Week Tonight with John Oliver, May 19, youtube/r-ERajkMXwo.

Orlowski, A. 2003, "Google to fix blog noise problem," *The Register*, May 9, www.theregister.co.uk/2003/05/09/google_to_fix_blog_ noise/.

Ortiz-Cordova, A., Yang, Y. & Jansen, B. J. 2015, "External to internal search: associating searching on search engines with searching on sites," *Information Processing and Management*, 51, pp. 718–36.

Ossola, A. 2015, "The race to build a search engine for your DNA," *IEEE Spectrum*, March 20, spectrum.ieee.org/biomedical/diagnos tics/the-race-to-build-a-search-engine-for-your-dna.

Page, L., Brin, S., Motwani, R. & Winograd, T. 1998, "The PageRank citation ranking: bringing order to the web," Stanford Digital Library Technologies Project, dbpubs.stanford.edu:8090/pub/1999–66.

Palfrey, J. 2015, *BiblioTech: why libraries matter more than ever in the age of Google*, New York: Basic Books.

Pan, B., Hembrooke, H., Joachims, T., Lorigo, L., Gay, G. & Granka, L. 2007, "In Google we trust: users' decisions on rank, position, and relevance," *Journal of Computer-Mediated Communication*, 12, 3, pp. 801–23.

Pandey, S., Roy, S., Olston, C., Cho, J. & Chakrabarti, S. 2005, "Shuffling a stacked deck: the case for partially randomized rank ing of search engine results," in *Proceedings of the 31st International Conference on Very Large Data Bases*, Norway: Trondheim, pp. 781–92.

Pandurangan, G., Raghavan, P. & Upfal, E. 2002, "Using PageRank to characterize web structure," in *Computing and Combinatorics: 8th Annual International Conference, COCOON 2002, Singapore, August 15–17, 2002. Proceedings*, Heidelberg: Springer, pp. 1–4.

Parekh, B. 2000, *Rethinking multiculturalism: cultural diversity and political theory*, Cambridge, Mass.: Harvard University Press.

Pariser, E. 2011, *The filter bubble: how the new personalized web is chang ing what we read and how we think*, New York: Penguin.

Parker, G. 1994, *Internet guide: Veronica*, Education Library, Vanderbilt University, web.archive.org/web/20040808093422/http://www. lib.umich.edu/govdocs/godort/archive/elec/intveron.txt.old.

Pasquale, F. 2015, *The black box society: the secret algorithms that control money and information*, Cambridge, Mass.: Harvard University Press.

Pasquale, F. A. & Bracha, O. 2007, "Federal search commission? Access, fairness and accountability in the law of search," University of Texas Law, Public Law Research Paper No. 123, ssrn.com/abstract=1002453.

Pass, G., Chowdhury, A. and Torgeson, C. 2006, "A picture of search," in *InfoScale '06 Proceedings of the 1st International Conference on Scalable Information Systems, Hong Kong, May 30–June 1*, New York: ACM Press, art. 1.

Pedone, M. 2005, "Google bowling: how competitors can sabotage you," Webpronews.com, http://archive.webpronews.com/expertarticles/expertarticles/wpn-62–20051027GoogleBowling-HowCompetitorsCanSabotageYouWhatGoogleShouldDoAboutIt.html.

Peet, L. 2015, "Appeals court rules Google book scanning is fair use," *Library Journal*, 140, 19, pp. 11–12.

Pennock, D. M., Flake, G. W., Lawrence, S., Glover, E. J. & Giles, C. L. 2002, "Winners don't take all: characterizing the competition for links on the web," *Proceedings of the National Academy of Sciences of the United States of America*, 99, 8, pp. 5207–11.

Penzias, A. 1989, *Ideas and information*, New York: Simon & Schuster.

Peters, J. D. 1999, *Speaking into the air: a history of the idea of communication*, University of Chicago Press.

Peters, T. 1997, "The brand called you," *Fast Company*, 10, p. 83, www.fastcompany.com/28905/brand-called-you.

Piejko, P. 2016, "The mobile web intelligence report for Q1 2016," DeviceAtlas, deviceatlas.com/blog/download-new-mobile-web-intelligence-report-q1–2016.

Pinkerton, B. 1994, "Finding what people want: experiences with the WebCrawler," presented at the Second World Wide Web Conference, Chicago, October 17–19.

Pirolli, P. & Card, S. K. 1999, "Information foraging," *Psychological Review*, 106, pp. 643–75.

Pitkow, J. E., Schütze, H., Cass, T., et al. 2002, "Personalized search: a contextual computing approach may prove a breakthrough in personalized search efficiency," *Communications of the ACM*, 45, 9, pp. 50–5.

Plato. 2002, *Phaedrus*, New York: Oxford University Press.

Plotz, R. 1997, "Positive spin: Senate campaigning on the Web," *PS: Political Science and Politics*, 30, 3, pp. 482–6.

Polanyi, M. 1998, *Personal knowledge* [1952], London: Routledge.

Pool, I. de S. 1983, *Technologies of freedom*, Cambridge, Mass.: Belknap Press.

Poor, N. 2005, "Mechanisms of an online public sphere: the Slashdot website," *Journal of Computer-Mediated Communication*, 10, 2, p. 4.

Poster, M. 2006, *Information please: culture and politics in the age of digital machines*, Durham, NC: Duke University Press.

Prensky, M. 2001, "Digital natives, digital immigrants," *On the Horizon*, 9, 5, pp. 1–2.

2004, "The emerging online life of the digital native," www.marc prensky.com/writing/Prensky-The_Emerging_Online_Life_of_ the_Digital_Native-03.pdf.

Primary Research Group. 2009, *The survey of American college students: student library research practices and skills*, New York: Primary Research Group.

Purcell, K., Brenner, J. & Rainie, L. 2012, "Search engine use 2012," Pew Internet and American Life, March 9, www.pewinternet.org/ 2012/03/09/search-engine-use-2012/.

Purcell, K., Rainie, L., Heaps, A., et al. 2012, "How teens do research in the digital world," Pew Research Center, November 1, www.pewin ternet.org/2012/11/01/how-teens-do-research-in-the-digital-world/.

Putnam, R. 1995, "Bowling alone: America's declining social capital," *Journal of Democracy*, 6, 1, pp. 65–78.

Quinn, A. J. & Bederson, B. B. 2011, "Human computation: a survey and taxonomy of a growing field," in *CHI '11 Proceedings of the SIGCHI Conference on Human Factors in Computing Systems, Vancouver, May 7–12*, New York: ACM Press, pp. 1403–12.

Rader, E. & Gray, R. 2015, "Understanding user beliefs about algorithmic curation in the Facebook news feed," in *CHI '15 Proceedings of the 33rd Annual ACM Conference on Human Factors in Computing Systems, Seoul, April 18–23*, New York: ACM Press, pp. 173–82.

Radlinski, F. & Dumais, S. 2006, "Improving personalized web search using result diversification," in *SIGIR '06 Proceedings of the 29th Annual International ACM SIGIR Conference on Research and Development in Information Retrieval, Seattle, August 6–11*, New York: ACM Press, pp. 691–2.

Rafiei, D., Bharat, K. & Shukla, A. 2010, "Diversifying web search results," in *WWW '10 Proceedings of the 19th International Conference on World Wide Web, Raleigh, North Carolina, April 26–30*, New York: ACM Press, pp. 781–90.

Ramirez, A., Walther, J. B., Burgoon, J. K. & Sunnafrank, M. 2002, "Information-seeking strategies, uncertainty, and computer-mediated-communication: toward a conceptual model," *Human Communication Research*, 28, 2, pp. 213–28.

Ratcliff, C. 2016, "Google search index set to go 'mobile-first' within months," Search Engine Watch, October 18, searchenginewatch.com/ 2016/10/18/google-index-set-to-go-mobile-first-within-months/.

Ratzan, L. 2006, "Mining the deep web: search strategies that work," *Computerworld*, December 11, www.computerworld.com/article/

2548609/networking/mining-the-deep-web--search-strategies-that-work.html.

Razlagova, E. 2013, "The past and future of music listening: between freeform DJs and recommendation algorithms," in J. Loviglio and M. Hilmes (eds.), *Radio's new wave: global sound in the digital era*, New York: Routledge, pp. 62–76.

Rees-Mogg, W. 2006, "Grow up, Google: you've accepted censorship, now confront copyright," *The Times*, January 30, Features, p. 21.

Regalado, A. 2013, "Stephen Wolfram on personal analytics," *MIT Tech Review*, May 8, www.technologyreview.com/s/514356/stephen-wolfram-on-personal-analytics/.

Rettberg, J. W. 2014, *Seeing ourselves through technology: how we use selfies, blogs, and wearable devices to see and shape ourselves*, New York: Palgrave Macmillan.

Return on Now 2015, "2015 search engine market share by country," returnonnow.com/internet-marketing-resources/2015-search-engine-market-share-by-country/.

Ribak, A., Jacovi, M. & Soroka, V. 2002, "'Ask before you search': peer support and community building with ReachOut," in *Proceedings of ACM Conference on Computer Supported Cooperative Work*, New Orleans: ACM Press, pp. 126–35.

Robins, K. & Webster, F. 1999, *Times of the technoculture: from the information society to the virtual life*, London: Routledge.

Ronfeldt, D. F., Arquilla, J., Fuller, G. E. & Fuller, M. 1998, *The Zapatista "Social Netwar" in Mexico*, Santa Monica, Calif.: RAND.

Ross, P. E. 2007, "What's the Latin for 'delusional?'" *IEEE Spectrum*, 44, 1, pp. 49–50.

Rowlands, I. & Nicholas, D. 2005, "Scholarly communication in the digital environment," *Aslib Proceedings: New Information Perspectives*, 57, 6, pp. 481–97.

Rowlands, I., Nicholas, D., Williams, P., et al. 2008, "The Google generation: the information behavior of the researcher of the future," *Aslib Proceedings: New Information Perspectives*, 60, 4, pp. 290–310.

Rowley, J. 2002, "'Window' shopping and browsing opportunities in cyberspace," *Journal of Consumer Behavior*, 1, 4, pp. 369–78.

Ruckenstein, M. 2014, "Visualized and interacted life: personal analytics and engagements with data doubles," *Societies*, 4, 1, pp. 68–84.

Rust, R. T. & Oliver, R. W. 1994, "The death of advertising," *Journal of Advertising*, 23, 4, pp. 71–7.

Salmerón, L., Macedo-Rouet, M. & Rouet, J. F. 2015, "Multiple viewpoints increase students' attention to source features in social question and answer forum messages," *Journal of the Association for Information Science and Technology*, 67, 10, pp. 2404–19.

Salton, G. 1975, *A theory of indexing*, Philadelphia: Society for Industrial and Applied Mathematics.

Scardamaglia, A. & Daly, A. 2016, "Google, online search and consumer confusion in Australia," *International Journal of Law and Information Technology*, 24, 3, pp. 203–28.

Schenker, J. L. 2006, "What Google can't do," *Red Herring*, December 25, sls.weco.net/blog/hubert7653/23-dec-2006/8384.

Schiller, H. I. 1971, *Mass communication and American empire*, Boston: Beacon Press.

1996, *Information inequality: the deepening social crisis in America*, London: Routledge.

Scholz, T. & Schneider, N. 2016, *Ours to hack and to own: the rise of platform cooperativism, a new vision for the future of work and a fairer internet*, New York: OR Books.

Schudson, M. 1978, *Discovering the news: a social history of American newspapers*, New York: Basic Books.

1997, "Why conversation is not the soul of democracy," *Critical Studies in Mass Communication*, 14, 4, pp. 297–309.

Schuler, D. 2001, "Computer professionals and the next culture of democracy," *Communications of the ACM*, 44, 1, pp. 52–7.

Schulman, E. 1999, "Can fame be measured quantitatively?" *Annals of Improbable Research*, 5, 3, p. 16.

Schulz, D., Burgard, W., Fox, D., Thrun, S. & Cremers, A. B. 2000, "Web interfaces for mobile robots in public places," *IEEE Robotics & Automation Magazine*, 7, 1, pp. 48–56.

Schwartz, B. 2014, "Google's Matt Cutts: we don't use Twitter or Facebook social signals to rank pages," Search Engine Land, January 22, searchengineland.com/googles-matt-cutts-facebook-twitter-pages-are-treated-like-any-other-web-page-on-the-internet-182370.

2016, "Within months, Google to divide its index, giving mobile users better and fresher content," Search Engine Land, October 13, searchengineland.com/google-divide-index-giving-mobile-users-better-fresher-content-261037.

Schwartz, M. F. & Leyden, P. 1997, "The long boom: a history of the future: 1980–2020," *Wired*, 5, 7, pp. 115–31.

Seetharaman, D. 2016, "Mark Zuckerberg's 2016 challenge: code an artificial intelligence assistant," *The Wall Street Journal*, January 4, blogs.wsj.com/digits/2016/01/04/mark-zuckerbergs-2016–challenge-code-an-artificial-intelligence-assistant/.

Segal, D. 2011, "The dirty little secrets of search," *The New York Times*, February 12, www.nytimes.com/2011/02/13/business/13search.html.

Sennett, R. 2008, *The craftsman*, New Haven: Yale University Press.

Shah, R. 2000, "History of the Finger Protocol," www.rajivshah.com/Case_Studies/Finger/Finger.htm.

Shakespeare, W. 1912, *Troilus and Cressida*, New York: The Macmillan Company.

Shenk, D. 1997, *Data smog: surviving the information glut*, San Francisco: Harper Edge.

Sherman, C. & Price, G. 2001, *The Invisible Web: uncovering information sources search engines can't see*, Medford, NJ: CyberAge Books.

Shneiderman, B. 2000, "Universal usability," *Communications of the ACM*, 43, 5, pp. 84–91.

Siegler, M. G. 2009, "Google Social Search: Twitter and FriendFeed highlighted. What about Facebook?" TechCrunch, October 26, techcrunch.com/2009/10/26/google-social-search-launches-twitter-friendfeed-but-not-facebook-highlighted/.

Silverman, C., Strapagiel, L., Shaban, H., Hall, E. & Singer-Vine, J. 2016, "Hyperpartisan Facebook pages are publishing false and misleading information at an alarming rate," BuzzFeed News, October 20, www.buzzfeed.com/craigsilverman/partisan-fb-pages-analysis.

Silverstein, C., Marais, H., Henzinger, M. & Moricz, M. 1999, "Analysis of a very large web search engine query log," *ACM SIGIR Forum*, 33, 1, pp. 6–12.

Simeonovski, M., Bendun, F., Rizwan, M., Backes, M., Marnau, N. & Druschel, P. 2015, "Oblivion: mitigating privacy leaks by controlling the discoverability of online information," *Lecture Notes in Computer Science*, 9092, pp. 431–53.

Simmel, G. 1964, *Conflict: the web of group-affiliations*, New York: Free Press.

Simon, H. A. 1956, "Rational choice and the structure of the environment," *Psychological Review*, 63, 2, pp. 129–38.

1969, *The sciences of the artificial*, Cambridge, Mass.: MIT Press.

1971, "Designing organizations for an information-rich world," in M. Greenberger (ed.), *Computers, communications, and the public interest*, Baltimore: The Johns Hopkins University Press, pp. 37–72.

Simone, S. 2015, "What's ahead for enterprise search in 2016?" *KMWorld*, December 21, www.kmworld.com/Articles/News/News/Whats-Ahead-for-Enterprise-Search-in-2016-108225.aspx.

Simonite, T. 2013, "A Google Glass app knows what you're looking at," *MIT Technology Review*, September 30, www.technologyreview.com/s/519726/a-google-glass-app-knows-what-youre-looking-at/.

Singel, R. 2006, "AT&T seeks to hide spy docs," *Wired*, April 12, archive.wired.com/science/discoveries/news/2006/04/70650.

Sinha, A. 2007, "Does India need a *National* search engine?" NextBigWhat, January 2, www.nextbigwhat.com/does-india-need-national-search-enginehtml-297/.

Siu, E. 2013, "A look at Google's 200 search ranking factors," *Entrepreneur*, June 3, www.entrepreneur.com/article/226884.

Sklair, L. 1995, *Sociology of the global system*, 2nd edn., Baltimore: The Johns Hopkins University Press.

Smith, A. 2014, "What internet users know about technology and the web," Pew Research Center, November 25, www.pewinternet.org/2014/11/25/web-iq/.

Smith, A. & Anderson, J. 2014, "Predictions for the state of AI and robotics in 2025," Pew Research Center, August 6, www.pewin ternet.org/2014/08/06/predictions-for-the-state-of-ai-and-robotics-in-2025/.

Smith, J. F. 1964, "Systematic serendipity," *Chemical & Engineering News*, 42, 35, pp. 55–6.

Smyth, B., Coyle, M. & Briggs, P. 2012, "HeyStaks: a real-world deployment of social search," in *RecSys '12 Proceedings of the Sixth ACM Conference on Recommender Systems*, New York: ACM Press, researchrepository.ucd.ie/bitstream/handle/10197/4353/heystaks-recsys-2012–SUBMIT.pdf.

Snyder, H. & Rosenbaum, H. 1997, *How public is the Web? Robots, access, and scholarly communication*, WP-98–05, Bloomington: Center for Social Informatics, https:// scholarworks.ice.edu/dspace/ html/2022/1099/wp98–05B.html.

Sokullu, E. 2007, "Competing with Google search," Read/WriteWeb, July 18, readwrite.com/2007/07/18/competing_with_google_search/#!.

Solomon, L. 2007, "LSD as therapy? Write about it, get barred from US," *The Tyee*, April 23, thetyee.ca/News/2007/04/23/Feldmar/.

Southern, M. 2016, "SEO jobs and salaries down in 2016, but why?" Search Engine Journal, March 31, www.searchenginejournal.com/ number-seo-jobs-decline-2016/160738/.

Spaink, K. & Hardy, C. 2002, *Freedom of the internet: our new challenge*, Organization for Security and Co-operation in Europe, www.spaink. net/2002/05/27/freedom-of-the-internet/.

Specter, M. 2007, "Damn spam: the losing war on junk email," *New Yorker*, 83, pp. 36–40, www.newyorker.com/reporting/2007/08/ 06/070806fa_fact_specter.

Spink, A. 2002, "A user-centered approach to evaluating human inter-action with Web search engines: an exploratory study," *Information Processing & Management*, 38, 3, pp. 401–26.

Spink, A., Jansen, B. J., Wolfram, D. & Saracevic, T. 2002, "From e-sex to e-commerce: Web search changes," *Computer*, 35, 3, pp. 107–9.

Spirin, N., He, J., Develin, M., Karahalios, K. & Boucher, M. 2014, "People search within an online social network: large scale analysis of Facebook Graph Search query logs," in *CIKM '14 Proceedings of the 23rd ACM International Conference on Information and Knowledge Management*, Shanghai, November 3–7, New York: ACM Press, pp. 1009–18.

Sterling, G. 2015, "It's official: Google says more searches now on mobile than on desktop," Search Engine Land, May 5, searchengineland.com/its-official-google-says-more-searches-now-on-mobile-than-on-desktop-220369.

Stevens, C. E., Xie, E. & Peng, M. W. 2015, "Toward a legitimacy-based view of political risk: the case of Google and Yahoo in China," *Strategic Management Journal*, 37, 5, pp. 945–63.

Suber, P. 2007, "Trends favoring open access," CTWatch Quarterly, 3, 3, www.ctwatch.org/quarterly/articles/2007/08/trends-favoring-open-access/.

Sullivan, D. 2000, "Invisible web gets deeper," Search Engine Watch, August 2, http://searchenginewatch.com/showPage.html?page=2162871.

2015, "Yahoo & Google together again in new search deal," Search Engine Land, October 20, searchengineland.com/yahoo-google-search-deal-233963.

2016, "Google now handles at least 2 trillion searches per year," Search Engine Land, May 24, searchengineland.com/google-now-handles-2-999-trillion-searches-per-year-250247.

Sunstein, C. R. 2001, *Republic.com*, Princeton University Press.

2006, *Infotopia: how many minds produce knowledge*, Oxford University Press.

Svensson, M., Höök, K., Laaksolahti, J. & Waern, A. 2001, "Social navigation of food recipes," in *Proceedings of the SIGCHI Conference on Human Factors in Computing Systems*, Seattle: ACM Press, pp. 341–8.

Swidey, N. 2003, "A nation of voyeurs: how the internet search engine Google is changing what we can find out about one another – and raising questions about whether we should," *Boston Globe*, February 2, Magazine, p. 10.

Tapia, A. H., LaLone, N. & Kim, H.-W. 2014, "Run amok: group crowd participation in identifying the bomb and bomber from the Boston marathon bombing," in *Proceedings of the 11th International ISCRAM Conference, University Park, Pennsylvania, May*, University Park: Pennsylvania State University Press, pp. 265–74.

Tatum, C. & Jankowski, N. 2012, "Beyond open access: a framework for openness in scholarly communication," in P. Wouters, A. Beaulieu, A. Scharnhorst, & S. Wyatt (eds.), *Virtual Knowledge*, Cambridge, Mass.: MIT Press, pp. 183–218.

Teevan, J., Collins-Thompson, K., White, R. W. & Dumais, S. 2014, "Slow search," *Communications of the ACM*, 57, 8, pp. 36–8.

Tene, O. & Polonetsky, J. 2013, "A theory of creepy: technology, privacy, and shifting social norms," *Yale Journal of Law and Technology*, 16, pp. 59–100.

Thelwall, M. 2008, "Extracting accurate and complete results from search engines: case study Windows Live," *Journal of the American Society of Information Science and Technology*, 59, 1, pp. 38–50.

Thelwall, M., Haustein, S., Larivière, V. & Sugimoto, C. R. 2013, "Do altmetrics work? Twitter and ten other social web services," *PLoS One*, May 28, dx.doi.org/10.1371/journal.pone.0064841.

Thelwall, M. & Vaughan, L. 2004, "A fair history of the web?

Examining country balance in the Internet Archive," *Library & Information Science Research*, 26, 2, pp. 162–76.

Thornton, C. and Du Boulay, B. 1992, *Artificial intelligence through search*, Norwell, Mass.: Kluwer Academic.

Thorson, K. & Wells, C. 2015, "Curated flows: a framework for mapping media exposure in the digital age," *Communication Theory*, 26, 3, pp. 309–28.

Tobin, J. 1998, "An American otaku (or, a boy's virtual life on the Net)," in J. Sefton-Green (ed.), *Digital diversions: youth culture in the age of multimedia*, London: Routledge, pp. 99–118.

Tönnies, F. 1957, *Community and society (Gemeinschaft und Gesellschaft)*, East Lansing: Michigan State University Press.

Trattner, C., Parra, D., Brusilovsky, P. & Marinho, L. B. 2015, "Report on the SIGIR 2015 workshop on social personalization and search," *ACM SIGIR Forum*, 49, 2, pp. 102–6.

Trielli, D., Mussenden, S., Stark, J. & Diakopoulos, N. 2016, "Googling politics: how the Google issue guide on candidates is biased," *Slate Future Tense*, June 7, www.slate.com/articles/technology/future_tense/2016/06/how_the_google_issue_guide_on_candidates_is_biased.html.

Tsui, L. 2007, "An inadequate metaphor: the great firewall and Chinese internet censorship," *Global Dialogue*, 9, 1/2, pp. 60–8.

Turkle, S. 1996, "Rethinking identity through virtual community," in L. Hershman-Leeson (ed.), *Clicking in: hot links to a digital culture*, Seattle: Bay Press, pp. 116–22.

Twist, J. 2005, "Looming pitfalls of work blogs," BBC News, January 3, news.bbc.co.uk/2/hi/technology/4115073.stm.

US Congress Committee on International Relations. 2006, "The internet in China: a tool for freedom or suppression," 2001–2009.state.gov/p/eap/rls/rm/61275.htm.

Vaas, L. 2005, "Blogger blocked at US border," eWeek.com, November 29, www.eweek.com/c/a/Messaging-and-Collaboration/Blogger-Blocked-at-US-Border.

Vadén, T. & Suoranta, J. 2004, "Breaking radical monopolies: towards political economy of digital literacy," *E-Learning*, 1, 2, pp. 283–301.

Vaidhyanathan, S. 2012, *The Googlization of everything (and why we should worry)*, Berkeley: University of California Press.

Van Alstyne, M. & Brynjolfsson, E. 1996, "Could the internet Balkanize science?" *Science*, 274, 5292, pp. 1479–89.

Van Couvering, E. 2007, "Is relevance relevant? Market, science, and war: discourses of search engine quality," *Journal of Computer-Mediated Communication*, 12, 3, pp. 866–87.

Vander Wal, T. 2005, "Folksonomy definition and Wikipedia," www.vanderwal.net/random/entrysel.php?blog=1750.

Varnhagen, C. K., McFall, G. P., Figueredo, L., Takach, B. S., Daniels, J.

& Cuthbertson, H. 2009, "Spelling and the web," *Journal of Applied Developmental Psychology*, 30, pp. 454–62.

Vascellaro, J. E. & Lacapra, L. T. 2007, "Ask.com hopes ads compute to buzz," *The Wall Street Journal*, Eastern edn., May 3, p. B8.

Vaughan, L. & Thelwall, M. 2004, "Search engine coverage bias: evidence and possible causes," *Information Processing & Management*, 40, 4, pp. 693–707.

Waddell, K. 2015, "The NSA's bulk collection is over, but Google and Facebook are still in the data business," *The Atlantic*, June 3, www.theatlantic.com/politics/archive/2015/06/the-nsas-bulk-collection-is-over-but-google-and-facebook-are-still-in-the-data-business/45849 6/.

2016, "Why Google quit China – and why it's heading back," *The Atlantic*, January 19, www.theatlantic.com/technology/archive/2016/01/why-google-quit-china-and-why-its-heading-back/424482/.

Walker, C. W. 2004, "Application of the DMCA safe harbor provisions to search engines," *Virginia Journal of Law & Technology*, 9.

Walker, J. 2005, "Links and power: the political economy of linking on the web," *Library Trends*, 53, 4, pp. 524–9.

Walter, P. 2014, "Google Penguin nearly killed my business," *The Telegraph*, December 1, www.telegraph.co.uk/finance/businessclub/sales/11265882/Google-Penguin-nearly-killed-my-business.html.

Walther, J. B. 1996, "Computer-mediated communication: impersonal, interpersonal, and hyperpersonal interaction," *Communication Research*, 23, 1, pp. 3–43.

Wang, F.-Y., Zeng, D., Hendler, J., et al. 2010, "A study of the human flesh search engine: crowd-powered expansion of online knowledge," *Computer*, 43, 8, pp. 45–53.

Wang, M., Yang, K., Hua, X.-S. & Zhang, H.-J. 2010, "Toward a relevant and diverse search of social images," *IEEE Transactions on Multimedia*, 12, 8, pp. 829–42.

Warf, B. & Grimes, J. 1997, "Counterhegemonic discourses and the internet," *Geographical Review*, 87, 2, pp. 259–74.

Webber, S. 2002, "Mapping a path to the empowered searcher," in C. Graham (ed.), *Online Information 2002: proceedings*, London: Learned Information Europe, pp. 177–81.

Weber, L. 2012, "Colleges pay to protect students from toxic Google results," *The Wall Street Journal*, December 17, blogs.wsj.com/atwork/2012/12/17/colleges-pay-to-protect-students-from-toxic-google-results/.

Weinberger, D. 2007, *Everything is miscellaneous: the power of the new digital disorder*, New York: Times Books.

Weinstein, L. 2007, "Search engine dispute notifications: request for comments," Lauren Weinstein's Blog, June 15, lauren.vortex.com/archive/000253.html.

Wells, H. G. 1938, *World brain*, New York: Doubleday.

Westerman, S. J., Hambly, S., Alder, C., et al. 1996, "Investigating the human–computer interface using the Datalogger," *Behavior Research Methods, Instruments, & Computers*, 28, 4, pp. 603–6.

Whetstone, R. 2006, "About the Google News case in Belgium," The Official Google Blog, September 25, googleblog.blogspot.com/2006/09/about-google-newscase-in-belgium.html.

White, A. 2013, "Search engines: left side quality versus right side profits," *International Journal of Industrial Organization*, 31, 6, pp. 690–701.

Wiggins, R. 2003, "The privilege of ranking: Google plays ball," *Searcher*, 11, 7, www.infotoday.com/searcher/jul03/wiggins.shtml.

Wingfield, N., Isaac, M. & Benner, K. 2016, "Google and Facebook take aim at fake news sites," *The New York Times*, November 14, www.nytimes.com/2016/11/15/technology/google-will-ban-websites-that-host-fake-news-from-using-its-ad-service.html.

Winner, L. 1980, "Do artifacts have politics?" *Daedalus*, 109, 1, pp. 121–36.

1995, "Who will we be in cyberspace?" *Information Society*, 12, 1, pp. 63–72.

1997, "Cyberlibertarian myths and the prospects for community," *Computers and Society*, 27, 3, pp. 14–19.

Wojcieszak, M. & Rojas, H. 2011, "Correlates of party, ideology and issue based extremity in an era of egocentric publics," *The International Journal of Press/Politics*, 16, 4, pp. 488–507.

Wong, J. C., Levin, S. & Solon, O. 2016, "Bursting the Facebook bubble: we asked voters on the left and right to swap feeds," *The Guardian*, November 16, www.theguardian.com/us-news/2016/nov/16/facebook-bias-bubble-us-election-conservative-liberal-newsfeed.

Wu, T. 2015, "What ever happened to Google Books?" *The New Yorker*, September 11, www.newyorker.com/business/currency/what-ever-happened-to-google-books.

Yanbe, Y., Jatowt, A., Nakamura, S. & Tanaka, K. 2007, "Can social bookmarking enhance search in the web?" in *International Conference on Digital Libraries*, Vancouver, BC, Canada: ACM Press, pp. 107–16.

Yates, J. 1982, "From press book and pigeonhole to vertical filing: revolution in storage and access systems for correspondence," *Journal of Business Communication*, 19, 3, pp. 5–26.

Yeo, G. 1995, "The soul of cyberspace," *New Perspectives Quarterly*, 12, 4.

Yuwono, B., Lan, S. L. Y., Ying, J. H. & Lee, D. L. 1995, "A World Wide Web resource discovery system," presented at The Fourth International World Wide Web Conference, Boston, December 11–14.

Zeller, T. 2006, "AOL executive quits after posting of search data,"

The New York Times, August 22, www.nytimes.com/2006/08/22/
technology/22iht-aol.2558731.html.

Zhang, J. & Ackerman, M. S. 2005, "Searching for expertise in social
networks: a simulation of potential strategies," in *Proceedings of
ACM SIGGROUP Conference on Supporting Group Work*, New York:
ACM Press, pp. 71–80.

Zhang, J. & Lin, S. 2007, "Multiple language supports in search
engines," *Online Information Review*, 31, 4, pp. 516–32.

Zhang, S. 2014, "A creepy website is streaming from 73,000 private
security cameras," Gizmodo, November 6, gizmodo.com/a-creepy-
website-is-streaming-from-73-000–private-secur-1655653510.

Zhang, Y. 2001, "Scholarly use of internet-based electronic resources,"
Journal of the American Society of Information Science and Technology,
52, 8, pp. 628–54.

Zimmer, M. 2008a, "The externalities of Search 2.0: the emerging
privacy threats when the drive for the perfect search engine meets
Web 2.0," *First Monday*, 13, 3, firstmonday.org/ojs/index.php/fm/
article/view/2136.

2008b, "Privacy on planet Google: using the theory of 'contextual
integrity' to clarify the privacy threats of Google's quest for the perfect search engine," *Journal of Business & Technology Law*, 3, 1, art. 8.

2011, "Facebook's censorship problem," Michael Zimmer, April 21,
www.michaelzimmer.org/2011/04/21/facebooks-censorship-probl
em/.

Zipf, G. K. 1949, *Human behavior and the principle of least effort: an
introduction to human ecology*, Cambridge, Mass.: Addison-Wesley.

Zittrain, J. 2014, "Is the EU compelling Google to become about.
me?" The Future of the Internet and How to Stop It, May 13, blogs.
harvard.edu/futureoftheinternet/2014/05/13/is-the-eu-compelling-
google-to-become-about-me/.

Zittrain, J. & Edelman, B. 2003, "Empirical analysis of internet filtering
in China," *IEEE Internet Computing*, 7, 2, pp. 70–7.

Zuboff, S. & Maxmin, J. 2002, *The support economy*, New York: Viking.

Index